Harvard Historical Studies, 111

*Published under the auspices
of the Department of History
from the income of the
Paul Revere Frothingham Bequest
Robert Louis Stroock Fund
Henry Warren Torrey Fund*

PERRY OF LONDON

A Family and a Firm on the Seaborne
Frontier, 1615–1753

Jacob M. Price

HARVARD UNIVERSITY PRESS
Cambridge, Massachusetts
London, England
1992

Library of Congress Cataloging-in-Publication Data

Price, Jacob M.
    Perry of London: a family and a firm on the seaborne frontier, 1615–1753 / Jacob
M. Price
        p.   cm. — (Harvard historical studies; v. 111)
    Includes bibliographical references (p.   ) and index.
    ISBN 0-674-66306-3 (acid-free paper)
    1. Perry of London—History. 2. Perry family. 3. Tobacco industry—Great
Britain—History. 4. Tobacco industry—Great Britain—Colonies—America—History.
5. Tobacco industry—Virginia—History. I. Title. II. Series.
HD9141.9.P47P75 1992
382'.41371'0942—dc20   91-36591
                              CIP

Contents

Preface   vii

Note on Names   xiv

Introduction   1

I. The Rise of the House of Perry, 1615–1721

  1. The Early Perrys and Their Wanderings   7

  2. The Emergence of Perry & Lane   19

  3. The Business of the Perry Firm   28

  4. The Public Role of Micaiah Perry I   52

II. The Fall of the House of Perry, 1721–1753

  5. The Challenge of the Third Generation   63

  6. The Perils of Politics   72

  7. The Family after the Fall   91

  Conclusion: Choosing a Frame for the Picture   95

Abbreviations   104

Appendix A: Draft Service Agreement   105

Appendix B: Goods Exported by Perry, Lane & Co. to Virginia and Maryland   107

Appendix C: The Hutchinson Connection   112

Appendix D: The Early Perys and Perrys: Some Problems   114

Selected Bibliography   121

Notes   139

Index   181

Tables

1. The Rise of Perry & Lane, 1672–1697   21

2. Commission Earnings of Perry & Co., 1676–1731   50

3. Tobacco Imports of Perry & Co., 1697–1732   78

4. Leading London Tobacco Importers, 1729, 1731   79

Figures

1. Antecedents and Siblings of Micaiah Perry I   10

2. Descendants of Micaiah Perry I   26

3. The Early Perys and Perrys According to Betham   115

4. The Early Perys and Perrys: An Alternative Account   117

Preface

At the beginning of the seventeenth century, participation in many a branch of English foreign trade was either monopolized by a favored joint stock company or restricted to members of a particular chartered society (for example, the Merchant Adventurers, the Eastland Company, the Levant Company). Very often these chartered companies restricted their membership to Londoners and to "mere merchants," excluding retailers, manufacturers and ship captains. By contrast, participation in the newly developing trades to North America and the West Indies—particularly after the termination of the Virginia Company in 1624—was open to all subjects of the Crown. With the gates ajar, a numerous and motley band of small venturers—including retailers and ship captains—pushed into these new and promising American trades. By the last quarter of the seventeenth century, it had become apparent that most of this huckster horde lacked the resources to carry on transatlantic trade efficiently and profitably, and that a contraction in the number of participating firms was already in progress. Thus, even though the merchandise turnover in all branches of the Atlantic trades continued to expand until the American Revolution, the number of English and later Scottish firms involved was progressively reduced, leaving such trades in the hands of much fewer but considerably stronger houses.[1] In eighteenth century London, these fewer and stronger American houses (even if collectively never as weighty as the firms trading to Europe and the Mediterranean) could cut most respectable figures. In the contemporary outports, their equivalents were even more important, dominating the commercial life of such places as Glasgow, Liverpool and Bristol.

Success in any open trade was not just success for an individual or a firm; it might also open new prospects of advancement for a whole family. Kin might help a growing firm with capital, credit, reputation and a useful circle of acquaintances in all sorts of places. In return,

the partners in a successful firm might help their kin with employment, orders for goods, credit, introductions, and opportunities for
advantageous investment, as well as with that subtle, indirect transfer
of prestige and business standing that might be thought of as
"reflection of the lustre of success." Conversely, of course, there was
the ever present threat that a declining or failing firm could drag
families down with it.

Many decades ago, when I first began my research in early modern
British foreign and colonial trade, I dreamed of finding somewhere,
perhaps in the muniment room of a country house, the complete
records of one of the more successful firms, one that had proved its
fitness by surviving for two or more generations in the hazardous
North American trade, particularly in its most important branch, the
trade to the Chesapeake. With the passing years, I came to perceive
that there was no reason why such a complete archive should have
been preserved anywhere. Business records are normally destroyed
after they have ceased to have any current or potential use. A few
items are, of course, spared the fire or the shredder because they
relate to some special circumstance, such as a lawsuit or a trust or
other inheritance.[2] Even those deliberately retained for a time are
likely to be preserved over the centuries more by chance than by
design.

Thus I learned that even the most energetic researcher is unlikely
to find a complete archive of any relevant seventeenth or eighteenth
century firm. When he or she does find business records that chance
has preserved, they are likely to be mere fragments: accounts without
the relevant correspondence, or vice versa. If some correspondence
turns up, it usually proves to be (outgoing) letterbooks without the
parallel incoming letters, or, in fewer cases, incoming letters without
the matching outgoing correspondence. Like other historians working on similar imperfect materials, I soon decided that one could
not wait for a perfect trove to turn up but had to work with the
material available; in this spirit, I published a number of articles on
seventeenth or eighteenth century firms based on characteristically
fragmentary evidence. In the course of preparing one such piece (on
the London Scottish merchant James Russell),[3] I realized that the
available fragments could be used to reconstruct not merely the
activities of a firm but the history of a family over many generations,
a family in this case whose history touched Scotland, England, Mary-

land, Virginia and India in the century and a half between the Union
of 1707 and the Mutiny of 1857.

My experience with the Russells led me to wonder whether an
equivalent reconstruction could be attempted for other London
mercantile families, particularly the Perrys, who were exceptionally
important in the trades to Virginia and Maryland almost a century
before Russell. (For four decades they appear to have been the most
important British firm trading to the continental colonies.) Elizabeth
Donnan had published an article on them in 1931, but, as she was
very much aware, it was only a beginning.[4] Her work was based
entirely on printed sources and, because of the chronological distribution of those sources, necessarily emphasized the later history of
the firm under Micajah Perry the younger, to the neglect of its earlier
and more important history under his grandfather, Micaiah Perry
the elder. This chronological imbalance also led to an interpretive
distortion, with an overemphasis on the importance of the planter
consignment trade and a relative neglect of other modes of mercantile operation used by the firm. I had reason to believe that enough
additional material was available to enable one to reconsider the
character of the firm presented by Donnan and place its story and
the saga of the Perry family in a much wider context.

A generation ago, three noteworthy studies appeared embodying
such a combination of business and family history: Richard Pares'
1950 study of the Pinneys of Bristol; Michael Flinn's 1962 study of
Crowleys, the great ironmongers; and Ralph Davis's 1967 study of
the Levant-trading Radcliffes.[5] The Pares and Davis studies were
based in good part on substantial bodies of business and family
papers preserved in country houses and transferred relatively recently to university and public libraries and county archives. Flinn,
however, found to his sorrow that all the Crowley business records
had long before been destroyed, but as partial consolation he did
have access to some family and estate papers. For the Perrys the
initial prospects were even more daunting. No cache of Perry business or family papers has been found, or, I fear, is likely to be found.
Nevertheless, a substantial amount of historically significant evidence
has turned up in a wide variety of places. Since Donnan wrote,
additional correspondence touching the Perrys has been published
by Virginia specialists. More important, though, are the large manu-
script collections in Virginia and the District of Columbia which were

found to contain scattered correspondence to and from the firm. In England, the most important sources, in addition to the obvious wills and Colonial Office series at the Public Record Office, proved to be court records, including those of Admiralty, Exchequer and Chancery. Of these, the richest for the Perrys was Chancery. Almost sixty years ago, George Sherwood alerted his fellow early American genealogists to the riches that could be found in Chancery bills and answers as well as in the better known Prerogative Court of Canterbury wills.[6] Sherwood devoted most of his attention to the first two-thirds of the seventeenth century. Since his time, the library of the Society of Genealogists (in London) has acquired a microfilm of the privately prepared Bernau Index to Chancery proceedings. This index, despite its technical difficulties, is extremely useful for the post-Sherwood period, particularly when one is dealing with as distinctive a name as Micajah Perry. In addition, the Society of Genealogists also possesses a valuable set of notes prepared by the late Major G. S. Parry, calendaring a great number of references to persons named Parry or Perry in Prerogative Court of Canterbury wills and Chancery proceedings of the sixteenth, seventeenth and eighteenth centuries. Of course, since neither George Sherwood nor Major Parry was automatically interested in topics that attract the attention of a modern economic or social historian, it was necessary in every case to go from their notes to the archival documents themselves to obtain or confirm the information needed. Other "leads" had to be generated and pursued by the usual methods of historical research.

After assembling a wide variety of scattered data surviving in repositories in England, Ireland and the United States, I realized how much of the story of the Perrys could now be told and where major gaps persisted. Almost no personal correspondence has come to light, nor have any balance sheets or similar general accounts of the firm. But historians, like archaeologists, are used to working with fragmentary evidence. Enough has survived to make possible the reconstruction of the complex rise and fall of the Perrys of London—family and firm.

When one attempts to write the history of a family, one necessarily becomes involved in its genealogy. I am aware, though, that for many professional historians, even one page of genealogy may be a page too much. I have nevertheless devoted a good deal of space (particularly in Appendices C and D) to the pedigrees of the Perrys and kindred families. In this I have not been particularly interested in what may be termed longitudinal or serial genealogy and have not striven to pursue the family lines of descent into the nineteenth and twentieth centuries. Similarly, I have investigated the antecedents of the Perrys only from the moment when their Exeter ancestor first became a merchant in the reign of Henry VIII. I was, however, much more interested, as the reader will discover, in what may be called the latitudinal or structural genealogy of the family: the contemporary relationships of the London Perrys and their partner Lane to other families in Devon, London, Northamptonshire, Ireland, Virginia and elsewhere. I hope that the fuller delineation of these connections will help the careful reader understand a good bit more about the world in which the Perrys lived and the character of some of their migratory and other major decisions.

I should like to thank the earl of Limerick for access to his family muniments, and Gerald Aylmer, Paul Clemens, Louis Cullen, John Hemphill, Henry Horwitz, Kenneth Lockridge, John McCusker, Thomas Power, John Shy and Christopher Smout for their much appreciated information, suggestions or comments.

As always, I am indebted to the archivists and librarians of the institutions mentioned in the notes and bibliography for their courtesy, efficiency and valued assistance. The Bodleian Library kindly granted permission to reprint the document that appears in Appendix A.

Concentrated work on this book began when I was a visiting fellow at All Souls College, Oxford, in 1984–85. I remain indebted to the Warden and Fellows of the college for their hospitality. My research has been assisted by fellowships from the National Endowment for the Humanities and at the University of Michgan by grants from the office of the Vice-President for Research and the Horace H. Rackham School of Graduate Studies.

Perry of London

Note on Names

Members of the family are identified in the text as Micajah (or Micaiah) Perry I, II, III, and Richard Perry I, II, III, IV. This usage is for historical clarity only and does not imply that such enumeration was used by the individuals concerned.

In the sixteenth century, the Exeter family and many of their kin most commonly spelled their name Pery or Perye. The spelling Pery has been continued by the Limerick branch to the present day. During 1615–1660, the London branch spelled their name both Pery and Perry (the spelling used by an unrelated family of a contemporary Lord Mayor of London). After 1660, Micaiah Perry I and his descendants uniformly spelled their name Perry as did his brother John and the Clonmel-Tipperary branch.

In the sixteenth century, the family name appears to have been pronounced "Püry," "Pirry," or "Peery," pronunciations similar to that now preferred by the family of the earls of Limerick. We do not know how the London family pronounced their name but suspect that by the eighteenth century it was commonly sounded to rhyme with "berry."

The founder of the major Perry firm in London signed his name Micaiah, corresponding to the spelling of the name of the prophet in the Authorized or King James version of the Bible (I Kings 22; II Chronicles 18). His grandson, however, spelled his given name Micajah, perhaps only because he preferred a distinctive signature for business purposes.

Introduction

Between the sixteenth and the eighteenth centuries, the effective political and commercial hegemony of English state and society were extended from the rather narrow confines of England to a far-reaching zone embracing all the British Isles and significant parts of North America, the West Indies, Africa and Asia. With this geographic expansion went an expansion of career and investment opportunities for persons from different strata of English (or later British) society. For students of colonial America, the new opportunity that comes most readily to mind was emigration. There were, however, less permanent overseas opportunities for well-connected army officers and civil administrators, for merchants and their employees, for ship captains and their crews. By the end of the seventeenth century, we can see developing among sections of the lesser gentry and trading classes a peripatetic, migratory or, in current terminology, expatriate subculture: that is, a network of families whose younger male members were normally prepared to consider careers that would take them for many years out of the home country but that also seemed to promise opportunity for a dignified, comfortable return later in life. The Union with Scotland in 1707 was to bring a noticeably large element of Scots into this migratory subculture. Of course, not everyone who went out to Ireland, North America, the East or West Indies returned. Some found an early grave on a distant shore; others married and settled overseas; still others were discouraged by poverty from contemplating a return. However, enough did return to create in Britain the subculture of families with overseas histories, connections and perspectives.

For members of merchant families, particularly in the seventeenth century, the instrumentality for the pursuit of these overseas opportunities was most commonly a family firm. For such families over many years the fate of the family and the fortunes of the firm were closely intertwined—closely but not inextricably. Family connections were often useful to a firm for mobilizing capital and for establishing credit at home and abroad. The success of a firm gave lustre and resources to a family and enabled it very often to establish prestigious and useful marital alliances with other desirable families. But the symbiosis between family and firm could be ruptured by death, withdrawal or commercial disaster. A family firm might go out of business, or the family might sell their share in a merchant partnership to others, enabling the firm to continue without them. Either way the withdrawing family liberated talents and resources which could be applied elsewhere. Finally, and all too frequently, a firm could be forced into bankruptcy, or—more commonly for overseas firms—be forced to turn its assets over to its creditors and go into a supervised liquidation. Either bankruptcy or forced liquidation meant disaster for many families, but others saved some resources through marriage contracts and other family arrangements. The departure of these unsuccessful firms and families cleared the way for other firms and families to pursue the opportunities (real or illusory) hovering on the seaborne frontier.

The full range of such opportunities and options can in part be understood by looking closely at a family whose history reveals the import of many of the new choices. The story of the upwardly mobile Perry family of London exemplifies the opportunities that were emerging during the seventeenth and eighteenth centuries in England, Scotland, Ireland, the Mediterranean, North America, the West Indies and eventually in the East Indies as well. For approximately half a century (ca. 1690–ca. 1740) the family firm, successively styled Perry & Lane and Micajah Perry & Co., were the acknowledged leaders among the Chesapeake merchants of London and for at least thirty years (ca. 1690–ca. 1720) were by a substantial margin the largest importers of tobacco into London or Great Britain. Since tobacco was then the most valuable British import from North America, this activity made them in market terms the most important British firm trading to North America in those years. Their importance was recognized by their fellow Chesapeake merchants and by the government, for both of whom the head of the firm was the natural spokesman for the Chesapeake trade.

One must not, to be sure, assume that the Perrys, because they stood at the head of the North American trades around 1700, stood also at the pinnacle of the London commercial and financial world. Neither they nor any other North American merchants occupied such a role then. For example, only a handful of North American merchants participated in the directorate of the Bank of England[1] or the New East India Company (founded 1698)[2] in the early years of those bodies, and the roles of that handful were usually quite obscure. The interest of the Perrys' story lies accordingly not in their reaching what might be considered the absolute top of the metropolitan heap, but rather in its suggestion of just how far upward the North American trades could carry a family and a firm, and what risks went with such success.

No one, I think, expects the history of any business family to proceed forever onward and upward. The house of Perry was still at the top of their own particular heap in 1719–1721; by 1745–1746 their name had disappeared from the Chesapeake trade and from the public life of the City of London. For a historian, business failure may be more difficult than success to analyze satisfyingly. In addition to the obvious questions about costs, prices, markets, efficiency, credit and capital resources, there are the further nagging musings or doubts about the possible effects of the circumambient culture and of inter-generational psychological differences and stresses. Did the assimilated or internalized values of the culture enervate the family's competitiveness over time? Did such values distract attention from the "bottom line"? Were the younger members of the family simply not as good businessmen as their fathers and grandfathers? Or were they rather too anxious to show how much better they could be? Failure, one should remember, is a more common economic phenomenon than success and should attract more attention than it does from sociologically as well as economically inclined historians.

Perhaps the classic literary investigation of the problem of bourgeois decline is Thomas Mann's *Buddenbrooks*, which significantly in its original German edition bears the subtitle "The Decay of a Family" *(Verfall einer Familie)*. Written before the end of the nineteenth century, it recounts the disintegration of a Lübeck merchant family whose roots go back to the eighteenth century. In the many decades since I first read the novel, I have often thought of it as the sort of book a historian would like to write but never could. The novelist can give the reader all the social detail needed to depict the family's place in society, their mode of living and the stages and causes of their decline. More than that, the novelist can open to the reader something of the mind of the actors and let the reader understand or imagine he or she understands the reasons why the story goes as it must. The historian can do little of this, and so can rarely pretend to get inside a subject in the way a novelist sees into protagonists. Thus the historian will probably never explain failure as fully as readers would like. The historian can instead often only ask questions or pose hypotheses.

For Mann in *Buddenbrooks,* a serious interest in the arts, if not demonstrably the cause, was at least a very visible symptom of the irresistible disease sapping the strength of one bourgeois family. Modern writers touching on the decay of equivalent nineteenth century British business families rarely devote much attention to art, but are much intrigued by the thesis of the country house malady, the attraction for the successful bourgeois of the landed estate with its great house, its appropriate style of living and attendant set of values, often so alien to those of the counting house. (The thesis remains attractive even though some recent work casts doubt on the frequency with which successful bourgeois acquired major landed holdings.)[3] Though the London Perrys acquired some scattered parcels of country property, they never assembled what is normally considered a country estate nor enjoyed any country residence beyond a villa in Epsom. For them the relevant symptom of cultural estrangement and irresistible decay was politics.

In the Buddenbrooks' Lübeck, or in pre-reform Liverpool or Glasgow, some participation in municipal affairs was the common experience of most successful businessmen, usually coming well after success had been established. But eighteenth century London was more than ten times the size of Glasgow, Liverpool or Lübeck, and its political strife not something to be entered into lightheartedly, or as a normal stage in the cursus honorum of success. Thus, the younger Micajah Perry's election to Parliament and the aldermancy when only thirty-two years old was a more than serious step; in retrospect, it was a portentous symptom. No longer fully absorbed by the challenge of the seaborne frontier, he was drawn instead to a different adventure with different risks.

I have therefore divided the history contained in this little book into two parts: the Rise of the House of Perry, and the Fall of the House of Perry.

Part I

The Rise of the House of Perry, 1615–1721

1 / The Early Perrys
and Their Wanderings

A traveller by water in 1696 approaching Jamestown, the hamlet capital of Virginia, would have immediately noticed, amidst the nondescript small wooden buildings of the town, two more imposing and relatively large brick structures. At the western end of the town was the new or fourth "state house" where the public affairs of the colony were transacted. A few hundred yards down the James was a partially derelict terrace of three brick buildings facing the river. The central edifice, by then burned and abandoned, had formerly served the colony as its first state house; that to its west had most likely been an inn, serving among others those coming to town for public business. The third structure in the terrace, the only one still in use, belonged to Perry & Lane, merchants of London, and was then occupied by Micaiah Perry's nephew John Jarrett; it was most likely the headquarters of the business of that firm in southern Virginia.[1] The conspicuous size of the Perry building and its site at the very center of the public life of the colony are symbolic of the more than prominent part played by that firm in the life and trade of Virginia. A discreet visitor to the Customs House in London that year could have ascertained that Perry & Co. were by a substantial margin the leading importers of tobacco in the metropolis, indeed in the country. From the well-informed in Whitehall, he could also have learned that most negotiations and communications between the Chesapeake trade of London and the Treasury or the new Board of Trade passed through the hands of the same Micaiah Perry.

The pre-history of even an important mercantile family is usually very difficult if not impossible to establish.[2] However, Micajah (or

Micaiah) Perry I (1641–1721) fortunately left us three quite meaningful, if seemingly inconsistent, clues to his family origins. When
the young Micaiah was admitted as an apprentice in the London
Haberdashers Company in 1656, he stated that his father then resided in Glasgow.[3] In a High Court of Admiralty deposition in 1692,
Micaiah Perry of the parish of St. Katherine Cree Church, London,
stated that he had been born in New England and was then fifty-one
years old.[4] A few years later, when the same Micaiah Perry applied
to the Heralds for arms, he stated that he believed that he was related
to the Perry family of Devon previously granted arms—but could not
establish the precise connection. Since the only such family known
in Heralds' Visitations (Pery of Water) had left no traces beyond the
mid-sixteenth century, the Heralds were cautious and gave him arms
similar to but not identical with that family's.[5] Of these three clues,
that for Devon goes back farthest in time and it is in fact amongst
the maritime mists of south Devon, the world of Hawkins and Drake,
that we begin to find other clues of our Perrys' antecedents.

Perry or Pery is a fairly common name in the southwest and among
many our attention is drawn in particular to three at first obscure
families of this name settled respectively at Plymouth, at Buckland
Monachorum (to the north of Plymouth) and, most relevant for this
history, at Exeter. They were almost certainly related to each other,
though we cannot yet establish with absolute certainty the precise
connection. Some of them may have been mariners. At least one
Perry commanded a Topsham ship in the Newfoundland trade ca.
1589–1594.[6] Topsham is the port of Exeter, where we early pick up
the trail.

The story of the Perrys as merchants begins in 1531–1532, when
one Roger Pery was admitted a freeman of Exeter by apprenticeship.
Whether or not he was, as alleged, sprung from the armigerous Perys
of Water, Roger was part of an extensive cousinhood, with kin in
Hampshire, Wiltshire and Somerset. Following in the footsteps of his
master, Roger became a merchant in Exeter, as did his two sons
William and Richard.[7] Both also became bailiffs of Exeter and appear
in the records of the local Society of Merchant Adventurers. There
we find William (city bailiff, 1578) an active if relatively small-scale
merchant in the 1560s, importing raisins, figs and wine ("sack"),
presumably from Spain and the Mediterranean. Richard can also be
found in the Exeter port books in the 1580s importing wine and

other goods from Spain or Portugal.[8] Both brothers were specifically named as merchants trading to Spain and Portugal and as founding members in Queen Elizabeth's charter of 1577 incorporating the Spanish Company.[9] But, as Roger and his sons William and Richard had rather low assessments for local taxes, the family was presumably not too prosperous in the sixteenth century. This would have made them particularly receptive to alternative career opportunities for their offspring in the expanding English world overseas, particularly when the outbreak of the interminable hostilities with Spain in 1585 created obstacles to continuing in their family's accustomed trade. Around 1600, William's son William settled as a merchant at Limerick in Ireland, where there was a significant Exeter element from the 1580s. There the younger William was later joined by his nephew Edmund (from Buckland Monachorum, Devon). Edmund was to marry the daughter of Stephen Sexton, mayor of Limerick, and found the prominent landed Pery family of Limerick, destined to play a very important part in Irish politics in the generation of the Union of 1800 and to acquire several peerages.[10] However, the subject of this study will not be the Pery family of Limerick, descendants of William Pery, bailiff of Exeter in 1578, but rather the Perry family of London, descendants of William's brother Richard, bailiff of Exeter in 1585.

During the years 1575 to 1595 Richard Per(r)y I resided in the heart of Exeter near the cathedral in the parish of St. Petrock, of which he was churchwarden in 1583–1585. Although a bailiff, he was not particularly prosperous; his assessments for 1577–1595 are below the average for his parish.[11] The parish register shows that Richard had nine sons, including Richard (christened 1580), John (1581), and William (1588).[12] Richard the father subsequently moved to the outlying parish of St. Edmund, Exeter, whose registers record his burial (1621) and those of his sons Roger (1618), Edward (1622) and William (1619).[13] The last named's death date makes it possible to avoid confusing him with another relevant William Pery (d. 1637) who appeared in Virginia in 1611, settled on the James River, served in the House of Burgesses and Council and founded a colonial family. It is more likely that the William of Virginia belonged to the Buckland Monachorum family and was only a distant cousin of the Exeter Perys.[14] The two sons of Richard I of Exeter who particularly interest us, the second Richard and John, settled as merchants in

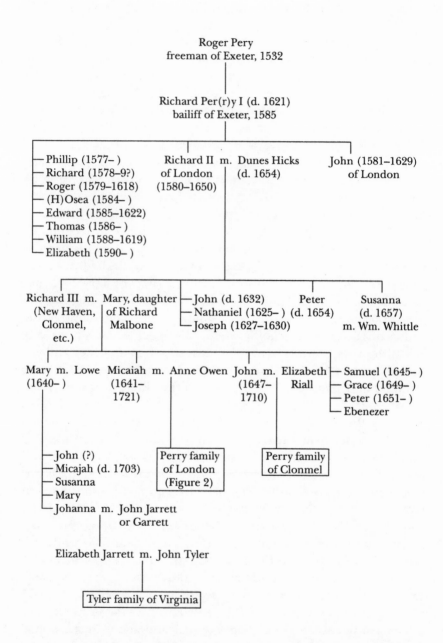

Roger Pery
freeman of Exeter, 1532

Richard Per(r)y I (d. 1621)
bailiff of Exeter, 1585

— Phillip (1577–)
— Richard (1578–9?)
— Roger (1579–1618)
— (H)Osea (1584–)
— Edward (1585–1622)
— Thomas (1586–)
— William (1588–1619)
— Elizabeth (1590–)

Richard II m. Dunes Hicks
of London (d. 1654)
(1580–1650)

John (1581–1629)
of London

Richard III m. Mary, daughter
(New Haven, of Richard
Clonmel, Malbone
etc.)

— John (d. 1632)
— Nathaniel (1625–)
— Joseph (1627–1630)

Peter
(d. 1654)

Susanna
(d. 1657)
m. Wm. Whittle

Mary m. Lowe
(1640–)

Micaiah m. Anne Owen
(1641–
1721)

John m. Elizabeth
(1647– Riall
1710)

— Samuel (1645–)
— Grace (1649–)
— Peter (1651–)
— Ebenezer

— John (?)
— Micajah (d. 1703)
— Susanna
— Mary
— Johanna m. John Jarrett
or Garrett

Perry family
of London
(Figure 2)

Perry family
of Clonmel

Elizabeth Jarrett m. John Tyler

Tyler family of Virginia

Figure 1. Antecedents and Siblings of Micaiah Perry I

London. Richard II had served an apprenticeship at Buckland Monachorum, perhaps in some branch of the local cloth trade. We next pick up his trail in 1611 when he was in Cadiz selling English woollen cloth for London merchants.[15] (His father and his uncle William had been importing "sack" or sherry in Elizabeth's time, so this activity implies a resumption of the Spanish involvement of the family.) Richard II had returned to England by 1615, when he married Dunes Hicks in the parish church of St. Pancras, Soper Lane, London.[16] That same year he was admitted by redemption to the freedom of the Company of Merchant Taylors of which he subsequently became a liveryman (1627), assistant (1643) and warden (1645).[17]

Richard Pery II early became interested in the Virginia Company of London and received at least one small land grant in the colony.[18] A lawsuit preserves the record of a venture of £300 worth of woollen cloth and other goods which he exported to Virginia in partnership with James Carter, a London shipmaster and trader, who went out with the goods only to die in Virginia. When Carter made his will there in 1626, he directed that all the tobacco remaining on hand at the time of his death be consigned for sale to his "kinsmen" Richard and John Pery, merchants of London.[19] Shortly thereafter, John went out to Virginia to look after the affairs of his firm in the colony, presumably including the Carter estate. He also died in Virginia, having first made his will there on 26 June 1628 at Perry's Point near James City with William Pery as witness. He left bequests of twenty shillings to the poor of the parishes of St. Antholins, London, where he resided, and St. Edmunds, Exeter, and the town of Plymouth (suggesting that he had resided there after Exeter). He also left middling bequests to various kinfolk, including the widow of James Carter, his cousin Susanne (née Pery), originally from Plymouth or its vicinity. The residue of his estate went to his brother Richard and children.[20]

After the abolition of the Virginia Company in 1624, Richard II and John Pery and then Richard alone had continued trading to the colony privately—sending out modest shipments of cloth and importing modest amounts of tobacco—at least until 1640.[21] (Around 1644, Richard II signed a petition of "Merchants, Grocers and others dealing for Tobacco.")[22] He resided in the parish of St. Antholins, London, from at least 1621 to 1650. Before moving there, his wife

Dunes (née Hicks) appears to have given birth to his first two sons, Richard III and John, the latter of whom died in 1632. After the move to St. Antholins, she had five additional children, only two of whom lived to maturity: Peter (b. 1621) and Susanna (b. 1623).[23] In 1638, Richard Pery of St. Antholins was rated for taxes at thirty pounds per annum. This put him in the fifteenth percentile of the householders of that middling parish.[24] He was more prosperous than his father, but, in the London context, only a minor merchant.

The religion and politics of Richard Pery II seem relatively middle-of-the-road, though our evidence is thin. He lived in St. Antholins, a very active ultra-Puritan parish (but later more presbyterian than independent), with more endowed "lecturers" than any other parish in London; to support such worthy preaching, Richard contributed in the 1620s to the characteristic Puritan activity, the "Feoffees for the Purchase of Impropriations" (that is, trustees for the acquisition of privately owned rights to tithes or other ecclesiastical income, with concomitant patronage). In the same decade he was involved in both the Virginia Company and the Massachusetts Bay Company. He was indeed elected an "assistant" of the latter company and so named in the charter of 1628 but did not emigrate with most of the others.[25] Although in 1640 he handled remittances of the king's ship money to London for the sheriff of Devon,[26] he nevertheless stayed in London in succeeding years, when many royalists left, and was rewarded by being made an assistant and warden of the Merchant Taylors Company in 1643–1645.[27] In 1648 he had to convince those in authority that he was no longer the London factor of a notorious royalist merchant of Totnes, Devon.[28] That same year he was named by Parliament a commissioner to collect taxes in his ward.[29] A mixed record, indeed.

By contrast, Richard Pery II's son, Richard III, was anything but a trimmer or fence-sitter. His record is ultra-Puritan: he showed the strength of his youthful convictions by emigrating in the late 1630s to New England and participating in the foundation of New Haven. That settlement was planted by a group of London Puritans led by John Davenport, a minister who had given up his benefice in the Laudian church, and Theophilus Eaton, an Eastland merchant of London. Davenport had been one of the original "Feoffees for Impropriations" in 1629, the contributors to which included Richard Pery II and one Richard Malbon(e), a kinsman of Theophilus Eaton and one of the original band that went out with Davenport to Boston in 1637. After less than two years in America, the Davenport group, including Malbon, left Boston and moved to the shores of Long Island Sound in 1639 to found the colony of New Haven. In this they were joined by others then in the Bay colony, including "Richard Perry of Charlestown."[30] We do not have any details of Richard Pery's emigration to Massachusetts Bay, but we do know that about the time of his removal to New Haven in 1639 he married Richard Malbon's daughter Mary. The registers of the First Church in New Haven record the birth of five of their children: Mary (1640); Micaiah (1641); Samuel (1645); John (1647) and Grace (1649).[31]

The maternal grandfather of these children, Richard Malbon, from the first held many positions of responsibility in New Haven Colony, including treasurer, magistrate and captain of the artillery company, though he gave up most of them around 1645 to devote more time to his shipping interests and to his life at sea as captain of a trading vessel.[32] His son-in-law Richard Pery occupied a respected if less prominent and not noticeably affluent place in the new colony and new society of New Haven. In an early list of the seventy persons constituting "all the Freemen of the Courte of Newhaven," he was one of only eighteen designated as "Mr." But a tax list of 1643 put his personal estate at £260, with 38.8 percent of heads of households (47 persons) assessed more. Perry got into trouble with the court several times over his dilatoriness in performing his common guard duties. In 1644 he accepted appointment as clerk of the train bands and was thereby "freed from trayning in respect of his weaknes." He was later elected secretary of the plantation (or colony) for several years. These honors do not seem to have counterbalanced the ill effects of the climate on Richard and his family. At the General Court meeting of 10 March 1646/7, "Richard Perry secretarie had liberty to goe a voiadge for the comfort of his familye." The following February he also gave up his position as clerk of the train band "being otherwise imployde." In November 1647 he sold ninety-two acres of upland and meadow that had been allotted to him, though he still retained his town house and barn; but these too were sold in 1649. We know little of his nonagricultural employments except that he appears to have been a part owner of a vessel, the *Phoenix*.[33] Richard Pery and family were apparently ready to leave the colony by early 1650 but were delayed by responsibilities for the affairs of

Pery's father-in-law Captain Richard Malbon. After Malbon left the colony on business in 1648 or 1649, his estate was attached for debt. Richard Pery stayed another year in the colony to try to get the attachment taken off, but finally left to rejoin his father-in-law in England in 1651 or 1652.[34]

There are hints of considerable tension between Richard Pery II of St. Antholins, London, and his son Richard III of New Haven. When Richard II died in January 1649/50, he left relatively little to his eldest son Richard. According to the custom of London, he bequeathed one-third to his widow Dunes; the one-third that normally would have gone to all the children went only to the children in London, Peter and "Susan," his son Richard having been fully "advanced" by an earlier gift of £250. From the remaining discretionary third, small bequests of forty shillings went to the poor of St. Petrocks and St. Edmunds, Exeter, St. Antholins, London, and Buckland Monachorum, where he had served his apprenticeship, while even smaller amounts went to the clerk, sexton and lecturers of St. Antholins, with the residue going two-fifths to Richard and three-tenths each to Peter and Susan. Nothing was bequeathed to his grandchildren in New Haven.[35]

A year or two after the death of his father, Richard Pery III returned to England where some sort of partial family reconciliation seems to have taken place. When Dunes Pery, widow of Richard II, died in the winter of 1653–1654, she left ten pounds to her son Richard III, five each to his children Mary and Micaiah and two each to his four other children unnamed. Everything else was left to her son Peter and daughter Susanna, with whom she was living.[36] When her son Peter Pery, merchant of St. Antholins, died the next winter, he left the bulk of his estate to his sister Susanna but included five pounds for his brother Richard and two pounds for each of Richard's children.[37] Susanna subsequently married William Whittle, merchant, by whom she had a daughter, Esther, before dying in 1657. By her will, in which she left one hundred pounds to Esther and most of the residue to her husband, she also left numerous small bequests, including ten pounds to her brother Richard and ten each to Richard's seven living children: Micaiah, Samuel, John, Peter, Ebenezer, Mary and Grace.[38]

Thus, these bits of our mosaic suggest that Micaiah Perry was born in New Haven in 1641 and brought back to England when he was about ten years old. In October 1656, when he was fifteen, the records of the Haberdashers Company (one of the great merchant guilds of London) show that Micaiah was bound apprentice to Robert Carter, citizen and haberdasher of London and son of John Carter of Middlewich, Cheshire.[39] It is tempting to think that these Cheshire Carters and the Perrys' Carter cousin in the 1620s, and the later great Carters of Virginia, with whom Perry was to have so much business, were somehow connected. There is, however, no evidence yet to tie them together and we must therefore be content with the reflection that Carter is a fairly common name in England.[40]

When Micaiah Perry was apprenticed in 1656, his father was described as "Richard Perry of Glascow in Scotl[an]d gent."[41] In an urban context, "gentleman" by the second half of the seventeenth century most often implied a rentier or someone following a respectable but middling profession or someone employed in a public post not lofty enough to merit the more honorific "esquire." In fact, Richard Pery III in 1656 was collector of customs and excise at Glasgow (where he had resided since at least 1654) at a salary of £80 per annum—the most highly paid collectorship in Scotland except for that at Leith, which also went to someone with probable New England connnections.[42] Richard Pery would appear to have been a pluralist, holding from 25 March 1656 to 29 September 1657, at a salary of £30 p.a., the further position in the central excise administration of "messenger itinerant for the Country Accompts," working under the Surveyor-General (Samuel Sandford).[43]

We know nothing of any useful political connections Richard Pery III might have had in London, except that his father-in-law Richard Malbon, another returner, became overseer of the Savoy Military Hospital at a salary of £140 p.a. As there is later evidence from the 1690s of a family connection between the Perrys and the family of Richard Hutchinson, Treasurer of the Navy under Cromwell, it is possible that this connection with Richard Hutchinson (who sat on the committee supervising the Savoy Hospital) accounts for the places acquired by both Malbon and Richard Pery.[44] The latter would also have been helped in acquiring his Glasgow collectorship by his access to some other of the returned New England Puritans who occupied prominent places in the administration of Scotland in the 1650s: from Massachusetts, Richard Saltonstall, Jr. (a commissioner of customs and excise in Scotland), and George Downing (scoutmas-

ter-general of the army in Scotland); from Connecticut, George
Fenwick, M.P. (military governor of Edinburgh and Leith); and from
New Haven, Samuel Desborough or Disbrowe, brother of Major-General
John Desborough, Cromwell's brother-in-law. S. Disbrowe and
Saltonstall were from 1652 commissioners for sequestrations (and
customs) in Scotland and, with Fenwick, "Commissioners for Visiting
and Regulating Universities and other Affairs relating to the Ministry
in Scotland." Of the four, the most important was Disbrowe, who had
lived in New Haven colony from 1639 to 1650—when Richard Pery
III also lived there—and whose superior connections made him a
member of Parliament, a member of Cromwell's council in Scotland,
a judge of exchequer, Lord Keeper and ultimately Lord Chancellor
of Scotland.[45]

But the Protectorate did not last forever and Richard Pery's wanderings were not over. Shortly after he disappears from the records
of the central excise establishment in September 1657, we find Richard Pery III in Ireland at Clonmel in county Tipperary, where he
became a merchant and held a minor post in the Cromwellian civic
administration.[46] Clonmel was a regional marketing center at the
juncture of a main north-south road between Dublin and Cork and
a main east-west road between Waterford and Limerick. Roundabout
was pastoral country where cattle were raised for the export markets
in Cork and Waterford. The move from Glasgow to Clonmel might
appear implausible until we recollect that Richard had family connections in Ireland. His cousin William Pery of Limerick spent part
of his time in London, where he had a residence in Stepney. Frequent small bequests from the 1620s through the 1650s suggest that
the Perys of Limerick and the Perys of London remained on close
and cordial terms in these years.[47] Richard III's brother Peter Pery
had been trading to Ireland in the 1640s and was deeply involved in
Irish affairs as London agent for numerous "adventurers" in the
reconquest and settlement of Ireland. As such, Peter was authorized
to "draw" for them when the confiscated lands were distributed.[48]

An even more interesting Irish connection is the one tying the
Perrys to their "kinsmen" the Hutchinsons, a family with conspicuous
branches in Massachusetts, England, and later Ireland. In the 1650s,
Richard Hutchinson (brother of William, the founder of the Massachusetts line) was Treasurer of the Navy under Cromwell. The profits
of this highly remunerative office as well as his earlier mercantile

gains he invested in lands both in England and in Ireland, particularly in county Tipperary. In 1658, Richard Hutchinson leased all his Irish lands for ninety-nine years to his son Edward, newly returned from New England. At about the same time Richard Pery and family moved to Tipperary, settling very close to their Hutchinson cousins. As one of Richard's sons was later to be involved in managing the Hutchinson lands in the county, one may reasonably wonder whether the move of Richard Pery III to Tipperary might have been encouraged by the Hutchinsons. In any event, in generations to come, the Perrys were to join their Hutchinson kinsmen and close neighbors as substantial landowners in the county.[49]

Thus, though the evidence is thin, it does seem to indicate that, ca. 1657–1660, Richard Pery III emigrated to county Tipperary with all his children except Micaiah (already apprenticed in London). In Ireland Richard and his son John appear to have devoted themselves successively to trade, cattle raising and the accumulation of land, which in the late seventeenth century could be acquired on most advantageous terms. In so doing, Richard and John established Tipperary branches of the family that were to last longer than the London branch.[50]

Meanwhile, back in London, Micaiah Perry's apprenticeship terminated at Michaelmas 1663, at the end of its seventh year. Shortly after his ensuing admission to the freedom of the Company,[51] Micaiah Perry of the parish of St. Mary-le-Bow, London, "haberdasher," obtained a license on 20 October 1663 to marry Ann Owen of the parish of St. Swithin, London, spinster. Micaiah said that he was about 23 years old when he was in fact 22; the young lady was "about 24" and, one suspects, did not have any better prospects.[52]

Her father was Dr. Richard Owen, a distinguished orthodox Anglican clergyman who had been deprived of his livings from 1643 but at the Restoration was rewarded with an Oxford D.D., a prebend at St. Paul's and the return of his living of St. Swithin.[53] The formation of such a royalist-establishmentarian alliance implies the rejection by young Micaiah of his New Haven upbringing and all that his father had believed in and still professed.[54]

Micaiah Perry's marriage and conformity to the Church of England was but one of the ways in which members of his family responded to the religious settlement of 1662. If the Restoration restored Dr. Owen to his livings, it had less happy results for Micaiah's

uncle, Samuel Malbon (his mother's brother). Samuel, educated at
Harvard when the families were in America, took an Oxford B.A. in
1651 and in the following years was successively vicar of Hensham,
Essex, and rector of Blofield, Norfolk. In 1660, he was ejected from
the latter living when the old sequestered Anglican rector was restored. Samuel Malbon was forced to emigrate to Amsterdam to serve
an English congregation there.[55] In Ireland, the Perys of Limerick
adhered to the reestablished official church, while the Perrys of
Tipperary, the family of Micaiah's father and brother John, turned
their back on the establishment and helped form a Presbyterian
church in Clonmel, which their descendants continued to support
till at least the latter part of the eighteenth century.[56]

Despite their religious differences, the London and Clonmel Perrys remained in touch with each other and cooperated on land and
other business transactions.[57] Since Dr. Owen had suffered so much
during the Interregnum and had a very large family, he could not
have given his daughter Ann a significant dowry. However, she must
have brought something with her, for, shortly after their marriage,
Micaiah and his wife, using her property, acquired rights to some
land in county Tipperary.[58] This was the beginning of the London
Perrys' interests in Irish lands, which lasted until the 1740s.

2 / The Emergence of Perry & Lane

A most immediate problem facing Micaiah Perry at the end of his apprenticeship in 1663 was earning a living. We do not know precisely when he went into business for himself or what his activities were during 1663–1666. We only know that by 1665 or 1666 he had embarked on the trade with Virginia.[1] We can only speculate about what sort of connections his family might have retained there from his grandfather's trading days in the 1620s and 1630s. The most lasting decision of Micaiah's early trading years was joining in partnership with Thomas Lane, an association that was in existence by 1673 and was to last until Lane's death in 1710.[2]

Micaiah Perry's commercial and obscure antecedents did not prevent him from finding a partner from a distinctly different milieu. Thomas Lane was sprung of the minor gentry, being the younger son of Thomas Lane of Dodford, Northamptonshire, where his family had been established at least since his great-grandfather's time. The family, if not noticeably affluent, was eminently respectable; his grandfather was a pluralist clergyman and his uncle a fellow of Exeter College, Oxford. (One imagines that the partners might have met through the Owens.) Northamptonshire was conspicuous among the counties of England for its numerous resident gentry. Some of them, like the Lanes of Dodford, had large families and it was reportedly very difficult for younger sons to establish themselves on the land in such a socially crowded county. Some younger sons, like the Lanes just mentioned, sought careers in the church; other in trade or colonization. Thomas Lane had an uncle who settled in Barbados and two brothers who settled in Jamaica. Other Northamptonshire gentry houses sent scions as planters to Virginia, including the Washingtons, Ishams and Stones, and the conciliar families of Bernard, Burwell, Lightfoot and Randolph. The Randolph connection was to be particularly important for the young firm of Perry & Lane.[3]

Thomas Lane acquired other connections whose importance is more difficult to assess. In December 1679, still a bachelor at the age of forty, he obtained a license to marry Mary Puckle, spinster and orphan.[4] The new Mrs. Lane came from a family oriented almost as much as the Lanes or Perrys toward the seaborne frontier. One of her brothers was to settle in Jamaica.[5] Her mother was the daughter of Richard Hutchinson, Treasurer of the Navy under Cromwell, and thus of a family whose history freqently touched that of their kinsmen, the Perrys. Her father, Major William Puckle, originally from Norwich, was rewarded for his services to the parliamentary cause by being named a commissioner of excise, 1656–1659.[6] At the Restoration, he lost any further chance of such comfortable provision and had to support himself as a merchant in London in partnership with his brother Thomas. Such employment could not have satisfied him because in 1674 he agreed for £300 p.a. to undertake a special mission of inspection of the East India Company's posts on the east coast of India between Madras and Bengal.[7] He obtained this appointment on the recommendation of Major Robert Thomson, deputy governor of the company, another ex-Cromwellian.[8] Major Thomson had been rewarded for his own military services by appointment as a navy and victualling commissioner in the 1650s, but had two zealot brothers rather more important: Colonel George Thomson, M.P. and member of the Council of State, and Maurice Thomson, erstwhile Virginia merchant and East India interloper but influential political figure and customs commissioner during the same years. (The Thomson family had extensive Virginia connections going back to the 1620s.)[9] Putting these pieces together, we see an "old Cromwellian" network still with some influence in the mid-1670s. The boon to Major William Puckle was not, however, unqualified, for he died in Bengal in October 1676, leaving his daughter, the future Mrs. Lane, an orphan with, one suspects, only a modest dowry.[10]

Perry & Lane started off in the Chesapeake trade on a rather restricted scale. The London port book for 1672 shows only 28,580 lb. of tobacco imported in the name of Thomas Lane and nothing in the name of Micaiah Perry.[11] (Either partner could handle this

Table 1.   The Rise of Perry & Lane, 1672–1697

| | Tobacco Entered at London in the Name of: | | | |
	M. Perry	T. Lane	The firm	Est. value (£)
1672	—	28,580 lb.	[28,580 lb.]	494
1676	132,966 lb.	55,125	[188,091]	2665
1677	86,950	153,975	[240,925]	3664
1686	—	—	1,734,876[a]	27,830
			(2,064,000 w/Cowes)	33,110
1697	—	—	4,723,200[b]	137,760[c]

a. Thomas Lane & Co. in London; Micaiah Perry (& Co.) at Cowes
b. 10,496 hhd. @ 450 lb. ea.
c. Based on high wartime prices prevailing before end of war in September.
Calculation based on "on board" or export prices with all duties deducted.
Sources: 1672: PRO E.190/56/1 and E.190/58/1 (courtesy P. Clemens). 1676: PRO
E.190/64/1. 1677: PRO E.190/68/1 (courtesy P. Clemens). 1686: PRO E.190/143;
E.190/834/9. 1697: London bills of entry (Beinecke Library, Yale). Values in last
column based on prices in Proctor's and Whiston's price-currents in Beinecke Library,
Yale, and Kress Library, Harvard.

customs house business, but it is possible that Perry was overseas
then.) Their rapid progress thereafter is summarized in Table 1. In
1676, the firm was twelfth in the London trade; by 1686, they had
become second, surpassed only by John Jeffreys & Co. With the death
of John Jeffreys in 1688 and the gradual withdrawal from the trade
thereafter by his nephews and heirs, Jeffrey and John Jeffreys, the
way was open for Perry & Lane to move into first place. That is where
they were in 1695–1697 and that is where, after the death of Thomas
Lane, the aged Micaiah Perry still was in 1719.[12] For at least thirty
years preceding his own death in 1721, his place at the head of the
trade was unassailable.

When Perry & Lane were starting out in the 1670s, one of the
leading names in the trade was George Richards. Originally from
Southampton, Richards had served an apprenticeship in London
and was free of the Weavers Company.[13] He was particularly active in
the tobacco import trade where he was second in London in 1672
and 1676 and fourth (in a much bigger trade) in 1686.[14] Richards
died in 1694, leaving £1800 to his daughter Sarah and at least £4000
to his son Phillip. However, Phillip died in April 1695, within a year
of his father, and at least another £1000 went automatically to Sarah,

who no later than 1694 had married Richard Perry IV, the only surviving son of Micaiah Perry. The Perrys would thus appear to have acquired much of the fortune and the business of George Richards in the 1690s.[15] Their firm was reorganized, with Richard Perry IV becoming a partner in what was now correctly called Perry, Lane & Co.

Down to this time Micaiah Perry and Thomas Lane appear to have kept almost all their resources tied up in the business. In 1698 Micaiah Perry was one of the commissioners for the two-million-pound subscription that provided the foundation for the establishment of the New East India Company—but did not actually subscribe himself to that company.[16] Richard Perry IV, however, after his marriage appears to have controlled funds outside the business (presumably his wife's inheritance), part of which he invested in the second subscription to the Bank of England (1697). Soon after, he became a director of that institution, 1699–1701.[17] Both Richard Perry IV alone and the firm of Perry, Lane & Co. had accounts at the Bank which they used in particular to settle bills of exchange and to pay customs duties. They also received frequent regular discount facilities from the Bank and special advances on occasion.[18] Only a handful of the Chesapeake firms of London had accounts and discount facilities at the Bank then; it may well have been a considerable advantage, and it certainly must have been prestigious.

Several minor occurrences suggest something of the distinction and affluence of the firm around 1700. By 1697, as Table 2 indicates, their position at the head of the tobacco trade was undisputed. Between 1690 and 1695 Micaiah Perry had moved up from a respectable tax bracket to the highest in the City.[19] In 1698, as just noted, he was named by the Crown a commissioner for the New East India Company subscription.[20] In 1701 he received armorial bearings from the College of Arms.[21] A map of Virginia was published about this time dedicated to him and bearing his arms.[22] In 1711, the London notary James Puckle (a cousin of Lane's wife) published *The Club*, an amusing collection of aphorisms and the like in the form of a dialogue, which he dedicated to Micaiah and Richard Perry and their late partner, Thomas Lane. The book went through several editions in the author's lifetime. In the last (1723), Puckle repeated the dedication to the partners, now all dead, "Whose Consummate wisdom, Matchless industry, and Perfect honesty, so justly made them

Live Beloved, and Die Lamented." The author further noted that, in the 1680s, the famous merchant Thomas LeGendre of Rouen had been ennobled by Louis XIV in part because he had paid the equivalent of £15,000 in customs—but that, in the years 1698 and 1699 alone, Perry & Lane had paid more than £260,000 in customs. (This is not as great as it might seem; most of the duties on tobacco were refunded if it was re-exported.) And, Puckle asked, "all things necessary for the use and ornament, pleasure and safety of mankind, (food excepted) being exported hence in purchase of Tobacco, to how many Thousand Artificers, Mechanics, Tradesmen, Mariners, &c. must those great Co-partners have afforded livelyhoods"?[23] Despite manifestations of respect, none of the partners ever received (or apparently sought) any municipal recognition.

The golden days of the firm came to an end with the death in 1710 of Thomas Lane. The prosperity of the firm had enabled him to withdraw some capital and he had in 1697 purchased for £6500 an estate in Charwelton parish in his native Northamptonshire, as well as some other land in that county. These holdings secured a £250 p.a. annuity which he left to his widow Mary (née Puckle) together with most of his personal estate (which would have included his share of the capital of the firm). In addition, he left his wife his one-third share in Chester's Quay, to go after her death to Richard Perry in trust for young Micajah Perry III. (The other two-thirds of Chester Quay were then owned by Micaiah I and Richard.) Lane also left his partners Micaiah and Richard Perry £1000 in recognition of the assistance he knew they would give his widow. He also left £100 each to Christ's Hospital, London (also remembered by George Richards) and St. Thomas's Hospital, Southwark, and to the London Workhouse in Bishopsgate Street, plus bequests of £100–200 each to eight named relations. On the death of his wife, his real estate and most of his personal estate (except for £2000, which his wife could dispose of by will) were to go to his nephew Valentine Lane, eldest son of his deceased older brother of the same name, with various reversionary interests to other nephews spelled out. When Lane's widow Mary died in 1727, the Chester Quay share and other parts of the estate she controlled went to her cousin Micajah Perry III. However, all of the Lane kin to whom Thomas's will had given reversionary interests in his Northamptonshire land died without heirs, so that in the end nephew Valentine Lane could leave the land inherited under that will to a Knightly cousin, related to him through his mother. (The Knightlys were a very old Northamptonshire gentry family.) Thus Thomas Lane failed in his efforts to establish a new landed branch of his own family in his native county.[24]

Legislation of 1667 recognized twenty-one legal landing keys or quays on the north bank of the Thames between the Tower of London and London Bridge. The first three of these, located between the Tower and the Customs House Quay and adjacent Wool-Dock, were Brewers Quay (73 feet wide), Chester Quay (51 feet) and Galley Quay (101 feet).[25] Their downriver location and their proximity to the Customs House Quay, where all tobacco had to be landed, made these three quays particularly valuable to tobacco importers. The Perrys by 1727 owned two of the three: Brewers Quay and Chester Quay, with their attached warehouses.[26]

The Perrys, though they lacked the immediate "county" antecedents of Thomas Lane, were not totally oblivious to the attractions of rural land. It will be remembered that after her marriage to Micaiah Perry I, Ann Owen's jointure was in 1667 invested in some land in County Tipperary. In 1683, Cooleagh, part of this land, was sold to Micaiah's brother John for £100.[27] Other land, however, was acquired in Ireland and England. In his will, Micaiah Perry I referred to the lease of the rectory and tithes at Eaton, in Bedfordshire, which he held from Trinity College, Cambridge, as well as the property in Leadenhall Street where the family resided.[28] Richard IV, who had married a wealthier wife, was more heavily involved in real estate. He held Brewers Quay alone, plus other houses in Leadenhall Street, Hatton Gardens and Moorfields, London. He also held property rights via a mortgage on the manor of Little Stanbridge or Stambridge in east Essex, plus some unspecified lands in Sussex burdened with an annuity to some Richards cousins of his wife. (The elder Micaiah had purchased Little Stanbridge in his own name, but mortgaged the property to his son Richard, who apparently had used his wife's money in the mortgage loan.)[29] Since the Brewers Quay property seems to have been more valuable than all the enumerated rural property combined, the wills would suggest that the Perrys remained essentially a City family. However, it is possible that other rural real estate, both in England and Ireland, passed intentionally to the heir at law (eldest son) without being mentioned in wills.

Micaiah Perry I had apparently maintained normal family bonds with his siblings in Ireland despite their possible religious differences. In the 1680s he appears to have helped his brother Peter settle as a merchant in York County, Virginia, making him his attorney (i.e., principal agent) there. For a time in the 1680s there was a firm active in Virginia styled Hill, Perry & Randolph, the partners most likely being Peter Perry and the councillors Edward Hill, Jr., and William Randolph. Since we do not hear any more of Peter Perry after 1694, we must assume that he died about then. Micaiah's older sister Mary had married someone named Lowe in Ireland. By the 1680s she also had emigrated to Virginia with all her children (except her son John). Her daughter Johanna Jarrett is believed to be an ancestor of President John Tyler (see Figure 1.)[30] The most important of Micaiah's Irish siblings was John, who acquired a substantial landed estate in county Tipperary and founded a family (with several branches) seated there until recently.[31] Of the remaining siblings— Samuel, Grace and Ebenezer—we know nothing. All of their generation except Micaiah and John were apparently dead by 1709, for none of the others is mentioned in John's will of 1709 or Micaiah's of 1720.

Micaiah lived to be eighty, surviving his siblings as well as his sons, Micajah II (who died at 22) and Richard, his partner. Richard, who died on 16 April 1720, was survived by two sons and three daughters, seven other children having died before him.[32] He had already provided for his eldest daughter Sarah (1702–1763) on her marriage in 1719 to William Heysham (1691–1727), M.P. for Lancaster, son of William Heysham (1666–1716), M.P. for Lancaster and London. Of an old Lancaster family, the senior William Heysham and his older brother Robert had become major West India merchants of London. To his next daughter, Mary, Richard Perry IV left £3000 in Bank of England stock, and to his youngest daughter, Elizabeth, £1000 in South Sea stock (which would have been worth many times as much in the first half of 1720). His half interest in the partnership with his father went one-third to his older son, Micajah III, one-third to his younger son, Phillip, and one-third to his wife, Sarah. His reversionary rights to the older Micaiah's house in Leadenhall Street he left to Phillip (subject to a life tenancy by his mother) along with the other leasehold properties in Leadenhall Street. His own one-third share in Chester Quay and the third left by Thomas Lane went to Micajah III. All the other real estate he left to his wife for life and then to their elder son Micajah III. The most important piece was Brewers Quay, which then produced £150 p.a. but which was expected to produce perhaps twice as much when the current lease expired in 1728. At that time, the widow Sarah was to give up her one-sixth interest in the firm to her sons Micajah and Phillip. In the meantime the partners together were not to draw more than £60–90 per month "allowance" (£720–1080 p.a.) from the firm.[33]

Less than a year and a half later, old Micaiah died on 1 October 1721 at age eighty.[34] He left his half of the business to his grandsons Micajah III and Phillip but his third of Chester Quay to Micajah only. To his unmarried granddaughters Mary and Elizabeth he left £750 each plus his lease of Eaton in Bedfordshire. Any real estate not

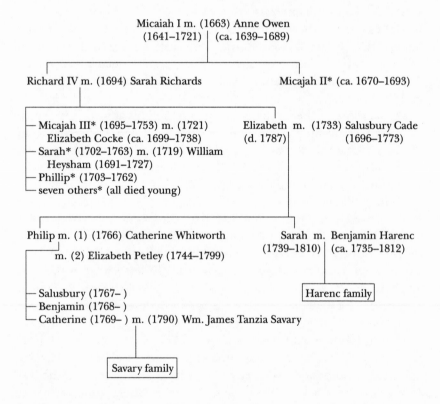

* died without known issue

Figure 2. Descendants of Micaiah Perry I

mentioned in the will, including that in Ireland, would have gone automatically to Micajah III as heir at law. In addition to some minor family bequests, old Micaiah like his partner Lane left £100 each to Christ's Hospital and the London Workhouse.[35]

Micaiah I had been living in the parish of St. Botolph Bishopsgate when his wife Ann died in 1689; she was buried in the church there.[36] Shortly thereafter he moved to Leadenhall Street in the parish of St. Katherine Cree, where he lived for the rest of his life. He asked, though, to be buried next to his wife in St. Botolphs.[37] A few years later the church was pulled down for rebuilding, thus obliterating both their graves. Their son Richard, however, was buried near his seven departed children in St. Katherine Cree Church, where his widow erected a handsome monument which survives (see Figure 2).[38]

On the death of Micaiah Perry I in October 1721, his firm, the largest private tobacco importing business in Britain and perhaps in the world, passed into the hands of his two grandsons: Micajah III, age twenty-six, and Phillip, not yet nineteen.[39] Micajah III had been very active in the firm well before his father's death. About half the firm's customs house entries for 1719 are in his name.[40] In 1721, a few months before his grandfather's death, young Micajah married Elizabeth Cocke, daughter of Richard Cocke, a prosperous London linen draper.[41] But the Perry firm had entered on a new phase.

3 / The Business of the Perry Firm

T he only previous extended work on the Perry firm was an important article by Elizabeth Donnan which appeared in 1931.[1] She was able to uncover relatively little about the family but presented an interesting account of the business, which she described almost entirely in terms of the consignment system. This is understandable in light of the material she used. In fact, most of the surviving correspondence touching the Perrys (including much not used by Donnan) is planter correspondence of the 1720s and 1730s, when the firm was owned and managed by the third generation, Micajah III and Phillip. In that generation the firm can reasonably be described as a house serving planter consigners. However, to acknowledge this is not to say that the firm had been such in the time of their grandfather, founder Micaiah I.

To understand what the business and market might have been like when Micaiah Perry I and Thomas Lane were starting out in the 1670s, one needs first to be reminded of the socio-economic hierarchy of the tobacco growing areas of Virginia and Maryland around 1670–1700. At the bottom of society were the slaves and indentured servants. Their labor produced much of the tobacco but they did not market what they produced. Hence they intruded into the world of Perry & Lane only when the firm ventured into the servant or slave trades. The next social level consisted of tenant farmers, most commonly former indentured servants. They frequently had to raise tobacco to satisfy their rent and taxes (commonly paid in leaf) but normally had a surplus to sell. All of them hoped and many of them eventually succeeded (if they lived long enough) in becoming independent proprietors or smallholders owning their own farms or small plantations, with perhaps a few indentured servants to help them. At a significantly higher level were those middling planters who owned up to twenty slaves. Higher still were the larger planters, owning more than twenty slaves. (One has to wait till after 1713 to find many grandees, or very large planters, owning over 100 slaves.)[2] Within the category of the larger planters was a subset that Paul Clemens has labelled merchant-planters. They were merchants who had succeeded in trade and had invested part of their commercial profits in land and slaves.

One must of course avoid labelling every planter who sold something to another planter as a "merchant-planter." The term is most usefully reserved for persons who appear in the record as merchants but who were conspicuously successful both in trade and as accumulators of land and slaves. Most middling and larger planters, though never thinking of themselves as merchants, had a room or outbuilding on their plantation called the "store"; the term still generally retained its older meaning of a place where supplies were stored or kept until needed. When the lesser neighbors and dependents of these middling and larger planters—particularly their tenants and former servants—urgently needed some supplies, in the absence of any handy peddlers or traders, they had to turn to their bigger neighbors. Such appeals for help with supplies were often satisfied by a friendly sale, thus reinforcing ties of neighborliness and the patron-client relationships that bound together that crude and still unformed society. Thus, among people who were clearly plantation owners, we can find traces of differing levels of trading activities. Some were genuine merchants (Clemens's merchant-planters) interested in shipping and importing and selling wholesale; others conducted primarily retail rural trading operations, modest affairs but undertaken for profit; while still others supplied their neighbors and dependents from time to time as a courtesy or as a fringe activity subordinate to the management of their estates, and did not consider themselves professional traders. As it is frequently difficult to distinguish among the different types of activity, one should pay particular attention to the way the vending planters described themselves in legal documents and the way their neighbors or correspondents addressed them.[3]

English merchants trading to the Chesapeake had to work within the restrictions created by this great range in scale and income of tobacco producers and by their highly dispersed pattern of settlement. There were hardly any towns in the seventeenth century Chesapeake except the "capitals" of Jamestown and St. Mary's City, and they were places of little commercial importance. Early trading ventures to the Chesapeake had often been entrusted to captains and supercargoes who could travel about and seek out business where settlers were to be found. The practice, however, was inefficient in its utilization of ship time and by mid-century had largely yielded to the factor system. The English merchant desiring to trade to the Chesapeake would either by himself or as part of an ad hoc syndicate or "adventure" send out an agent, usually known as a factor, who would sell goods and buy tobacco on the account of his principals, the metropolitan merchants, and receive in return a salary or a commission of ten percent (five percent for selling the trading goods and five percent for buying tobacco).[4] The factor normally rented a room from a planter at a place convenient for keeping his goods; most of his time, however, was spent travelling about, meeting planters, arranging sales and purchases, and related details. He might be at his "store" as seldom as one day a week. Most of the factors appear to have remained in the colony only a few months (like the protagonist of the contemporary humorous poem, "The Sotweed Factor") or at most a few years.[5] But some settled permanently. As members of this last group accumulated a bit of capital of their own, they became the peddlers, country traders and even merchants of the colony. A very few of them might even become the affluent merchant-planters described above. As such, in their dealings with merchants in England they could act more as equals than as employees or dependents.

Some of the larger planters were not satisfied with the local market provided by this motley crew of ship captains, factors, peddlers, country traders and the occasional local merchant. They preferred to ship their tobacco on consignment to a merchant in England, particularly in London or Bristol, to be sold on their account and the proceeds returned to them in goods or available as credits against which they could draw bills of exchange. We can find traces of such consignments as early as the 1650s but available evidence would suggest that the planter consignment trade remained quite secondary to the direct trading mode down to the start of the Nine Years War in 1689. Even as late as 1717, "several Virginia Merchants" of

London (including Micaiah Perry, Richard Perry and William Byrd II, then in London) could submit a memorial to the Board of Trade asserting that "The trade to Virginia is usually carryed on by sending Factors with their goods from Brittain, who had been brought up [in the trade] and understood the different nature of Tobacco: by which means they made return in Exchange for their goods in such sort of Tobacco, as was proper for that Market, for which it was designed. . . ."[6]

Two developments during the 1690s stimulated the hitherto rather minor planter-consignment system. First of all, the war at sea interrupted shipping between the Chesapeake and England, depressing tobacco prices further in the Chesapeake but pushing them up in Europe, where American tobacco became at times quite scarce. The normal spread between American and European prices widened. Trying to get some benefit from this widening gap, more planters ventured on consignments, despite the attendant great risks, doubled freight rates and astronomic rates for insurance (when available) during war years.[7] Second, the war greatly reduced the supply of indentured servants choosing or able to go to the Chesapeake. The resulting labor shortage created an enhanced demand for slaves who from the 1690s were increasingly imported directly from Africa instead of, as heretofore had been more common, from the West India colonies.[8] However, while indentured servants were normally sold for tobacco, slave importers tried wherever possible to sell their cargoes only for money. Since coin was always in short supply in North America, this usually meant bills of exchange. But only merchants and consigning planters could draw bills of exchange on their English correspondents. Other planters needing bills of exchange to buy slaves would have had to try to procure such paper in the local market and could be assured neither of a ready supply nor of an attractive rate of exchange. One could escape this dilemma only by consigning one's tobacco too. Thus, rising demand for slaves gave an additional impetus to the consignment trade after 1689.[9] However, despite its marked growth during the Nine Years War, in volume of tobacco shipped the planter consignment or commission trade never surpassed the direct trades.

At the Virginia end, the scale of these various modes of production and exchange are suggested by several estimates made around 1700 by William Byrd II. "On every River of the Province," he wrote, "there are Men in Number from ten to thirty, who by Trade and Industry have got very compleat Estates [that is, merchant-planters]. These Gentlemen take Care to supply the poorer sort with Goods and Necessaries, and are sure to keep them always in their Debt, and consequently dependant on them. Out of this Number are chosen her Majesty's Council, the Assembly, the Justices and Officers of the Government."[10] (William Byrd II should have known a good bit about this element, for his father was one of them.) As increasing numbers of the more substantial planters came to consign after 1689, they in part liberated themselves from dependence on the plutocratic merchant-planters. Byrd estimated "that there is at least 400 or 500 of the Inhabitants that trade to England [i.e., consign tobacco there] and have Goods & Merchandizes hence."[11] (Including Maryland would perhaps raise his total closer to 1000.) Below them, of course, there remained the many thousands of lesser planters who did not consign but sold their tobacco and bought their needed supplies "in the country." These minor cultivators remained important in the aggregate. Down to the middle of the eighteenth century, they accounted for well over half of tobacco production.[12]

Modes of Operation

This then was the unstable, rapidly changing Chesapeake trade into which Perry & Lane ventured in the late 1660s and 1670s. At that stage of the trade's evolution, the firm could not specialize in the planter consignment business. There simply weren't enough substantial consigning planters then. The scraps of evidence we have suggest that the firm tried every variety of the trade. They reached the smaller planters through the "Sotweed Factor" type of direct trade. They acted as correspondents for independent merchants in the Chesapeake. Finally, when consigning became more common after 1689, they, as the largest (and presumably the safest) house in the trade, attracted a good share of the consigning planters' business. Since no original records of the firm of Perry & Lane have survived, we have to form our picture of their varied business from scraps of evidence that do survive, mostly in the records left behind by lawsuits.

Our earliest bit of evidence concerns the direct trade carried on by the young firm of Perry & Lane in the 1670s. Although they were primarily a Virginia firm they decided then to join with Edward

Bleeke (Bleke, Bleake, Blake), merchant of London, in sending an "adventure" to Maryland entrusted to one Joseph Sayer or Sayres as factor. Sayer not giving satisfaction, they subsequently empowered one Edward Gunnell to take over the adventure. Gunnell and Sayer, working together, rented a room for six months in the "dwelling house" of Jonathan Sibrey "to keep a Store in". (This may well be the earliest surviving recorded use of this phrase.) For the rent of the room and for "dyet washing & lodging" they were to pay 1500 lb. of tobacco for the first two months and 1000 lb. monthly thereafter.[13] The small scale of the operations of a single factor is confirmed by other contemporary examples[14] including another case involving Perry, Lane & Co. In 1693 they sent Edward Bathurst, the brother-in-law of Thomas Lane, out to Maryland with a cargo of "linnens and woolen haberdashery wares shoes stockings" and the like, together worth £334. The disreputable Bathurst later established some sort of commercial liaison with Robert Dunckley, merchant of London, but failed to settle his accounts with Perry, Lane & Co., who had to sue in 1705.[15] The stores of the factors of the 1690s, it is clear, were small affairs, particularly when compared with the much larger Scottish operations after 1740.

We have somewhat more data on the dealings of Perry & Lane with the independent merchants in the Chesapeake—including two of the largest, Robert ("King") Carter and William Byrd I. Almost none of Carter's correspondence has survived for the years before 1720 but we know that he was close to Perry, who had obtained from the proprietor the agency for the Northern Neck of Virginia, which he managed from London while delegating the Virginia end to Robert Carter. This comfortable arrangement lasted until 1713, when the proprietress, Lady Fairfax, took the business away from them and entrusted it to Thomas Corbin, a London merchant with family ties in Virginia, who then delegated the Virginia end to his brother-in-law Edmund Jenings and his nephew Thomas Lee. On Lady Fairfax's death, the trustees of her estate consulted the Perrys and were persuaded to resume the former Perry-Carter connection. (Carter thereafter leased the whole Northern Neck proprietorship for £400–450 sterling p.a.)[16]

In the 1720s, when evidence becomes a bit fuller, we find that the closeness of Carter and the Perrys was commercial as well as political. He consigned to them for sale much tobacco, however acquired, and ordered from them goods both for the use of his plantation and for sale. When Carter received big consignments of slaves from the West Indies to sell on the usual high commission, Perry & Co. acted as his "guarantees" and had to cover any remitted bills of exchange not honored by their addressees.[17] The Perry house was also able to assist Carter with payments for land acquisitions.[18]

William Byrd I could represent the classic merchant-planter.[19] He was a third-generation Virginia merchant, his business having been founded by his grandfather, Thomas Stegge. He continued its original long-distance traffic with Indians to the southward, based on a trading station at the falls of the James River in Henrico County. He later moved his residence downriver to Westover in Charles City County, but kept the trading station at the falls, from which his expeditions ranged several hundred miles to the southward. Byrd had originally inherited from his uncle Thomas Stegge, Jr., 1800 acres, which he had expanded to over 26,000 acres by 1704. He was deputy auditor-general of Virginia from 1687; when his correspondence refers to bills of exchange remitted to or drawn on Perry & Co., it is not always clear whether they were on official or private account. From Perry & Lane he ordered goods suitable for both the Indian trade and the general local trade. To them he remitted, besides bills of exchange and some furs, considerable quantities of tobacco (200–300 hogsheads per year in 1688–1691). He sent another hundred hogsheads during each of those years to Arthur North, who shared his London correspondence. Byrd at that time claimed that he could have sent at least five hundred hogsheads yearly if shipping were not so scarce in wartime. Most of the hogsheads were bought on the open market by Byrd, who constantly complained of the quality of what was offered him, alleging that he had to look at four hundred hogsheads to buy eighty or ninety.

William Byrd was never satisfied with the shipping situation. In the still peaceful summer of 1688, he quarrelled with a ship captain who claimed that he could not break even at the prevailing freight rate of £6 per ton (of four hogsheads). During the war years 1689–1691, Byrd complained that the trade would be ruined by the high wartime freight rates of £16–17 per ton. He frequently recommended that Perry & Lane not confine their shipping business to large London ships that took relatively long to load and were routinely instructed to wait for convoy, but also charter some small West Country vessels that would need little time to take on cargo and could sail as soon as loaded without waiting for "the fleet." He appears to have been advising Perry & Lane to forget about insurance on unconvoyed ventures and divide their risks (that is, self-insure). But Perry & Lane, who wanted their tobacco brought to London, thought that the return voyages of such unconvoyed vessels were too risky and appear not to have accepted Byrd's advice.

In addition to the well-known Robert Carter and William Byrd, Perry & Lane corresponded with a number of other merchants in Virginia who have left only a few faint tracks in the records of lawsuits: Colonel William Wilson (burgess, Elizabeth City County, 1684–1702), Colonel William Leigh (burgess, King and Queen County, 1691–1704), James Wallace and Samuel Wilson, all described as merchants, entrusted Perry & Lane around 1704–1706 with the payment of a bequest;[20] Colonel Samuel Bridger (burgess, Isle of Wight County, 1705–1706) and Edmond Godwin entrusted the firm with the affairs of a ship as well as its cargo.[21] While the suits suggest conflict, other evidence suggests confidence. Captain Christopher Morgan had been a ship's master in the service of Perry & Lane, a part owner of several of the vessels they employed and a small merchant in Virginia on the side. When he retired, he lent £3000 (about two-thirds of his personal estate) on bond to his former employers.[22]

In general we know next to nothing about the various smaller merchants in Virginia and Maryland with whom Perry & Lane appear to have had dealings around 1700. One interesting exception is Robert Anderson, Jr., a small merchant at "the Narrow of Yorke River in New Kent County," whose letterbook for 1698–1715 survives.[23] He was the son of Robert Anderson, Sr., who died in March 1711.[24] The father was most likely a planter, but in the opening years of the letterbook the son appears only as a merchant. His principal correspondents at first were the minor London merchants Cuthbert Jones and Samuel Clarke.[25] Anderson was involved in a "joynt stock" or "joynt account" with them. This apparently did not work out to their mutual satisfaction and in 1701 or 1702 they dissolved the joint venture and corresponded thereafter on the more common commission basis. Jones sent small "cargoes" of goods (not more than a few hundred pounds worth at a time) which Anderson sold, remitting the proceeds in tobacco.[26] Anderson also received in 1702 a similar small cargo from one John Lang (of no known address) to be sold on the usual conditions.[27]

When the war started in 1702, freight rates and other expenses soared. With European goods becoming scarcer in the Chesapeake, Anderson in 1706 invested in some land and slaves and set up a "shoemaking trade," probably one of the many short-lived manufactures we hear about during the war years.[28] The slaves may also have been used to cultivate tobacco, for in 1708 for the first time Anderson sent Jones six hogsheads "of my own."[29] However much or little tobacco Robert Anderson, Jr., was raising in 1708, he must have become something of a landowner and tobacco producer after the death of his father in 1711.[30]

Even before then, Anderson appears a more substantial figure in his letters. Early in 1710 he started to receive consignments of European manufactures, rum and other West Indian goods from John Page, a substantial Virginia merchant-planter who had in 1709 taken his family to England where he settled as a merchant. Anderson was able to sell the goods within Page's price limits and obtain payment in tobacco.[31] But before he could develop this new, most promising correspondence, Page died suddenly, about December 1710, whereupon the firm of Micaiah Perry & Co. assumed responsibility for Page's estate and children. Thus Anderson had to ship the tobacco acquired for Page to Perry & Co. and found himself in correspondence with that now great house, to whom he sent 107 hogsheads of Page tobaccco in 1711 and at least 30 in 1712.[32]

The year 1711 saw the first of a series of crises and failures that hit the London tobacco trade toward the end of Queen Anne's reign. Anderson apparently had reason to question the commercial survivability of Cuthbert Jones[33] and in 1712 began to correspond on a large scale with Richard Lee III of the eminent Virginia family, a partner in the London house of Corbin & Lee, who sent him large cargoes of goods to sell on their account. He had hardly started this new correspondence when he was instructed that Richard Lee was in trouble and was not to hold Page funds.[34] Anderson was therefore rather grateful to have access to Perry & Lane, with whom he began a reciprocal commission correspondence in 1714.[35] Before much could come of this, Anderson himself died in early 1716.[36] His correspondence is, however, a rare insight into the world of the small to middling independent merchants in the Chesapeake at the turn of the eighteenth century, merchants whose business brought them into correspondence with Perry & Lane.

Thus far, I have had almost nothing to say about the planter consignment business of Micaiah Perry & Co. (or its predecessor,

Perry & Lane), though some writers on the subject have described correspondence with planters as the characteristic business of the firm. Instead, the evidence has tended to suggest that, whatever may have happened later, in the lifetime of Micaiah Perry I correspondence with merchants in the colonies and direct trade there via petty factors were more important in the firm's business. Planter consignments did increase after 1689, stimulated by the widened gap between colonial and metropolitan prices during the wars and by the relatively high prices prevailing in Europe during the peace years 1713–1725.[37] As already noted, William Byrd II, writing ca. 1700–1705, had estimated that four or five hundred planters in Virginia sent tobacco to England on their own account and imported goods from thence. Fewer than a hundred of these could have been included among the "great men" on each river (the merchant-planters) whom Byrd described elsewhere.[38] The rest must have been smaller trading planters or pure planters. The activity of such consigning planters (sometimes called "freighters" at the time) was beginning to be felt. In 1706, Cuthbert Jones asked Robert Anderson to get him some of their consignments. Anderson tried, but warned Jones that the desirable consigning planters expected a lot from the merchants to whom they shipped their tobacco. They were not satisfied with the prices for European goods shown on Jones's invoices and noted that comparable goods shipped by others, particularly by Perrys, often came at prices up to 25 percent less. Perry, Lane & Co. were evidently the standard by which others were judged.

Anderson also reminded Jones that it would be necessary to be complaisant and pay bills of exchange drawn by consigning planters even when, by the custom of merchants, one was not strictly obliged to do so.[39] This meant being more indulgent than Perrys. In one case, recorded in a lawsuit, a number of Virginians, following normal practice, drew bills of exchange on Perry, Lane & Co. to pay for the purchase of slaves. Each bill was secured by or drawn against the anticipated value of tobacco shipped by the Virginian drawing the bill to the merchant on whom the bill was drawn. However, in this case, the uninsured ships carrying the tobacco were lost at sea (perhaps to French privateers) and Perry, Lane & Co. refused to pay the uncovered bills. From the deposition of Micaiah Perry it seems evident that he was used to having such bills drawn on him by both planters and merchants.[40]

Data survive of three large blocks of bills of exchange on London drawn and remitted from Virginia between 1695 and 1710. In all three cases, one is immediately impressed by the substantial proportion of such bills drawn on Perry & Lane. The least surprising example is a group of 53 bills from 1702 to 1705 remitted them for the account of the estate of the Rev. Cope Doyley, late rector of Williamsburg. Of these, 22 (41.5 percent) were drawn on Perry & Lane.[41] (In remitting to Perry & Lane, the executor in Virginia may well have preferred buying bills on Perry & Lane, assuming that this would minimize difficulties in collection.) Almost as impressive is the list of bills remitted by John Sheffeild to his partner Thomas Starke in London between 1697 and 1703. The surviving records show that Sheffeild remitted bills from Virginia and Maryland on 38 English houses, including 35 in London. Sheffeild, when still Starke's apprentice, was sent to Maryland to sell goods and collect sums owed there primarily from local traders; subsequently Starke sent Sheffeild several shiploads of slaves to be sold for bills of exchange. Even though Maryland was not the primary area of activity for Perry & Lane, over 17 percent of the bills Sheffeild obtained there were on that firm. However, of the bills (on 32 different addressees) received for the slaves sold (mostly to planters in Virginia), about 31 percent were on Perry & Co.[42] Equally impressive are the lists of bills remitted from Virginia to the Royal African Company, 1703–1708: of 283 bills sent from Virginia during those years, 250 were on London; of these, 76 (30.4 percent) were on Perry & Co.—almost exactly the same percentage as on Starke's slave bills.[43] Such figures are impressive but are only what we we might expect when we remember that in 1697, Perry & Lane accounted for about 25 percent of the tobacco imported into London from Virginia and that the bills on big houses of good reputation should have been more acceptable to the Royal African Company and its agents (who were contractually responsible for collections) than those on relative unknowns. (Bills drawn on houses outside of London were usually unacceptable unless made payable in London.)[44]

It is sometimes argued that the frequency with which the name of Perry & Lane occurs as drawee on Virginia bills implies not only that the firm was important in the trade, but also that the bulk of its business was now coming from planter consigners. The logic of this argument is hardly persuasive. One must remember that most of the relevant evidence comes from slave trade bills and planters buying slaves would draw their own bills (rather than buy) wherever possible. But the slave trade was only a small part of total Chesapeake trade. Moreover, the assumption of such arguments seems to be that bills for any purpose were drawn only by planter consigners. We must remember that bills passed from hand to hand by endorsement, so that planters could remit bills drawn by merchants and merchants remit those drawn by planters. As yet we know very little about most of the people who drew or endorsed bills on Perry & Lane. Micaiah Perry himself had deposed that bills were drawn on him by both merchants and planters.[45] By themselves the surviving slave trade bills of exchange merely confirm the impression drawn from other evidence that Perry & Lane were an imposing presence in the Chesapeake.

Thus, even if it cannot be stated with any certainty exactly what was the share of the planter consignment trade in the total Virginia business of Perry & Lane, the evidence does suggest that such consignments were of increasing importance to the firm after 1690 and were very likely relatively more important to them than to most smaller firms.

Only a handful of letters or accounts survive to cast light on the planter consignment business of Micaiah Perry & Co. before the death of Micaiah I in 1721. The single major exception is the letter-book (starting in 1717) of John Custis IV, prominent planter and the third of his family to serve on Virginia's council.[46] He had married a daughter of Daniel Parke the younger, who had also corresponded with Perry & Co., and thus was continuing an established connection.[47] Custis was a very big York River planter and an atypically astute manager. Between 1717 and 1721 he divided his consignments (ca. 50 hogsheads annually, all to London) between Perrys and Dee & Bell and could draw bills of exchange for £300 or £500 when needed. In his youth Custis had served some sort of clerkship in London and in 1718 reminded his correspondents Dee & Bell, "I was not almost 7 yeares with Mr Perry to know nothing of the Methods of your business."[48] His letters show an unusual mastery of the details of London commerce; he was one of the few planters of his generation who kept a substantial cash balance in the hands of his London correspondents which could be used to pay customs duties early and thereby earn a 7 percent p.a. rebate from the Crown (at a time when the legal rate of interest was five percent).[49] This discount for early

payment of duties was an option only for the superior Virginia to-
baccos suitable for the British home market—the re-exported tobacco drew back all or most of the duty—and Custis was sure that
his shipments were "as good as [any] you will receive . . . this year."
Despite his constant complaining about the poor quality of the goods
sent him and lack of appreciation for the merit of his best York River
tobacco, Custis stuck with the Perrys for decades while dropping
other correspondents, such as Dee & Bell, after only a few years. This
would suggest that one of the shrewdest planters of his generation
at bottom found the services of Perry & Co. satisfactory.[50]

Few other planter correspondents of Micaiah Perry I could have
been as rich or as well connected as Custis. The affairs of the others
have left little record except for an occasional mention in a will or
lawsuit. Since many of them, however, trusted Micaiah Perry I as
executor or trustee, they too—like Custis—must have judged that
they could not do any better.[51]

To summarize, there is no way to establish precisely the relative
share in the business of Micaiah Perry & Co. of the different trading
systems employed by the firm: the factor or direct-trade mode (which
Perry himself agreed was the most common for the trade as a whole);
correspondence with the substantial merchants (or merchant-planters) in the Chesapeake; or the more familiar planter-consignment
commission system. Given the size and rank of the firm, one must
assume that all three modes were important for them. I can therefore
be quantitatively precise on only two topics: for many decades this
firm came first in the London tobacco import trade; and their tobacco came overwhelmingly from Virginia—88 percent in 1697, and
97 percent in 1719. In the former year they entered almost three
times as much tobacco as their nearest London rival and 2.6 times
as much in imports from Virginia. In 1719 their total tobacco imports
were more than twice those of their closest rival while their leaf
imports from Virginia were at least three times those of number two.

The Tasks of a London Trading House

Regardless of the relative importance of the different trading modes
used by Perry & Lane in their traffic to Virginia and Maryland, at
the London end of their business, they had to perform basic functions necessary in all overseas trading houses: mobilize capital; obtain

credit; arrange for shipping and related services; purchase export goods; and sell the tobacco and other returns received from America.

Because no balance sheet of the Perry firm has survived, we are totally in the dark about their capital or stock-in-trade throughout the many decades of their existence. It must have been quite small when they were starting out in the 1660s and 1670s. The very rapid increase in their tobacco import activity between the 1670s and 1690s (Table 1) implies a very substantial and necessary increase in their stock-in-trade over these decades. Most of this probably came from the reinvestment of profits, though Richard Perry IV's marriage to the Richards heiress doubtless brought a significant infusion of outside capital into the firm when most needed in the challenging 1690s.[52]

Most successful businesses of the time supplemented their own capital by long-term borrowing, frequently but not necessarily on bond. Perrys obtained one such £3000 bonded loan from Christopher Morgan, a retired ship captain formerly in their service.[53] Other funds came their way as temporary deposits, including the substantial sums they held as London financial agents of the colony of Virginia. We have already noticed the funds which their rich Virginia planter correspondent, John Custis, left in their hands. Similar private deposits on interest were then and later to come to the house from at least two other notably affluent individuals in the Chesapeake, Robert Carter and Richard Bennett, and from a respectable number of less well-known figures.[54] Though still other deposits may have been left with them by further well-to-do persons in America, it is likely that Perry & Co. were able to borrow more from persons in England (such as Morgan) than from even the most prosperous of their American correspondents. However, in years when the public funds deposited with them were large, the total Virginia deposits may have been larger than their home borrowing.

An import business of their magnitude necessarily made the Perry firm a great user of shipping. In 1719 the house imported tobacco alone on some fifty different vessels.[55] We have no evidence that, in the lifetime of Micaiah Perry I, the firm normally owned or even chartered whole vessels.[56] Instead, they appear to have held shares in many vessels and chartered space as needed. This dispersed their risks at a time when insurance was both difficult to find and expensive. Usually the shipping shares owned (from one-thirty-second to one-sixteenth) were in the names of the individual partners (for example, Micaiah Perry, Richard Perry and Thomas Lane would each own one-thirty-second of a ship); chartering, however, was done in the name of the firm. When the house's partners were the largest shareholders in a vessel, one of them would normally act as ship's husband (or manager). Of course, the firm also received cargoes on vessels which they did not manage. Vessels built and owned in the Chesapeake might also be entrusted to them as agents when such vessels visited London.[57] The name of the firm was inevitably as well known in the High Court of Admiralty as it was at the Customs House.

In the war years after 1689 Perry & Lane seem to have preferred relatively large vessels, including two at 250 tons: the *Pennsylvania Merchant* (built in Pennsylvania), partly owned by them through participation in the fur trading Pennsylvania Company, and the New England–built *Exeter Merchant* of Exeter—a reminder that the Perry family retained some Exeter connections after almost a century.[58] Much more impressive was the 400-ton *America* (Thomas Wilkins, master) with 24 guns and 70 men, for which letters of marque and reprisal were taken out in 1695.[59] Despite the size of the crew, this was probably an armed merchantman and not a career privateer. Almost as impressive are some other vessels in which the firm held shares and for which letters of marque were taken out in the 1690s: *Perry and Lane* (C. Morgan, master), 360 tons, 40 men, no guns(?); *London Merchant* (W. Orton), 300 tons, 40 men, no guns(?); *Culpepper* (J. Wynn), 460 tons, 40 men, 26 guns; and the *Anne and Mary* (R. Tibbott), 200 tons, 40 men, 16 guns.[60] The repeated figure of 40 men is rather suspicious, suggesting a maximum rather than an actual crew size. Even so, the high tonnages and crew sizes suggest that the larger and stronger London firms were able to meet the challenge of French privateers in the 1690s and to extract some benefit from the very high freight rates of that decade and the widened gap between Chesapeake and European tobacco prices. Such vessels could, despite very high insurance rates and large crews, earn something on freight and enable their shippers to earn something selling tobacco.

Closely allied to shipping then and in later years was the provision of insurance. Marine insurance was routinely used in the North American trades later in the eighteenth century, even during the wars of 1739–1763.[61] There is, however, a striking infrequency of references to insurance in the Chesapeake trade during the wars of 1689–1713; even when available, rates were presumably prohibitively high. In at least one well-known case, the executors of a Virginia merchant refused to pay insurance when it apppeared in Perrys' accounts, *temp. Anne*, and were supported by a local jury.[62] With insurance not available, or too expensive or too controversial, Perrys, like others in the trade, were forced to put their primary trust in the great convoys from the Chesapeake characteristic of these years. This meant that their vessels were frequently involved in long and expensive delays in the bay, waiting for the time appointed for the fleet's sailing; at home, Perrys led the London mercantile battalions in a vexatious battle with the outports about the proper timing of the convoys' departures from Britain. We noted above that William Byrd I thought that these long waits for the fleet were uneconomic and suggested to Perrys—to no avail—that they employ smaller vessels and risk them without convoy in a "run" to a western port. The uncertainties and vagaries of convoying also meant that severe shortages of American produce (with very high prices) could develop in the middle of a war, to be succeeded on arrival of a too large convoyed fleet by sudden glut and precipitously lower prices. But even convoys could not guarantee the safe arrival of Perrys' vessels. I have estimated elsewhere that in the war of the 1690s French privateers in an average year captured ten to twenty vessels from the Chesapeake with up to two million pounds of tobacco. In the next war, losses were slightly lower (51 vessels in the Chesapeake trade between 1702 and 1707).[63] Even so, a cluster of uninsured tobacco vessels bound for London was taken at one time by the French, forcing the Perrys to refuse to pay a considerable number of bills of exchange drawn against the lost tobacco.[64] Self-insurance may be attractive in theory but carried a particularly heavy load of risk during the corsair wars of 1689–1713.

After shipping, the most important activity of the firm at the London end was the purchase of goods to be sent out to America, either on the company's own account or on commission for merchants and planters in the Chesapeake. Appendix B lists all the goods which Perry & Lane entered for export at the London Customs House in the year ending Lady Day 1698. As all the outward entries in question were made between December 1697 and March 1697/8, that is, after the end of the Nine Years War in September 1697, this can be considered the activity of a peace year. The list is most impressive, with about 140 varieties of goods. These range in splendor from two coaches and luxurious silks to utility fabrics and common nails. The most valuable single category was English woolens, worth over £6600, but for physical volume we cannot but be impressed by the over 30,000 yards of ozenbrigs and other German linens. Also impressive are the 19,000 lb. of shoes and other wrought leather, the almost 7000 hats and the great variety of groceries and other comestibles, with over 18,000 pieces of glassware and earthenware to help with their consumption. Less expected are the industrial tools and raw materials, including 40 dozen wool-cards (used for carding or combing wool before spinning), smalts (a dye) and other colors and coloring, 2 cwt. of alum (used to fix dyes on fabrics) and 358 lb. of brimstone (which could be used to bleach fabrics). It would appear that even in the 1690s there was more local industry in the Chesapeake than we usually imagine. By contrast, the grindstones, quern stones and plows are much more expected in an agricultural economy.[65]

To the firm, a great challenge came in the range of these 140 different commodities. Price and credit terms demanded much attention, for export goods could normally be purchased on 12–18 months' credit, with a discount of 10 percent p.a. for cash or early payment. We know from the Anderson correspondence cited above that Perry & Lane in this generation had a reputation for buying at very attractive prices.[66] This meant that at least one of the partners had to be good at bargaining with the big wholesale woolendrapers, linendrapers, haberdashers, grocers and ironmongers who between them supplied a large proportion of the goods purchased for export; it also meant that someone in the firm had to examine the "bills of parcels" or "shop-notes" as they came in and make sure that the prices and specifications were as agreed. (The parcels themselves were normally not opened when confidence existed between the seller and buyer.) James Puckle, it will be remembered, had saluted the firm for the great amount of employment its impressive export orders created.[67] It appears that, in the lifetime of Micaiah Perry the elder, such a rapport existed between the firm and its suppliers and guaranteed satisfactory quality and competitive prices on the goods purchased.

The other great commercial task of the firm was, of course, selling the tobacco and other goods that came to them from America. Their tobacco sales fall into three categories. The best Virginia tobacco, particularly that from York River, was sold to local manufacturers and dealers for the home market. The Oronoco tobacco of Maryland and some varieties from northern Virginia were sought out by London merchant-buyers for export to Holland, Germany and the Baltic where such leaf was preferred. The London buyers could be acting on commission for correspondents on the Continent, or could be speculating on their own. Tobacco which could not be sold advantageously in London could be exported by Perrys or any other importing firm on their own account for sale by a merchant-factor abroad, particularly in Rotterdam, Bremen or Hamburg.

In 1686, Perry & Lane imported (as far as we can know) about 84 percent of their tobacco at London and 16 percent at Cowes on the Isle of Wight. The latter was leaf destined for the Continental market; it was entered at Cowes only to satisfy the navigation acts and then immediately reloaded for export, usually to Rotterdam. The tobacco imported at London, however, was intended primarily for the domestic market; Perry & Lane do not appear to have been active exporters at London at this time. As late as 1689, they exported only 1342 lb. of tobacco from London.[68] Many other big importers, particularly George Richards, Samuel Groom, Arthur North and William Paggen (also very active at Cowes) were similarly inactive then as exporters at London. The situation changed during the Nine Years War, when danger from enemy privateers made it quite impractical for any tobacco vessels to leave convoy at Cowes, whose tobacco transit trade after 1689 withered to nothing.[69] This forced the firm to rethink the way they conducted their business.

In the 1690s, with all their tobacco now arriving in London and with their imports growing substantially, Perry & Lane were now in a more precarious position. By 1697, their house accounted for 18.34 percent of the tobacco imported at London from all sources (compared with 12.25 percent in 1686), and almost 25 percent of that imported from Virginia. Thus, their sales were potentially of sufficient volume to influence the market. If they exported some tobacco on their own account, they might well be avoiding depressing their local market. Thus, while Perry & Lane in 1689 had exported (in their own name) only the aforementioned insignificant 1342 lb.

of tobacco (around three hogsheads), in 1690 they exported 79,817 lb. and in 1697, 705,282 lb.(about 90 percent to Rotterdam, the rest to Hamburg, Bremen, Flanders and Spain). This came to almost 15 percent of their importation in 1697, but was in no sense extraordinary.[70] It was, for example, slightly less than the 16 percent of their total imports that the firm re-exported from Cowes in 1686.

When I examined (in the same sources) the activity of the top fifteen tobacco firms in London in 1697 (entering at least 1000 hogsheads each and accounting for almost 60 percent of imports then), I found a discernible pattern. With one exception, the firms importing exclusively or primarily from Maryland re-exported in their own names from 64.8 to 93.6 percent of their imports.[71] This reflected the north European preference for the lighter Oronoco leaf of Maryland. By contrast, the firms importing primarily from Virginia were more varied in their export activity. At one extreme, four of them exported from 58.9 to 79.7 percent of their imports that year—proportions approaching those of the contemporary Maryland houses.[72] At the other extreme were three firms that exported little or none of their tobacco imports.[73] Perry & Lane with re-exports of 14.9 percent were thus between the two extremes of the Virginia houses. The variations in exports by the Perrys and the other Virginia houses can probably be accounted for by two considerations. Firms that imported the superior York River and James River Virginia leaf would find their best market in England and not abroad; while firms that received consignments might believe it advisable to sell their consigned tobacco locally, even to an exporter, rather than ship it to a foreign market not understood by the consigning planters. However, the relatively low percentage of the imports of Perry & Lane re-exported by the house in 1697 would also suggest their caution about such ventures.[74]

Ancillary Activities

Though the business of Micaiah Perry & Co. and predecessor firms was heavily concentrated in the Chesapeake trade, that commerce, when conducted on their scale, inevitably involved them in other trades, though not necessarily of equivalent magnitude. They were not specialists but dabbled—probably fairly frequently—in the trade in indentured servants.[75] There is, however, no record of them engaging in the interloping slave trade to West Africa before 1700. Instead on occasion they contracted with the Royal African Company to take delivery of 50–200 slaves in Virginia, paying for the same with bills of exchange drawn by their agent there on themselves and payable in three installments at two, four and six months after presentation in London.[76] After the interloping slave trade was regularized by legislation of 1698, there is record of their sending only one vessel to the Guinea coast during the years 1702–1712.[77] However, we have already seen that countless slaves purchased by planters in the Chesapeake were paid for by bills of exchange drawn on Perry & Lane and that they guaranteed the bill remittances for the slaves sold by Robert Carter.[78] In this limited sense, the firm could be described as bankers to the slave trade.

Elsewhere in the Atlantic world, the Perry firms had correspondents in Madeira where their outward bound ships could stop for supplies and take on small cargoes of wine for the American colonies.[79] They similarly had correspondents in the West Indies from whom they could order shipments of rum and other West Indian produce to help "assort" the trading stock of their factors and correspondents in the Chesapeake. They also received West Indian sugar consignments at London, particularly from Barbados, Jamaica and St. Kitts, though they never pretended to be a major West Indian house. Even so, they acted as the London representatives of the St. Kitts settlers who acquired French lands after the peace of 1713.[80]

Less obviously connected was their interest in the Indian fur trade. We have already noted Perry & Lane's close connection with William Byrd I, the greatest Indian trader in late seventeenth century Virginia. Of the 251 importers of tobacco in London in 1697, only thirty also imported "skins." Although seven of the top nine tobacco importers (including Perry & Lane) imported skins or furs from Virginia or Maryland, only a scattering of the smaller houses did so.[81] Micaiah Perry had still other interests touching the fur trade at points between New York and South Carolina, either through Perry & Lane or through other ventures of his own.[82] The most conspicuous of these side ventures was a London-based syndicate called the New Pennsylvania Company, whose principal partner he appears to have been. Perry & Co. had other sustantial dealings with Philadelphia merchants, but the activities of this New Pennsylvania Company centered on North Carolina. From the records of some lawsuits involving the company in the North Carolina courts during 1705–1713 we know that they used the factor system there and on at least one occasion had to sue a factor to get him to settle his accounts. The European and West Indian goods sold in that colony were sometimes paid for in fur, but, in dealing with the small settlers in northeast North Carolina, more often in pork.[83] There was then a considerable market for North Carolina pork in the Chesapeake for local consumption and particularly for provisioning homeward bound tobacco vessels. For such ships the North Carolina pork trade filled a function similar to that of the Cork provision trade for outward bound vessels.[84] In Virginia, of course, the North Carolina pork could also be exchanged for tobacco, and some tobacco was shipped from Virginia in the name of the New Pennsylvania Company. Insofar as it supplied either tobacco or provisions for the return voyages of the house's tobacco carriers, Perrys' trade in North Carolina, like that in the West Indies, can be thought of as ancillary or complementary to, rather than competitive with, their Chesapeake trade. Elsewhere in North America, Perry & Co. have left no trace of commercial activity.

Profit and Loss

We now know something about how the business of Perry & Co. was conducted, but how successful were they? How much money did they make? In the absence of any annual accounts of the firm, such questions are virtually impossible to answer unequivocally. We can only make some rough guesses.

The single solid piece of evidence that touches on the profitability of the house is the previously noted provision in Richard Perry's will that his wife and two sons, to whom he was leaving his one-half share in his father's business, should not between them and his father (who held the other half) withdraw from the firm for their living expenses more than £60–90 per month "allowance," or £720–1080 p.a. If this was all the firm was earning, its prosperity, though comfortable, would not appear outstanding. However, other examples indicate that successful and well-run firms tried to retain and reinvest as much of their profit as possible. For example, during 1760–1768, the London Chesapeake firm of James Buchanan & Co. distributed only 23.5 percent of its profits as "allowances" to its partners while reinvesting or adding to their "capital stock" the remaining 76.5 percent.[85] Such a high retention rate was usually necessary because much of the book profit consisted of balances owed by overseas correspondents and thus not immediately available for distribution. The Buchanan example may be extreme, but if the Perry firm retained a less Spartan two-thirds of their book profits, then their total annual earnings in 1719 would have been somewhere between £2160 and £3240; if they retained three-quarters, their earnings then would have been around £2880–4320. A figure in either range is not totally implausible for the years 1697–1719.[86]

The nature, if not necessarily the scale, of earnings of such firms varied with their mode of operation. A London merchant-factor house charged a 2.5 percent commission for selling the American produce sent for sale by their American correspondents (whether planters or merchants) and the same commission for buying and shipping goods ordered by the same colonial "friends." The selling commission, however, earned much more than the buying commission because it was calculated on the total sum involved in a transaction, including the customs duties that might at entry be bonded (rather than paid in cash) and then for the most part cancelled if and when the tobacco was re-exported. Because of this method of calculation and the level of duties, after 1685 an English firm's earnings from commissions on tobacco sales were normally at least 2.5 times as much as earnings from commissions on returns purchased for the same "principals" in the Chesapeake.

The situation was reversed in direct trade. The goods exported in "adventures" to America (commonly purchased on at least twelve months' credit) were normally sold there at retail mark-ups of 100 percent or more—though much less on wholesale transactions. But, to cultivate the firm's customers in the Chesapeake, their factors there had to offer the current local market price for tobacco. In peacetime, this closely followed metropolitan prices, after due allowance was made for transport and related costs. However, when too many vessels were in the Bay at one time looking for cargo, competition could force up the local market price so that tobacco returns might be made at no book profit or even at a book loss. Thus, from an accounting standpoint, the mark-up or profit margin on trade goods sustained the profitability of the direct trading firm. In both modes, there would be losses from uncollectable debts, but these were likely to be more intractable in the direct or retail trade than in the consignment trade.[87]

Given the absence of any accounts of the Perry firm, there is no way to estimate their profits from direct trade. However, one can make a stab at estimating—or guessing—earnings on their commission trade, inasmuch as we know imports, current prices and rates of commission for a few years. To get some idea of the general area of their earnings, I have in Table 2 made an artificial calculation based on the nonfactual assumption that all their trade was on commission. In other words, I asked what would their earnings have been if all their tobacco had come to them on consignment.

In the table, column 1 lists the known tobacco imports by the firm,

Table 2.   Conjectural Reconstruction of Commission Earnings of Micaiah Perry & Co.'s Tobacco Import Trade, 1676–1731

	(1)	(2)	(3)	(4)	(5)	(6)
			2.5%		2.5%	Total hypothetical
	Tobacco imports	Full price (per lb.,	commission on sales	Net price (per lb.,	commission on returns	commission earnings
Year	(lbs.)	in pence)[a]	(£)	in pence)[b]	(£)	(£)
1676	188,091	5	98	2.6	51	149
1677	240,925	5.25	132	2.85	72	204
1686[c]	2,064,000	[8]	1720	3.05	656	2376
1697	4,723,200	10.5	5166	4.2	2066	7232
1719	3,419,000	[9.5]	3383	3.42	1218	4601
1731	1,435,277	7.75	1159	1.67	250	1409

a. Includes all duties (net and assuming bonded). Even if tobacco was reexported and most of the duties were refunded, the commission was calculated on the full price, including duties.

b. From full price (column 2), deduct net duty (1.6d in 1676–1677; 4.15d in 1686; 5d in 1697; 5.28d in 1719 and 1731); freight (1d per lb. in 1697, 0.5d per lb. in other years); and miscellaneous (0.3d per lb.). This suggests the net price received by the Chesapeake consigner and available for "returns" (merchandise ordered), on which the firm charged another 2.5 percent commission (col. 5).

c. Includes activity of firm at both London and Cowes this year.

Sources: Column 1: See Tables 1 and 3. Column 2: 1676–1677: Robert Woolley, *The Prices of Merchandise in London* (1676–1677), in Kress Library, Harvard Business School; 1697: [James] *Whiston's Merchants Weekly Rememberancer of the Current Present-Money-Price of their Goods Ashoar in London* (1697) in Beinecke Library, Yale; *Proctor's Price-Courant* (1697) in Beinecke and PRO C.O.104/178/ 68; 1731: *Proctor's London Price-Courant Reviv'd*, no. 182 [1 July 1731] in BL. Figures in square brackets are estimates only. Other prices generally based on mean between low price for top grade and high price for "middling" grade of York or James River tobacco.

column 2 the known or reasonably estimated prevailing prices (including duties), and column 3 the calculated earnings of a 2.5 percent commission on the sales of such imports at such prices. In column 4, I have deducted from the full price amounts for duties, freight and miscellaneous charges. This subtraction yields the net price available for the purchase of "returns," the merchandise ordered by and shipped to the consigning correspondents in America. Column 5 gives the yield of a 2.5 percent commission on such "returns," while column 6 gives the total commission earned both on tobacco sales (column 3) and purchases of associated goods exported to America (column 5). In addition to this income, the firm would also have had some earnings from its ancillary trades but they were unlikely to have been very large. Moreover, from the gross earnings in column 6 would have been deducted overhead for the counting-house, uninsured losses by hazards of the sea (including enemy privateers) and losses on uncollectable debts. In a strictly commission business, all uninsured losses of cargo at sea would have been borne by the "principals" in America, though the firm or their partners would have had to bear part of the equivalent losses of shipping.

These hypothetical calculations do not yield secure figures for the earnings of the Perry firm in any specific year. They do suggest, though, that earnings for their tobacco business in the vicinity of £5000 p.a. or more were distinctly possible by the 1690s. It was, of course, the reinvestment of such earnings that made possible the very rapid expansion of the firm's activity in the 1680s and 1690s. The earnings figure for 1719 (£4601) is clearly consistent with the figures suggested by Richard Perry's will. Finally, these calculations support the inference derived from James Puckle that the business of the firm was at its zenith in 1697–1699.

4 / The Public Role of Micaiah Perry I

The tobacco import trade at London, like so many other trades, needed some effective structure for collective action even though it possessed no chartered form of organization. In 1685 the nominal import duty on tobacco had been raised from 2d. to 5d. per lb.; by 1704 that duty had reach 6.33d. per lb. There were various deduction from the nominal duty, but, even when all allowances were subtracted, the effective burden of taxation—when the duties were bonded (rather than being paid in cash)—was 4.15d. per lb. in 1685 and 5.28d. in 1704. These were duties of roughly 100 percent at the time of adoption[1] and could be much heavier (over 200 percent) whenever tobacco prices in Europe declined. These very high import duties, almost all drawn back (refunded) at re-exportation, involved the trade in frequent negotiations with the Treasury on the details of payment and bonding. For its part, the Treasury was none too happy about the various stratagems which less upright importers might use to avoid or delay paying the duties. To plug these loopholes, the Treasury frequently found it necessary to obtain from Parliament supplementary legislation altering the rules governing the importation of and the payment of duties on tobacco—such as the clause of 1699 which forbade the importation of bulk or loose tobacco. Between 1689 and 1723 there was an act of Parliament affecting the tobacco trade approximately every other year.[2] In addition, the tobacco merchants of London had frequently to intercede with the secretaries of state, the Privy Council and the new Board of Trade on matters concerning the tobacco colonies of Virginia and Maryland and foreign markets for re-exported tobacco. In wartime they had also to remonstrate most strenuously with the Admiralty about convoys. In the very difficult war years of the 1690s sailings to the American colonies were particularly restricted and each trade given a quota of sailors which it could not exceed.[3]

To handle these difficult negotiations with various branches of government, tobacco importers at London in 1685 or shortly thereafter developed an organization for lobbying. In the 1720s, when we have details of its operation, the importers' association elected a committee of twelve, six from the Virginia trade and six from the Maryland trade. The presiding officer of the committee and association was called the Treasurer. To him was paid a toll of 3d. per hogshead on all tobacco imported at London. On the 57,225 hogsheads imported in 1697, this would have come to £715, enough to pay for stationery, postal charges, a few handbills a year for distribution to members of Parliament, frequent travel to Westminster and back, and perhaps gifts to government clerks and the counsel of a solicitor. Much more important were the unpaid services of members of the committee in appearing before various government boards and in less public lobbying.[4]

There must inevitably have been a great amount of jealousy in the trade between the numerous small importers who were being squeezed out and the relatively few bigger importers who were coming progressively to dominate.[5] The smaller importers might have expressed their resentment by packing the Virginia-Maryland trade committee with their own representatives. We do not know the electoral system used, but in fact we find no such populist politics in the trade. The committee from 1685 down to the American Revolution appears to have been composed of a mixture of leading figures in the trade (the top five importers) and some respected figures from old established firms, less active as importers but still important enough to rank in the top thirty.[6] Among the the first or leading group, some names recur so regularly as to stand out as the recognized spokesmen for the trade. When one scrutinizes the names of committee members that appear on memorials to government authorities or on delegations to various boards, the particular name which appears most consistently in the years between 1689 and 1733 is not surprisingly Micaiah Perry, whether it be the grandfather or the grandson. In these years that name appeared almost religiously in the same position of honor, the upper right-hand corner of the signatures, a position presumably reserved for the Treasurer or head of the trade.

It had not always been so. During the reigns of Charles II and James II, an equivalent leadership role had been performed by John Jeffreys, whom we can trace back in the trade to 1641–1642, and whose prominence therein had been recognized as early as 1660 when he was proposed (as a representative of the Chesapeake trade) for membership on a committee of merchants advising the lords of the committee of council on matters relating to foreign trade.[7] Jeffreys' Brecknockshire family connections were royalist (and later Tory) but he prospered in the Virginia trade both in the Interregnum and after the Restoration.[8] Available data indicate that he was first in the trade in 1672, 1676, 1677, 1679 and 1686, even though he was reported to have lost £20,000 in tobacco during the Great Fire of London.[9] Jeffreys was very much part of the older *gemeinschaftliche* world of great London merchants. He was an alderman (briefly) and auditor of London, a commissioner of lieutenancy for the City as well as master of the Grocers Company. In his last years, John Jeffreys conducted his business in partnership with his two nephews, Jeffrey and John, sons of his brother Watkin (or Walter) of Bailie, Brecknockshire. At his death in 1688, John Jeffreys left his business and most of his estate to these two nephews.[10]

The brothers Jeffrey and John Jeffreys were even more conspicuous in their public roles than their uncle John. They were on the commission of lieutenancy of London (as good Tories) from at least 1690 and Jeffrey later served as sheriff and alderman of London and Colonel of the Yellow Regiment of the Train-bands; he was knighted in 1699 and would have been elected Lord Mayor in 1708 had he not then been terminally ill. Years before, Jeffrey had purchased the substantial property of The Priory at Brecon and thereby established an interest that enabled him to represent that borough in Parliament during 1690–1698 and 1701–1709.[11] His brother and partner John was less active in the public life of London, but was M.P. for Radnorshire (1692–1698), Marlborough (1701–1702, 1705–1708) and Brecknockshire (1702–1705). Sir Jeffrey's son Edward was also M.P. for Marlborough, 1705–1708, and for Brecon, 1709–1713; while John's son John, M.P. for Brecknockshire, 1734–1747, and Dartmouth, 1747–1766, became a professional politician, or what Sir Lewis Namier called a "parliamentary beggar." He obtained the places of Joint Secretary to the Treasury, 1742–1746; Secretary to the

Chancellor of the Exchequer, 1752–1754; Warden of the Mint, 1754–1766; and Deputy Ranger of St. James's Park.[12]

While Sir Jeffrey Jeffreys and his brother John in the 1690s were beginning that course of public involvement that brought to them and their sons so many public honors, they were less inclined to continue their uncle John's intense involvement in the Chesapeake trade. They did not withdraw abruptly from trade but gradually transferred their chief center of interest away from the Chesapeake. Other heirs to firms in the tobacco trade were doing much the same in the war-tossed 1690s. The Jeffreys brothers continued to hold shares in ships, including privateers and other letter of marque ships, some of which traded to the Bay,[13] but imported little tobacco themselves. Their uncle John Jeffreys had been an original member of the Royal African Company, mentioned in its charter, and had served as one of its "assistants" (directors) in 1672–1673 and 1675. His nephews continued this interest with Jeffrey serving as assistant in 1684–1686 and 1692–1698 while John held that office in 1690–1691 and 1693, as did Sir Jeffrey's son Edward in 1702. However, after the interloping trade was legalized, Sir Jeffrey Jeffreys became active as a "separate trader," sending out three slavers on his own in 1702–1704. He was also developing trading interests with Iberia, the Wine Islands and the West Indies, and became a government contractor for victualling the navy in Jamaica, 1692–1694, and for remitting funds to the garrison in New York, 1702–1709.[14] His more passive investments included shares in the old East India Company and in the "Mine Adventure."[15] But his Chesapeake trade soon withered away to nothing. On surviving lists for 1695 and 1697, Jeffrey Jeffreys appears as only the forty-fifth or forty-sixth largest tobacco importer in London. His name is missing from a 1702 list of tobacco bonds due.[16] His fortune did not suffer from this redirection of interest: in 1696, Narcissus Luttrell estimated that he was worth £300,000.[17] The bulk of his estate passed ultimately to his granddaughter Elizabeth, who had married the lawyer Charles Pratt, subsequently first Earl Camden.[18] The Jeffreys name disappeared from London—except for traces on the map in Jeffreys Square in the City and Jeffreys Street in Camden Town, an early nineteenth century development on one of their sometime properties.

With the withdrawal of the Jeffreys brothers from the tobacco trade in the 1690s, the way to the top in that business was left open to men of rather more obscure backgrounds such as Perry and Lane. As head of what was now the most important firm in the North American trade, Micaiah Perry was naturally called upon to occupy the place left vacant by the death of John Jeffreys as public spokesman for the trade. While Jeffreys' royalist and Tory antecedents and connections were most likely helpful in Restoration London, Perry's Whig and even nonconformist connections were no great disadvantage in the post-Revolution capital. But, first and foremost, Perry had to prove himself—and prove himself he did most unquestionably—as an effective but quiet representative of the interests of those who entrusted him with their public concerns, starting with the governments of the tobacco colonies.

Both Virginia and Maryland had export duties on tobacco which were normally paid in sterling bills of exchange. To realize the value of such paper and for other business, the colonies required a financial agent in London. From the 1690s, Micaiah Perry I was such an agent for Virginia and, for shorter periods, for Maryland also. He was on occasion asked to act as political agent for Virginia as well.[19] Such recognition and responsibility, however, did not prevent him from joining with other merchants to protest against colonial measures of which they disapproved. These included laws of North Carolina discriminating against Nonconformists and laws of both Virginia and North Carolina compromising the position of creditors.[20]

Not confining themselves to such obvious colonial trade issues as convoys, customs regulation and debts, Micaiah Perry and his colleagues on the Virginia-Maryland trade committee at London were also prepared to convey to the government their views on matters of considerable political or even diplomatic sensitivity. They saw in the visit of Peter the Great to England an opportunity both to request the English government to use its influence to persuade Peter to permit the use of tobacco in Russia, and to encourage Parliament to end the privileges of the Muscovy Company and open the English trade to Russia. When a group of major figures from the Bank of England and the New East India Company elbowed them aside and obtained from Peter a monopoly of the new Russian tobacco import trade, the Chesapeake traders of London accepted defeat calmly, for they saw a promising market opening up. One-half of the tobacco sent to Russia by the new company was provided by Perry & Lane.

When, however, the new monopolists sent skilled tobacco workers to Russia (seemingly to oblige Peter), Micaiah Perry led the protest which resulted in an order-in-council for the workers' recall. This order-in-council of 1705 can be viewed as the most relevant precedent for the subsequent legislation of 1719 prohibiting the sponsored emigration of British skilled artisans.[21] A few years later, Micaiah Perry conveyed to the Board of Trade the merchants' controversial opinion that tobacco exports to France (in exchange for wine) should be permitted despite the war. In 1709, he was also consulted by the board about the trade's ideas for points to be sought in a future commercial treaty with France. The suggestions of the colonial trades were not incorporated into the subsequent commercial treaty of Utrecht, an omission which helps to explain part of the general hostility of port merchants toward that treaty.[22]

In addition to his public role as colonial agent and spokesman for the trade, Micaiah Perry I performed less public but equally appreciated work as personal agent (financial and political) for important people in the colonies. His firm were "merchants" for Governor Francis Nicholson of Maryland and Virginia, among others.[23] As already noted, he did what he could to advance the careers of his correspondents, obtaining for Robert Carter the agency of the Northern Neck and for William Byrd I the posts of deputy-auditor and receiver-general of Virginia. After Byrd's death, Perry obtained the receiver-generalship for his son, William Byrd II, and (from auditor-general William Blathwayt) the deputy-auditorship for Phillip Ludwell "without any gratification or premium but 2 1/2 p' C[en]t St[erling]." When a post involved custody of public moneys, Perry received and paid the funds remitted to London and was willing and able to stand as surety or bondman for the appointed, including William Byrd I and Governor William Keith of Pennsylvania. Acceptance as surety required the concurrence of the Treasury and thus constituted a form of public recognition as well as the foundation of considerable private obligation to them.

Appointments to Virginia's council of state were successfully solicited by Perry for Robert Carter (1694), John Custis III (1700), William Byrd II (1708), William Cocke (1713) and Nathaniel Harrison (1714). Similar appointments in Maryland were also procured by Perry in 1709–1711 for John Dorsey, Philemon Lloyd and Richard Tilghman. There undoubtedly were other successful patronage intercessions by Perry that have left no trace in the records. That a single councillor, Phillip Ludwell, was reported to be related to six or seven other councillors affords some further sense of how intimately Micajah Perry was associated with the highest circles in the colony, so many of whom he had helped get appointed to the colony's council.[24]

By comparison, neither Micaiah Perry I nor his partner received much public recognition in London from neighbors, fellow citizens or fellow guild members. Their relative neglect here stands in marked contrast to the honor-laden experience of the Jeffreys. Perhaps the politics of the Perrys and Lane were too Whiggish for the mounting Tory sentiment among the lesser voters in London and for the mixed ministries so common under William III and Anne—at least until 1708. Nor did they derive the importance others did from financial services to the government. Micaiah Perry's two million pounds paid in customs apparently counted for much less than the services of the directors of the great moneyed companies.[25] The political situation changed, at least for the moment, under the heavily Whig ministry of 1708–1710. In preparation for the election of 1708, the Whig ministers reconstituted the prestigious lieutenancy of London (the commissioners who exercised within the City the functions of a county lord lieutenant). Among the new names added to the lieutenancy were Micaiah and Richard Perry, as well as Peter Paggen and John Hyde, the next largest tobacco importers in 1697.[26]

Micaiah Perry acquired status of a different sort by charitable activities that made him the collaborator of prominent persons in the establishment of the day. In 1691, the assembly of Virginia named him one of the five persons in England charged with raising money for the intended College of William and Mary. Also on the commission was the bishop of London. (Micaiah Perry contributed to the college and served as receiver of its English income. The Perrys continued to serve the college for three generations.)[27] In 1701–1702, the archbishop of Canterbury, as sponsor of a fund for the relief of Protestant refugees from France, employed Micaiah Perry to remit relief funds to both Ireland and Virginia.[28] Under the Whig ministry of 1708, Micaiah Perry was named to the controversial board of "Commissioners and trustees . . . appointed by her Majesty . . . for the collecting, receiving and disposing of the money to be collected for the subsistence and settlement of the poor Palatines lately arrived in Great Britain." The other commissioners included establishment figures such as White Kennet, dean of Peterborough, and City grandees such as Sir Alexander Cairnes, bart. (one of "the most Wealthy and Eminent Bankers of this City") and Sir Theodore Janssen, knight, director of the Bank of England (1694–1701) and the New East India Company (1698–1709). As a commissioner, Perry was involved in making the contract to settle six hundred of the refugees in North Carolina.[29] He was also employed by the Treasury to remit to New York relief funds for needy Palatines there and missionary funds for the Society for the Propagation of the Gospel in Foreign Parts.[30]

At no time between the mid-1690s and his death in 1721 was anyone likely to deny the leading role of Micaiah Perry I and his firm in the London-Chesapeake trade, indeed in the British-North American trade. But was it really secure? And for how long?

Part II

The Fall of the House of Perry, 1721–1753

5 / The Challenge of the Third Generation

W hen octogenarian Micaiah Perry I died in 1721, his firm, then styled Micaiah Perry & Co., was indisputably the leading tobacco importing firm in London and all Britain—and probably in the world.[1] It had been in business from about 1665 and had enjoyed its leading position from the early 1690s. The old man's role as the acknowledged spokesman of the Chesapeake trade before government agencies and ministers had been almost uniformly recognized during those same same years of market leadership.[2] The crucial problem then facing his firm—and indeed all family firms at equivalent stages of their history—was whether this preeminent and remunerative market position could be passed on from one generation of the family to another.

The transition was made all the more difficult for the Perrys because Richard, Micaiah's only surviving son and partner, had died in April 1720, a year before his father.[3] Thus the business, in default of other partners, passed to Richard's two sons, Micajah III, twenty-six years old, and Phillip, eighteen. They also inherited most of the family's other property, though their mother Sarah (née Richards) had substantial dower rights, and respectable provisions were left to their three sisters, Sarah (wife of William Heysham, M.P. and merchant), Mary and Elizabeth (later to marry Salusbury Cade, a court official).[4]

When Robert Carter, the Virginia councillor, heard of the death of Richard Perry, he wrote to the aged Micaiah, "I heartily condole with you for the loss of your son, so great and good a prop to our trade. The mercy you enjoy in having a grandson to step into his room is beyond compare." But what "King" Carter really thought of the change was expressed more candidly in a letter to his own son John: "The death of Mr. Richard Perry . . . [is] a great loss in the Virginia trade. The old gentleman [Micaiah] holds on, to a wonder; whenever he goes it is much to be feared the young men [Micajah III and Phillip] will never come up to his spirit in business."[5] But it was more than a matter of spirit. In a subsequent letter, Carter explained his reservations further: "I'm afraid the grandson hath not a head calculated to [get] through such a multitude of business with that dexterity that they [the firm] have hitherto done."[6]

That remained to be seen. In the short run, given Phillip's youth, it was inevitable that the business should almost automatically come under the dominant management of the elder brother, Micajah. He appears to have been sent out when in his teens to spend some time as a clerk in a counting-house in Philadelphia and learn something about the colonists and their business ways. On his return to London, young Micajah, perhaps because of his father's illness, early took an active part in the management of the firm. In 1719, about half the firm's Customs House entries were in the name of Micajah Jr.[7] We find little trace of Phillip upon the records in the 1720s except for an occasional signature on a petition from the trade to the government; in the 1730s, though, he handled some of the firm's correspondence.[8]

The Perry firm had outlying trading interest in North Carolina, the West Indies and Madeira,[9] but its primary trade continued to be with the tobacco colonies of Virginia and Maryland. Almost at once there were signs that all was not going well for the firm in this trade. The years between the end of the War of the Spanish Succession in 1713 and 1725 were years of relatively short or static crops and relatively high prices. They were also the years when Scots, particularly Glaswegians, made their first major foray into the trade. Our limited evidence suggests that Scottish shipmasters, supercargoes and factors in the Chesapeake were authorized to pay for tobacco whatever was necessary (in goods or bills) to send their vessels home fully loaded. Partly as a result of this aggressive Scots competition and more obviously as a result of the frequent short crops, English merchants who sent vessels out to solicit consignments but who did not authorize their Chesapeake representatives when necessary to buy tobacco for bills frequently found that their vessels returned without full loads. Merchants so affected complained that the Scots could pay such prices only because they were successful at evading customs. Eventually there was to be something of a customs "crackdown" in Scotland. Before that, however, the entire matter was brought to the attention of the House of Commons, then considering what was to become the Tobacco Act of 1723.[10] A committee of the house heard a considerable delegation of London and Bristol merchants complain of the current state of the trade. Among the complainants was the young Micajah Perry, who informed the committee:

> that his father [Richard], who died in 1719 [actually early 1720], paid, upon the importation of tobacco, to the crown, for duties, from 80,000*l.* to 100,000*l.* per annum; and that he does not now pay above 30,000*l.* per ann. because the North Britons give greater prices in Virginia to his correspondents [consigning planters and merchants] there, than he is capable of rendering them here:
>
> That he sent out 5 ships the last year, none of which came home above half laden, although the last crop but one was greater than had been for these two seven years; and that he lost 1,500*l.* by that voyage: that, the same year, the North-Britons sent out above 51 sail, all of which returned home full-freighted.[11]

This interesting statement suggests a fundamental shift or change of policy in the Perry firm in the early 1720s. In the heyday—ca. 1680–1710—of old Micajah's firm, Perry & Lane, the house used all three of the major organizational modes in the commerce between Britain and the Chesapeake: direct trade, merchant correspondence, and planter consignment.[12] After 1720 or thereabouts, the modes used by the firm became more limited. Previously existing stores were almost certainly discontinued, for there is no longer evidence of stores or factors in the Bay maintained by the Perry concern.[13] There are also fewer traces of correspondence with independent merchants there, though some such connections continued, particularly that with the major trader Richard Bennett of the Maryland Eastern Shore.[14] Instead, the surviving evidence relates overwhelmingly to the firm's correspondence with planters. This makes young Micajah's admission in 1723 that his ships had been coming back half-empty a particularly ominous portent.

One danger for a business concentrating more and more on planters' consignments was the darkening stormcloud of mounting debt. The smaller planters did not attempt much in the way of consignments but most often sold their tobacco and obtained their necessary supplies locally. William Byrd II estimated around 1700 that only about four or five hundred Virginia planters then consigned.[15] The middling planter-consigners could be held on a short credit leash by the Perrys and other great firms, and their bills of exchange could be refused acceptance when not covered by sufficient "effects in hand." But the very greatest planters, whose trade the Perrys were particularly desirous of attracting, required careful handling and often expected and received a considerable degree of credit. The biggest debtors in the Chesapeake were likely to be merchants,[16] but the larger planters may have started out as merchants—or their fathers did—and often extracted credit comparable to that furnished merchants.

Some idea of the volume of credit that the Perrys might extend to a major planter comes from the records of a lawsuit, Lloyd v. Perry. In 1690, John Lloyd, a successful merchant-planter, was the proprietor of a substantial plantation in Richmond County (on the Rappahannock River) in northern Virginia, which he valued at £10,000. He had been dealing with the London firm of George Richards and his son Phillip. When both died in the 1690s, Lloyd transferred his business to Perry & Lane, in part because Richard Perry had married George Richards' daughter Sarah and had in effect taken over the Richards business. In 1694, John Lloyd returned to Britain as a merchant at Liverpool, but eventually retired to a property he had acquired in Denbighshire, North Wales. He left his brother Thomas in charge of his Virginia plantation from which he continued to derive a substantial income. At the time of Phillip Richards' death, the Richards firm owed John Lloyd about £2000. But Lloyd was soon in debt to Perry & Lane and others, most likely because of land purchases in Denbighshire. For whatever reason, Lloyd borrowed from Sarah Kent, a widow, £1000 on a bond for which the Virginia merchants Micaiah Perry and Francis Willis were sureties. Shortly afterward Lloyd gave Perry and Willis a mortgage for £2000 on his Virginia estate to cover both the £1000 bond to Mrs. Kent and a £1000 line of credit his Virginia plantation enjoyed with Perry &

Lane. In fact the sums owed Perry & Lane by Lloyd on the annual accounts regularly exceeded this £1000:[17]

	1706	£1425.
1 Sept.	1709	1472.12.11
14 Feb.	1709/10	1509.14.0
19 July	1711	1720.14.0
18 Sept.	1711	1757.7.5
10 June	1713	1924.5.10
15 May	1714	1624.13.4
8 Nov.	1715	1957.8.2

Perhaps most, although definitely not all, of the larger planters were as debt-prone as John Lloyd. There was a sprinkling of very large planters or planter-merchants who knew how to manage their affairs prudently, and who even let some cash accumulate in the hands of their London correspondents, particularly Perrys[18]—cash which could be used to obtain an attractive discount of 7 percent per annum for the early payment of customs duties on tobacco sold for inland consumption in Britain.[19] Among Perrys' correspondents, the two who most obviously belonged to this prudent category were John Custis and Robert Carter. Both were councillors and among the wealthiest planters in Virginia and both kept balances of several thousand pounds in the hands of Perry & Co. in London. Both expected Perrys to use this money to obtain the discount for the early payment of tobacco duties. Custis, in fact, fretted when any of his fine York River tobacco was sold for export and thereby lost the discount. Custis, who in his youth had spent almost seven years in Perrys' counting-house learning the business, also expected that his London factors would use his cash in their hands to buy goods for him at the cash price (usually at least 10 or 15 percent below the credit price), but he gradually became convinced that Perrys, like Dee & Bell earlier, were buying his goods at the same eighteen months' credit on which they bought goods ordered by "the meanest planter." Both Carter and he came to prefer investing part of their idle balances in Bank of England stock or government annuities and lending the rest to Perrys at 4 percent p.a. Such worthies did not need credit from Perrys.[20]

However, John Custis and Robert Carter were exceptional in Virginia, even in their own families. One of the most complicated imbroglios with which the Perrys had to deal was the estate of Colonel Daniel Parke, a substantial planter and merchant in Virginia who had chosen to leave his family there and return to England in 1697. His abandoned family included his two daughters and ultimate heiresses: Frances, the elder, who subsequently married John Custis, and Lucy, who was to marry William Byrd II. Parke served with distinction in Marlborough's army after 1702 and was rewarded with the governorship of the Leeward Islands in 1705. This proved hardly a boon, for he was killed there in a riot in 1710.

In his will, Parke named Micaiah Perry the elder and Richard Perry as his executors in England and his two sons-in-law as executors in Virginia. They all knew each other quite well, for both the sons-in-law had served clerkships in the Perry counting-house in London: almost seven years in the case of Custis, less than two for Byrd. Parke left a complicated estate with land, effects and debts scattered over England and its colonies. His estate in the West Indies was left to his mistress and his illegitimate child there. Only £1000 of his estate in Britain and Virginia was left to his younger daughter, Lucy Byrd; the residue went to his older daughter, Frances Custis. With this, however, went the obligation to pay all the debts of the estate in England and Virginia. An act of the Virginia legislature was obtained permitting the executors to sell certain lands there to pay these debts. However, the ever prudent John Custis was reluctant to take on the obligation of paying Parke's debts. The rasher, land-proud William Byrd II, for his part, was reluctant to see these family holdings sold. By an agreement between Byrd, Custis and the Perrys, all the Parke lands in Virginia and England were transferred to Byrd, who assumed responsibility for paying all the estate's debts.

Among the Parke debts assumed by Byrd was an item of £2400 owed to Perrys. Other evidence suggests that Perrys lent Byrd additional sums to pay some of the other Parke creditors. Thus Byrd appears to have come out of this settlement owing Perrys something in the range of 4000–6000 pounds sterling.[21] He had hopes of reducing this quickly by the sale of Parke's Hampshire lands (reportedly worth £4000, but burdened with a £2100 mortgage plus interest). In the end the Hampshire lands were to lead to complex litigation and could not be speedily liquidated.[22] When Micajah Perry III came into his inheritance in 1721, he found it very difficult to retain the friendship and custom of William Byrd II and still exert enough pressure on him to get him to reduce the total owed. In 1731, James Bradby, a ship captain in Perry's service, let it be known that Colonel Byrd and Colonel [Mann?] Page (both councillors) each owed Perrys £4000.[23] Byrd did make an effort thereafter to reduce the debt, but it was slow going.

It would be difficult to think of anyone in Virginia who over many decades was closer to the Perry family than William Byrd II. He had lived with them as youth in the 1690s and a generation later his own daughters, during their sojourn in London, lived with Richard Perry and his wife. To him Richard Perry was "Dick" and his son "Mike." Byrd's London diary shows that between 14 December 1717 and 22 November 1721 he dined or supped with one or another of the Perrys over eighty times—not counting numerous tea visits.[24] It is then not surprising that for many years the younger Micajah Perry, like his father and grandfather, was prepared to indulge William Byrd II on his Parke debts as long as interest was paid and as long as Byrd continued to send him tobacco on which the Perry firm earned commission. The debt was relatively safe, for Byrd at his death in 1744 "owned . . . no less than 179,440 acres of the best land in Virginia." Byrd, as a councillor, could also do other favors for the Perrys in the colony. But, when he stopped consigning tobacco to Perrys in the late 1730s, Byrd realized that he had taken a serious step and would have to reduce his debt to them as speedily as possible. Even so, in 1740 (fully thirty years after the death of Parke), Byrd still owed Perrys £1000.[25]

Another famous Virginia family caused trouble to Micajah Perry III much sooner and to much worse effect. The Perry firm—and its predecessor, Perry & Lane—had dealings with William Randolph, colonel, councillor, planter and merchant, going back to 1686. In the 1680s, William Randolph appears to have been for a time partner with Colonel Edward Hill, Jr. (another councillor), and Peter Perry, brother of Micaiah I, in a Virginia firm styled Hill, Perry & Randolph.[26] Colonel William Randolph, for all his success as merchant, planter and politician, apparently never fully mastered the workings of compound interest. In August 1709, William Byrd II, making a social call, found the colonel, his fellow councillor, not at home, but could record that "Mrs. Randolph and I talked of the debt which the Colonel owes to Mr. Perry." The colonel himself raised the matter a

few weeks later and Byrd "promised to be the mediator." Randolph
made much of the fact that in his debt to Perry, "the interest was
twice as much as the principal." But in a letter to Perry & Co., he
recorded his understanding that interest would be charged on his
balance. When the colonel died in 1711, his widow once more appealed to Byrd for his "good offices with Mr. Perry on her behalf,"
but Byrd, whose own debt to Perrys was growing at this time because
of the Parke inheritance, was unable to accomplish much.[27]

When Colonel William Randolph died in 1711, his debt to Perry
& Co. stood at £3259.15s. In his will the colonel provided that his
plantation at Pigeon Swamp, Surry County, should be entrusted
either to his second son, Thomas, or to his fifth son, Henry, then
both unmarried, on condition that the son so entrusted devote the
net income of the plantation to paying off the debt to Perry & Co.
and acquire title to the said property only when the debt was
cleared.[28] We do not know how the sons reacted to this opportunity,
but, over the next few years, William Randolph's executors (his
widow Mary and his sons William and Thomas) were able to reduce
the total owed Perrys to £2465.1s.8d. by 1717. After that they made
no further effort to lower the debt (though they may have paid some
interest to prevent it growing) and old Micaiah let the matter rest.
However, as soon as the old man died in 1721, his grandsons Micajah
and Phillip and their mother Sarah (as executor of her late husband,
Richard) made renewed application to the Randolphs for payment.
When this proved ineffective, they commenced suit in the General
Court of Virginia in April 1722. The court consulted referees familiar
with the trade who reported that, if interest and insurance were
counted, as the three Perrys insisted should be done, then the Randolphs owed the Perrys the £2465.1.8 claimed; but, if "interest on
interest" were deducted, the amount owed dropped to £1324.16.9,
and, if insurance too were deducted, it dropped further to £1112.8.3;
if all interest were disallowed, the Perrys would end up owing the
Randolph estate £80.8.1. The court referred the matter to a jury
which found for the Randolphs by disallowing all sums claimed for
interest and insurance.[29] The Perry executors appealed to the Privy
Council, which in turn consulted merchant referees in London; a
majority reported that the interest and insurance claimed by the
Perrys were "fair and just and agreeable to what is always Charged,
and allowed in Accounts of this nature by the constant usage of

Merchants trading to the Plantations." The Privy Council committee on plantation appeals found for the Perrys and their recommendations were accepted by the Lords Justices in Council on 20 July 1725. The decision was very ill received in Virginia and in July 1726 evoked an address of protest to the king from the two houses of the colony's legislature. The Virginians claimed that it had been their constant practice to recognize automatically claims for interest arising from bonds, mortgages and other specialties but not interest on book debts unless specifically awarded by a jury. The Privy Council judgment stood. Councillor Robert Carter, acting governor of Virginia, in a semi-private letter to the Virginia agent, Peter Leheup, observed: "If the Merchants can wurry us out of our Estates by loading us with interest upon Interest we Shall be in a bad Condition[.] The best remedy will be not to go into their Debts."[30] In Carter's case, this was not sanctimonious cant, for, as noted above, he had a healthy credit balance with Perrys, even if few others did.

A fundamental question involved in the Randolph case was determination of the applicable body of law and custom. Correspondence and consignment were longstanding arrangements among merchants for their mutual benefit. Disputes therefore were generally settled by the "custom of merchants." Planters could utilize such inter-merchant institutions, but, in so doing, placed themselves within the authority of normal mercantile practice. If there was any doubt, the Privy Council here made it clear that disputes would have to be settled by the "custom of merchants" and not by such other criteria as a Virginia jury might choose to find applicable.

The young Perry brothers had then won their case against the Randolph estate, but at a considerable cost. Their grandfather had always cultivated his image as the friend, agent and protector of Virginia. One way or another, he had managed to avoid situations in which his firm would stand alone as the conspicuous antagonist of the tobacco colonies. Much had obviously changed in the few years since their grandfather's death. The name Perry by itself was no longer enough to intimidate the Randolphs or overawe the House of Burgesses of Virginia. Some serious reconstruction of the repute or, as we now say, the image of the firm was needed. Young Micajah's solution was to go into politics and to stand for Parliament.

6 / The Perils of Politics

T he political option marked a fundamental break in the family's observable behavior. With their Nonconformist antecedents, the family were natural Whigs and it was in fact the Whig ministry of 1708 that placed Micaiah I and his son Richard on the lieutenancy of London. In 1713–1717 the elder Micaiah is listed as a member of a Whig club.[1] Nevertheless, during the politically unstable years of 1689–1714, Micaiah the elder was probably not the only businessman who thought it expedient to keep his politics as much to himself as possible, for his American business would frequently make it necessary for him to lobby and petition Tory ministers as well as Whig. In the changed political situation after 1714, the less experienced young Micajah may have thought it less risky to play the political card. Any demonstration of political weight would, he may well have imagined, show the Virginians that he was someone they would do well to respect and cultivate.

After a generation of intense and inconclusive squabbling between Whigs and Tories, the political control of the City of London appeared to have shifted decisively toward the Whigs and ministerialists after the Hanoverian succession. In the City of London parliamentary election of 1715, three Whigs and a moderate Hanoverian Tory defeated four extreme Tories. However, the Tories remained an important outlet for popular dissatisfaction in the City and soon showed increased electoral effectiveness. In the parliamentary election of 1722, all four seats were taken by anti-ministerialists, including two or three Tories. Among the Whigs defeated in this election was a sitting member for the City, Robert Heysham, a West India merchant and mild anti-ministerialist, who died the next year. His nephew and partner, William Heysham the younger, M.P. for Lancaster since 1716, had in 1719 married Sarah, sister of Micajah Perry III, but was to die in April 1727. Thus, the former City friends and followers of Robert Heysham found themselves in the spring of 1727 free to follow the Heyshams' new "connection," Micajah Perry III.

The Walpole ministry took very seriously its political weakness in the City of London. One response was the unpopular London Act of 1725 which gave the Court of Aldermen a veto over the legislative actions of the Tory dominated Court of Common Council, and restricted the franchise somewhat.[2] The ministry also needed stronger parliamentary candidates to support. One of these was Micajah Perry III. Though hitherto politically inactive, he had some assets as a candidate. The Perrys, like the Heyshams, were export merchants and ship managers. That meant that over the years they had given valued business to hundreds of firms among those London tradesmen who sold export goods or ships' stores and gear: drapers, ironmongers, sailmakers, ropemakers, and the like. This commercial benevolence was pointed out most specifically in the preface to the 1723 edition of James Puckle's *The Club,* dedicated to the memory of the deceased Micaiah Perry I, Richard Perry and Thomas Lane (to whose wife, the author, a City notary and man of letters, was related). "All things necessary for the use and ornament of mankind, (food excepted) being exported hence in purchase of Tobacco," Puckle reminded his readers, "to how many Thousand Artificers, Mechanics, Tradesmen, Mariners, &c. must those great Co-partners have afforded Livelyhoods"?[3]

Nevertheless, there is much to suggest that the decision of Micajah Perry to stand for parliament with the support of the pro-ministerial Whigs in the City was taken rather suddenly in the spring of 1727, after the death of William Heysham the younger. Up to then, he hadn't even bothered to take up the freedom of the Haberdashers Company to which he was entitled by patrimony. This lack of interest was to change very suddenly when word reached London of the death in Germany of King George I, necessitating an early parliamentary election.

George I died on 12 June 1727. On the twenty-first, Micajah Perry, not yet a freeman, appeared before the Court of Wardens of the Haberdashers Company and agreed both "to take the clothing [livery] of this Company" and to become one of their assistants. On 7 July he was admitted to the freedom by patrimony and on the fourteenth took his oath as a member of the Court of Assistants.[4] The very next day, his parliamentary candidacy was announced, creating some difficulty for the slate of four aldermen who were already standing as court friends. In the event, by the twenty-fifth the very rich and aged Sir Gilbert Heathcote withdrew in favor of Perry. (Sir Gilbert was returned instead for St. Germans, a Cornish pocket borough of the Eliots made available to supporters of administration.) This game of musical chairs and the speedy advancement of a "new boy" suggest a considerable degree of behind-the-scenes activity. In the ensuing autumn parliamentary election, the City's four seats were divided between two ministerial Whigs (including Perry), one anti-ministerial Whig and one Tory. Perry came in third, ahead of the Tory, a most respectable performance for a novice. In recognition of the honor arising from his election to Parliament, the Haberdashers Company chose him its master in December, allowing him to fine for the privilege of omitting the intermediate grade of warden. The following February, he was also elected an alderman for Aldgate Ward, in which he resided—a lifetime position and a considerable honor for a thirty-three-year-old who had hitherto played little part in the City's civic life.[5]

These various electoral successes were striking honors for Micajah Perry III but ought not be thought of as unparalleled in the politics of the contemporary mercantile community. Successful eighteenth century businessmen very often took an active part in municipal affairs (particularly outside of London) and a good number were sent to the House of Commons: 198 "merchants" (including bankers and brewers) were elected to Parliament between 1715 and 1754, with 59 chosen for the Parliament of 1727 and 57 for that of 1734.[6] There were, however, some unusual features to Micajah's selection. During 1734–1832 the average age of M.P.s on first election to Commons was 34.6 years (or 32.6 years for 1754–1790), ranging from 31.9 years for country gentlemen to over 40 for those in the "commercial interest." Thus, Micajah Perry III, at 32, was noticeably young for a merchant M.P.[7]

Micajah Perry III differed from the other London M.P.s not just in age. In the Parliament of 1727 they included Sir John Eyles, subgovernor of the post-crash South Sea Company and formerly director of both the Bank of England and the East India Company; Sir John Barnard, whose independence was buttressed by a secure income of at least £4000 p.a. from his wine business; and Humphry Parsons, a wealthy Tory brewer who had married into the great Crowley iron family.[8] Alderman Micajah's private affairs were hardly as solidly based as theirs. Nor were his likely motives for getting into Parliament as clear-cut as those of many other merchant members. About three-sevenths of the "merchant" M.P.s sitting between 1715 and 1754 were government contractors or directors of major chartered companies (Bank, United East India, South Sea, Royal African).[9] But Micajah Perry was none of these. Most likely, though, he expected or hoped his election to Parliament would do some good for his none too solid Chesapeake business.

In his first years in Parliament, Micajah Perry, if not an ardent ministerialist, at least avoided any too flagrant break with the Walpole administration. His opposition on the "Spanish depredations" in the West Indies and hostility to the East India Company were only to be expected from a member from a major port. He devoted particular attention to colonial questions and, as agent for Pennsylvania, needed the benevolence of the ministry to get anything done. The peace years between the Treaty of Seville (1729) and the start of the War of the Polish Succession (1733) provided a seemingly calm interlude in which parliamentary time could be found for a variety of colonial questions advanced by one interest or another. In 1730, there was the act permitting the direct export of rice from Carolina to southern Europe, as well as the law for the direct importation of European salt into New York. In 1731 there was an act for the importation of nonenumerated plantation goods into Ireland. In 1732 there was an "act for the encouragement of the growth of coffee in America" and, in 1733, the famous Molasses Act.[10]

Micajah Perry was involved in the parliamentary progress of a few, if not the most important, of these measures. In 1727, even before his election to Commons, to encourage the local fisheries he helped obtain an act (13 Geo. I c. 5) permitting the importation of European salt into Pennsylvania, the colony for which he was then acting as agent.[11] Once in the house, he served in 1730 as committee chairman and rapporteur for another salt act (3 Geo. II c. 12) for New York, though the New York agent, Peter Leheup, an influential Treasury clerk, claimed credit for its enactment. In 1731 Perry tried unsuccessfully to get a similar act passed for Virginia.[12] In 1729, however, working with Virginia's special agent, John Randolph, he

was able to obtain an act repealing a clause in the Tobacco Act of
1723 prohibiting the importation into Britain of parts of tobacco leaf
stripped from the stalk. (The planters wanted the freedom to strip
in order to save weight and freight on certain grades of tobacco.)[13]
In addition, Perry was on the drafting or select committees for the
Carolina rice and colonial hats bills, though he does not appear to
have been a prime mover in either.[14] His role in the Jamaica coffee
bill was more important but that ended up a government measure.[15]

Perry, at least, thought that his legislative record was impressive
and was perhaps a little annoyed that the world did not pay more
attention to it. He felt that he alone had defended the interests of
the continental colonies when the first sugar bill was under consideration in 1731. He wrote to Cadwallader Colden, a New York merchant and old acquaintance from the days when both appear to have
been young clerks in Philadelphia: "it was a good deal of surprize to
me to find no advocate in the House of Commons for the Continent
but my self, & I very unequal to such a task." Even so, he was able in
debate to show from the records of his own firm that, both in taxes
paid and in exports, the continental colonies were much more important to the mother country than the West Indian lobby would
admit. He continued his defense of the continental colonies during
the later debate on what became the Molasses Act of 1733—but to
much less effect.[16]

To impress his important "friends" in Virginia, Alderman Perry
not only had to be an effective legislative lobbyist but also had to
show them that he had influence in patronage questions, an area
where his quieter grandfather was noticeably successful. Here he had
various new obstacles to circumvent, not the least of them Peter
Leheup, the pluralist Treasury clerk and agent for Virginia and other
colonies, who was also connected by marriage to Horatio Walpole,
secretary to the Treasury (to 1730), Auditor-General of Plantation
Revenues and brother of the prime minister, Sir Robert Walpole. The
lieutenant governor of Virginia, William Gooch, also came from the
Walpoles' home county, Norfolk, and was the brother of Dr. Thomas
Gooch, an influential cleric, master of Gonville and Caius College,
Cambridge and later to be successively bishop of Bristol, Norwich
and Ely.[17] Governor Gooch thus had many channels through which
to make clear his own preferences in appointments besides the
authorized ones through the secretary of state and the Board of

Trade. Perry had enough influence to get someone appointed Surveyor of Houses in Lancashire,[18] but apparently not enough to override that of Governor Gooch and Peter Leheup on appointments to Virginia places. In 1731–1732, with the concurrence of Governor Gooch, he was able to obtain the appointment to the Virginia council of John Tayloe, a great Rappahannock planter.[19] However, a few months later, the alderman's comparative political insignificance was made particularly clear in an anecdote relayed to Gooch by the visiting captain of a man-of-war with friends in the Treasury: "[Perry] goes one morning into the Treasury, fell into discourse with Mr. Leheup about the appointment of a Councillor for Virginia, and finding it was not like to be as he would have had it, flew into a great Passion, said you [Governor Gooch] had deceived him in the recommendation . . . and that he would have you out of your Government upon which Leheup, Mr. Christopher Lowe and the rest of the Clerks in the office, sett up an Horse laugh at him, telling him it was not in his Power, so away he went."[20]

The limited political effectiveness of Micajah Perry, M.P., was in marked contrast to that of his grandfather, who had never held public office. We know of at least five Virginia councillors whose selection was advanced by the efforts of Micaiah I between 1699 and 1714, as well as three others in Maryland.[21] Micajah III doesn't appear to have tried as hard. Between 1704 and 1713, Micaiah I appeared before the Board of Trade fifty times; between 1723 and 1731, Micajah III appeared there only nine times, and never thereafter.[22]

Within the London community of merchants trading to Virginia, Perry's prestige appears quite high during 1721–1734, partly because of the longstanding leading role of his firm, more obviously because of his position as a member of Parliament and an alderman. When the association of merchants in these trades was revived in the mid-1720s, Perry was named Treasurer or head of the trade, the person to whom was entrusted the voluntary fund of 3d per hogshead which the trade assessed itself for political lobbying. This "honor" was not an unmixed blessing, for tobacco prices were declining in the late 1720s and some people in Virginia and Maryland thought that part of the trouble was the excessive market power of the purchasing agent of the French tobacco monopoly and the failure of the trade's own organization to obtain better prices from him. Since Perry among others was known to sell to the French agent for ready cash, his prominent role in the association attracted undesirable attention, particularly in the Maryland press.[23]

Even so, Perry appears to have been treated with considerable respect by his American correspondents in the years immediately following his election to Parliament in 1727. Compared with what was to come later, the surviving correspondence for these years—with Byrd, Carter and Custis in particular—is noticeably civil. This politeness should not, however, lead one to surmise that all was going well in the tobacco consignment business of Micajah & Phillip Perry. The limited hard data on the firm's tobacco imports, assembled in Table 3, suggest that the Perry business peaked in the late 1690s, when, according to Puckle, the firm paid the Crown £260,000 in customs during 1698 and 1699.[24] In 1719, the firm was still first in the London tobacco import trade (and hence first in the kingdom) but was no longer so dominant. In 1697, the house accounted for 18.34 percent of all tobacco imported into London; in 1719, though still in first place, their share was only about 15 percent. After the death of old Micajah in 1721, the slippage accelerated. By 1732 the

Table 3.   The Tobacco Imports of Perry & Co., 1697–1732

Year	Hogsheads	Pounds Weight
1697	10,496	4,723,200 (est.)[a]
1719	—	3,419,000 (est.)[b]
1729	1,656	1,293,435
1730	1,598	1,191,906
1731	1,836	1,435,277
1732	1,506	1,219,683

a. The number of hogsheads shown in the source has been multiplied by 450 (the average weight of a hogshead at this time) to obtain the estimated pounds weight.

b. The 1719 source shows tobacco imports for Perry & Co. that year of only 2,719,529 lb. However, as this port book is very likely defective, this figure has been corrected. The book's principal defect is the omission by a careless clerk of whole days scattered through the year, though rather more frequent in the second half. For tobacco, this means that the total pounds shown in the book as imported in 1719 are about 20 percent less than the London totals for the same years in the Ledger of the Inspector-General of Exports and Imports (PRO Customs 3). This omission is compensated for in the estimate shown.

Sources: 1697: printed bills of entry, Beinecke Library, Yale University; 1719: Leeds City Library (Sheepscar Branch), Archives Department, Newby Hall MSS., NH 2440, (London Waiters') Port Book, 1719; 1729–1732: Cambridge University Library, Cholmondeley (Houghton) MSS. 29/29(3).

firm was importing only 36 percent as much as in 1719 or 26 percent as much as in 1697. Its earnings shrank even more, for tobacco prices in 1726–1739 were considerably lower than in 1697–1725. The estimates in Table 2 show hypothetical commission earnings in 1731 at only about 20 percent those of 1697. Under the circumstances, one is not surprised to find that by 1729–1731 the house had dropped from first to fourth place in the London tobacco import trade (Table 4).[25]

This decline in the firm's import business and earnings at the very least checked the growth of the house's capital; when combined with the difficulty of collecting debts from Chesapeake planters, it should also have led to serious cash flow problems. To satisfy the firm's liquidity needs (and perhaps the family's needs for dowries as well), Alderman Perry and his mother, Sarah, were evidently forced to sell some—probably most—of the real estate accumulated by Micaiah I and his son Richard IV from the 1690s. We do not have full data on their real estate holdings and transactions but the pattern after 1730 is clear. In that year, Micajah III and his mother made two substantial sales: for £887 they sold a group of eight small structures on Petticoat Lane near the corner of Stony Lane (on the City's eastern boundary); and for £2813 they disposed of a more valuable group of properties immediately to the west along Stony Lane and Gravel Lane, including "that Great Warehouse or Storehouse commonly called the Tobacco Warehouse" and several other "Great Warehouses

Table 4. Some Leading London Tobacco Importers, 1729, 1731 (two years combined)

Name	Hogsheads imported	Pounds wt. (000's)	Rank 1719
John Hyde & Co.	8845	6,342	5
John Hanbury	6447	4,332	—
Joseph Adams	4611	3,209	32
Micajah & Phillip Perry	3492	2,729	1
William Black	2917	1,590	—
Robert Crookshanks	2371	1,591	33
John Peele	1653	1,012	—

Source: Cambridge University Library, Cholmondeley (Houghton) MSS. 29/12, 29/29(3).

or Sugar houses."[26] With the decline in the firm's import activity, there was obviously less need for warehouse space. In 1734 Micajah found it necessary to sell the larger of his two residences at Epsom, a house stately enough to be rented for a time to the earl of Galloway. An even greater shadow was cast upon the firm's prestige when in 1735 for £9500 he sold Chester's Quay by the Tower of London with the abutting Pretty's Quay, together with their warehouses, cranes and other appurtenances.[27] By 1744, his principal Irish landholdings in County Tipperary and his remaining Epsom property were to go too.[28] Long before that, the direction in which his fortunes were moving was all too clear.

As his business withered away in the 1720s, Micajah Perry was pulled in different directions by the conflicting imperatives of his various political and business careers. Down to 1732 he avoided an extreme break with the government. A rupture with his friends in Virginia could not be postponed as long.

Perry's position was made more difficult by the decline in European tobacco prices after 1725,[29] evidently caused by production rising much more rapidly than demand, particularly during 1725–1739. Underlying this rise in production was the growth in the Chesapeake during these same years of rural population, both slave and free. The higher prices of 1713–1725 had enabled planters to buy more slaves and, as the children of these slaves came of working age, their labor recreated the problem of overproduction after 1725.[30] Since the reduction of cultivation through "stint" acts proved unenforceable, Governor Gooch pushed instead for compulsory inspection, which the Virginia legislature adopted in their Tobacco Act of 1730. Inspectors were to destroy all tobacco they considered below a certain minimum quality, thus reducing the quantity and raising the reputation of the Virginia produce reaching the market. The English consignment merchants were for the most part hostile to this act because it would reduce their earnings from both freight and commissions. Perry persuaded the customs commissioners to make a hostile report on the Virginia act, but the colony's agent, the more adroit Peter Leheup, interceded with the Board of Trade (and perhaps others) and the law was not disallowed.[31] Perry's unsuccessful opposition, so narrowly based on the earnings potential of his own business, could not have endeared him to the Virginians. It made all too evident his apparent acceptance of the impossibility of reconciling his own interests with those of the tobacco planters.

Even more damaging was the fierce dispute over debt legislation. This was long a most sensitive issue in the colonies. In 1716–1718, the Virginia merchants of London (led by old Micaiah) had obtained disallowance by the Crown of a Virginia act of 1663 which made it almost impossible for a British creditor to use the local courts to collect from a debtor who had moved to that colony.[32] When Gooch was appointed governor in 1727, he received the standard instructions to ask the legislature for a law "whereby the creditors of persons becoming bankrupt in Great Britain and having estates in our . . . [overseas] provinces" may collect the debts owing to the bankrupt. The Virginians thought such a law unnecessary but, as a slight concession, passed a law in 1728 weakening previous legislation declaring slaves to be real property for certain purposes, hence more difficult to use for paying debts.[33] The merchants, led of course by Micajah III (so recently aggrieved by the Randolph case), then took the initiative and complained to the Board of Trade against a Virginia act of 1705 that provided time limits within which suits could be brought for sums owing on judgment, bond, note, bill, or open account (book debts). On advice of counsel and the Board of Trade, the Crown in 1731 disallowed the 1705 Virginia act on the grounds that it was contrary to an English act of 21 James I, by which rights created by judgment or bond were unlimited in time. This disallowance created new problems, for there were other noncontroversial clauses in the 1705 act which were thereby disallowed too, including one establishing a procedure whereby a British creditor could prove his claims in Virginia courts by sending over a certificate sworn before two magistrates in the place of his residence.

Angered by the subsequent failure of the Virginia legislature to reenact this desirable clause (as recommended by Gooch), the Virginia merchants of London joined with their neighbors trading to Jamaica, and with similar merchants in Bristol, to petition the king on the debt problem. On reference, the Board of Trade recommended new legislation by Parliament and more explicit instructions to governors not to consent to colonial legislation discriminating against British residents. The lobbying challenge was taken up by merchant delegations from London, Bristol and Liverpool, who made their grievances clear to the House of Commons. Although the resulting measure affected all the colonies in North America and the West Indies, only Virginia and Jamaica appear to have been discussed in Parliament and only Virginia petitioned against it, sending over

Isham Randolph to argue their case. (He was a son of the late Colonel William Randolph whose debts had given the Perrys so much trouble just a few years before.) On the merchants' side, it was Micajah Perry who from the first took the lead in pushing for the bill which was in fact drafted by himself and John Scrope, secretary to the Treasury (and from a Bristol merchant family).

By the resulting Colonial Debts Act of 1732, British creditors could thenceforth prove their claims in colonial courts by taking an oath before any "chief magistrate" in Great Britain; and the land, houses, chattels, and slaves of debtors in the American colonies became liable for the satisfaction of debts "in the like manner as Real Estates are by the Law of *England* liable to the Satisfaction of Debts due by Bond or other Specialty." (This appeared to mean that real estate and slaves in the colonies were liable for debts as if secured by bond or other specialty, even though they were not in fact so secured.) The second provision was particularly offensive to the Virginians even though their own acts of 1705 and 1728 theoretically let slaves be seized for debts. Very likely it was the comprehensiveness and procedural simplicity of the British act of 1732 that seemed threatening to the bigger planter–slave owners.[34] Of Alderman Perry's central role in procuring the act they could have had no doubts.

The excitement and anger over the Colonial Debts Act of 1732 were to prove but curtain-raisers for Micajah Perry's greatest hour, the excise crisis of 1733. For at least twenty years the Treasury and the Chesapeake trade had been considering various warehousing proposals under which imported tobacco would be placed in the king's warehouse (without bonding or paying duty) until either re-exported or removed for internal consumption with full duty paid. In 1731–1732, the Treasury, disappointed with the current yields of the rather high taxes on tobacco, decided to seek legislation combining such a warehouse arrangement with the transfer of tobacco taxation from Customs to Excise. The Excise commissioners (who collected many indirect duties, including those on beer and spirits) had agents in all parts of the country with search powers broader than those available to Customs. Thousands of small manufacturers and retailers all over the country had been upset by the extension of Excise's authority to coffee and chocolate in 1724 and were quite hostile to any further expansion. The big tobacco consignment merchants were more disturbed by the warehouse provisions, which would cut into their commission earnings. Merchants or factors receiving tobacco consignments charged their 2.5 percent commission on the full sale price of the tobacco including duties, whether the duties were paid in cash or bonded, even when the unpaid bonds were cancelled on the re-export of the tobacco. Under a warehouse scheme, with no duties to be paid or bonded on the two-thirds or more of imported tobacco ultimately re-exported, their commissions would be substantially reduced. The consignment merchants or factors, of course, realized that their threatened commissions aroused little sympathy in the political nation. Therefore, their propaganda and that of their allies, Walpole's political foes, stressed the grievances and fears of the smaller manufacturers and retailers.

The excise scheme was concocted at the Treasury in 1731 and confidentially sent out to Virginia—almost certainly by Leheup—where it was considered by the council in December 1731. When it was ascertained that the colonial council was sympathetic, London asked for a formal address to the king and petition to the House of Commons from the council and House of Burgesses of Virginia requesting such a transfer of tobacco duties from Customs to Excise. By June 1732 the Virginia bodies were all the readier to cooperate because they had just received word of the passage of the distasteful Colonial Debts Act. Thus, by the spring of that year, well-informed people on both sides of the Atlantic knew about the excise proposal and those whose interests were involved had a year to plan their tactics.[35]

The Virginia petitions were brought to London in the fall of 1732 by John Randolph (soon knighted), the attorney-general of Virginia and another son of Colonel William Randolph, the memory of whose debt history continued to haunt the Perrys. The emerging excise scheme forced Micajah Perry to break decisively with the ministry with whom he had only recently been able to cooperate in the drafting of the Debts Act of 1732. Starting in January 1733, however, he was in the thick of the meetings, petitions and demonstrations against the excise scheme proposed for wine and tobacco. His great hour came when the bill was finally introduced and debated in the House of Commons. After the prime minister, Sir Robert Walpole, introduced the idea on 14 March in a committee of the whole, the principal speech for the opposition to the scheme came from Alderman Micajah Perry. Again on 4 April Perry made a major speech against the bill. Meanwhile, from the beginning of the year, the more literate of the parliamentary and other political opponents of the regime, led by Pulteney and Bolingbroke, had been busy writing articles and pamphlets against the proposal. Working with less publicity, the various committees of merchants, tobacco manufacturers and vintners were busy both distributing these writings and corresponding with their hundreds or thousands of business connections all over the country, urging their provincial friends to write in opposition to the bill to members of Parliament. No great number of Walpole's normal Commons supporters deserted to the opposition on this issue, but enough of them absented themselves (at a time when the opposition was very successful in getting their most irregular followers to attend) to shrink Walpole's majority dangerously and induce him to abandon the excise bill on 11 April.[36]

Perry's political career was at its zenith. In 1734 he was triumphantly reelected to Parliament by London as an anti-ministerialist. He was to be chosen sheriff of London, 1734–1735; lord mayor, 1738–1739; and colonel of the city's Orange Regiment, 1738–1745.[37] But there were to be other, sourer acknowledgements of his success in thwarting Sir Robert over the excise. Tobacco merchants dealt in a very heavily taxed commodity and thus were liable to very close fiscal supervision. In 1723 Perry and a number of other leading London tobacco merchants (William Dawkins, Robert Cary and James Bradley) had sold substantial quantities of tobacco to three obscure traders (Richard Corbett, J. C. Desmadril and Nicholas French) allegedly for export to Cadiz and Bayonne. It was later established that the leaf had instead been illegally relanded in Ireland. In 1733, shortly after Walpole's retreat on excise, new information suddenly came into the possession of Customs about this old case and suit was begun in the Court of the Exchequer for recovery of the drawbacks of duties allowed at exportation, now forfeited because the tobacco had not been exported as claimed. In the ensuing trial, which attracted a lot of public attention, a special jury found for the Crown on the facts of the case, but the court kept postponing final judgment. In 1737, Perry and the survivors of the other merchants involved petitioned the Treasury for a "composition" (or compromise lump sum payment). Such was finally conceded by the Treasury in January 1739 during Perry's lord mayorship. The burden of his lawsuit helps explain Perry's reconciliation with the government, which probably began about this time.[38]

Walpole's Treasury was not the only hostile wind battering Perry in the years following the excise affair. For decades the Perrys had been the London financial agents of the government of Virginia. In the now changed political atmosphere, John Grymes, the colony's receiver-general, transferred the colony's business from Perry to Robert Cary, a London merchant more acceptable in Virginia. Governor Gooch also ceased entrusting his private affairs to Perry.[39] Even the Bank of England grew cool.[40] Since Perry's relations with those in power were now so strained, he could do little to get favors for correspondents in America. As he wrote to Colden in 1734, "it is my misfortune at present to be so much out of favour, that my apearance at the Council board would rather do you harm than good."[41] Since his purely commercial services now gave less and less satisfaction, he found himself progressively deserted, one by one, by some of his firm's oldest friends in the tobacco colonies, ending in some cases connections going back fifty years and more.

Robert Carter, thought to be the greatest planter in the Virginia of his time as well as a part-time merchant, died in 1732. As noted before, he made financial investments in London through Perrys and kept balances of several thousand pounds in their hands to be used to get the "cash price" on purchases and discounts on the early payment of customs duties. But, though Perrys were very much his bankers, they were hardly the sole vendors of his tobacco. They had to share Carter's London consignments with William Dawkins, while much of his tobacco also went to the outports, including Weymouth, Lyme Regis, Bristol, Liverpool and Glasgow. After his death, Carter's executors continued to use Perrys as bankers but appear to have sent most of the estate's London tobacco to others, particularly Robert Cary.[42]

The Carters were not the only Virginians pulling back from Perrys in the post-excise years. In 1737, William Byrd II wrote them: "I am sorry to see your ships so long in loading. I have thrown in my mite to help both the Rappahannock and the Micajah and Phillip, but alas! your friends like those of the great Koulikun, are fallen off with a general defection. Had you taken the advice which the old councellor gave to Rehoboam and sooth'd the people with good words, they woud have been your servants for ever. But the Israelites were very stout, and so are we Virginians." One suspects that it would have taken more than "good words" to satisfy the "lost tribes" of Perrys' departing Virginia correspondents. Byrd himself was not satisfied with the prices he got from Perrys' sales and had ceased consigning to their house by 1739, when his debt to them had been reduced to £1000.[43]

An ever diminishing handful of Virginia planters stayed with the Perrys. Among the last loyal few were the Beverleys, who had close associations with the Perrys going back at least to the 1680s. Robert Beverley, the historian of Virginia, had boarded with old Micaiah in London and later performed legal and other services for him in the colony. His son, William, dealt with young Micajah till 1743, though relations were quite strained at the end.[44] The ebbing of the tide was clear. Perhaps the most telling loss was that of John Custis. Like Carter, Custis had money and investments in the hands of Perrys. He had known young Micajah Perry since 1712, when he had lived in the Perry household as a quasi-apprentice learning the tobacco business. When Perry became a member of Parliament in 1727, Custis wrote to congratulate him in a most friendly manner. Their relations began to show signs of stress with the passage of the Colonial Debts Act in 1732. Custis thought it unfair for the gentlemen of the British Parliament to make Virginia land seizable for book debts when lands in England could be attached only for debts secured by specialties (bonds, mortgages, and notes).[45] As the thirties wore on, Custis became increasingly impatient with Perry. He told him in 1733 that "you have a generall Character here of buying goods the dearest of any Merc[han]t in England."[46] This weakness in bargaining on purchases may have been associated with Perry's political desire to cultivate the goodwill of the numerous tradesmen-voters of London. Custis suspected as much and began to wonder whether Perry's political career could in the post-excise years be viewed as a good thing for his correspondents in Virginia. In 1735, Custis wrote but did not send a brutally frank letter to his old friend Perry: "I shall not trouble you with any more Tob: till you have more leisure to attend the Virg[ini]a business; w[hi]ch all mankind beleives lies much [neglected?] by your being in so much publick business in the Parliam[en]t and Citty; and it is the opinion of most if not all of your friends that it had bin superlatively more for your interest if you had only minded your Merchandise."[47]

In the years that followed, Custis complained ever more insistently of the inadequate prices received for his tobacco, and of Micajah Perry's neglect of correspondence. His advice unheeded, Custis ceased sending tobacco to Perry by 1739, though he appears to have left funds in his hands until at least 1741.[48]

In 1738–1739, Perry as lord mayor presided over many impressive ceremonies, including the laying of the foundation of the new Mansion House.[49] But less happy events were to trouble him in that year of public pomp. In October 1738, his wife, Elizabeth Cocke, died and was buried in the church at Epsom, where they still had a suburban villa.[50] In 1739, Micajah Perry's brother Phillip withdrew from the partnership and, with what was left of his capital, went to live the quiet life of a rentier in East Greenwich, where his sisters and mother also resided.[51] As the business had not been doing well, the withdrawal of Phillip's share of the capital must have put a great additional strain on Micajah and perhaps accounts for his renewed energy in collecting outstanding debts at this time.

Perry's private embarrassments made it increasingly difficult for him to keep up with the radicalization of anti-ministerial politics in the City of London. In 1739 he took a very conspicuous role in the House of Commons in opposition to the convention with Spain and was thanked by the livery. But by early 1741 he voted with the ministry on a motion for Walpole's removal. In the election of that year, only strong anti-ministerialists were returned by the City and Perry (now considered pro-court) was decisively defeated.[52]

Alderman Perry did not have the physical stamina or health to bear this strain. In 1743, it was reported that, "Dying of Dropsy," he had withdrawn to Bath and was "Not able ever to attend" the London aldermen's meetings.[53] What was left of his business affairs then was handled by his chief clerk, James Johnston, who even signed the current accounts sent out to overseas correspondents.[54] Johnston could not, however, accept bills of exchange, which consequently had to be sent to Bath for Micajah's signature. Everyone was soon aware of what was going on. When Walter King arrived in London from Virginia in December 1743, he wrote immediately to his stepfather-in-law, Colonel Thomas Jones, in the colony: "Your bills on Mr: Perry after delays are both accept[e]d; things seem very much on the decline there. I shall tell you more when I see you, but this to your Self: I have been w[i]th Mr. Phil Perry who lives at Greenwich, but business seems to be so much out of his road, that its a burthen to him to talk about it, so that I look Elsewhere to get mine done."[55]

Micajah Perry appears to have realized by 1744 or 1745 that, after taking into account the uncollectability of many debts outstanding in America, he was in fact insolvent. He did not go bankrupt but apparently called in his creditors and in an amicable settlement turned over all his assets to them.[56] The details of this settlement are unknown, except that he had by 1744 turned over to his competitor John Hanbury responsibility for collecting sums owed the Perry firm in America.[57] Once he had settled with his creditors, something could be done for him. He resigned his alderman's gown (25 November 1746) and was voted a pension of £200 p.a. by the Court of Aldermen of the City of London.[58] Despite his dropsy, later described as "palsy," Micajah Perry survived until 22 January 1753. In his last years he was so "utterly Incapable of Transacting any Business whatsoever" that Chancery had to appoint a guardian for him.[59]

Although Micajah Perry appears to have reached a satisfactory settlement with his English creditors by 1745, his overseas creditors were not equally mollified. Two of them, Richard Bennett, great merchant and planter of Wye,[60] Maryland, and the executors of James Pope, merchant of Madeira,[61] began Chancery suits against both Micajah and Phillip Perry to recover what they claimed was owing them. By this time the Court of Chancery had appointed a guardian to answer for Micajah. What the suitors really wanted was some compensation from Phillip, of whose withdrawal from the firm, they alleged, they had not been properly notified. These suits dragged on for many years until all the parties on both sides were dead. Nothing found indicates that the suitors ever recovered anything from Phillip or his estate.

Why was the firm of Micajah and Phillip Perry so unsuccessful? Without balance sheets or other accounts of the firm, this is a question to which only speculative answers can be given. Under Micaiah Perry I, the firm had used a variety of institutional and financial arrangements in their trade to the Chesapeake: they dealt through factor-storekeepers; they corresponded with independent merchants in the tobacco colonies; and they received consignments and other business from planters there. To get their tobacco back, the older firm preferred chartering needed cargo space on a large number of vessels, some of which they partly owned. Such diversification spread the firm's risks both as shipper and shipowner in peace and war. When they chartered cargo space on several dozen ships to and from the Bay, they knew that there was more than one way to fill those vessels. Some of the return cargo would be the firm's own tobacco acquired by the direct trade of their factors in the colonies; some would be bought for them or consigned for sale by their merchant correspondents; other lots would be consigned for sale by planters. If the planters consigned less than expected, the factors and merchant correspondents could be counted on to exert themselves and by purchase or otherwise make sure that the chartered space was filled.

The young Micajah Perry, however, from the first emphasized the planter consignment trade to the neglect of the other trading modes and, it would appear, preferred the prestige and ease of sending out whole vessels owned or chartered by his own firm. If such vessels could not obtain full return cargoes from the firm's planter "friends" in the Chesapeake, alternative ways of filling a vessel might not be readily available. Huge losses on shipping could result, as Micajah Perry himself averred in 1723.[62] In later years, when consignments and other freight would not fill one of the firm's vessels, authorization was sometimes given to obtain a full cargo by purchasing tobacco, but significant shipping losses continued. John Hanbury, who succeeded Perrys and Hydes as the largest tobacco importer in London in the 1740s and 1750s, was very cautious about investing too heavily in shipping, particularly in wartime, when high freight charges received could be more than consumed by high insurance rates and high wages. Hanbury expressed his reluctance to continue sustaining such risks in a letter to John Custis in December 1745: he would not "go on and do as Mr Perry & Mr [?] had done who . . . have lost by their ships within this 12 Years past near 30,000 £ between them."[63]

In addition to the losses on shipping, there was for consignment merchants like Perrys the ever threatening quicksand of planter debt. Merchants in the Chesapeake, even in the time of Perrys, probably owed British merchants more than planters did; but planters were much less dependable and much slower in paying. When a planter was insufferably late in making returns, a merchant creditor could seek to convert book debt into bonded debt and then perhaps get a court judgment on the bond, if only to force the indebted planter to give a mortgage. Perrys had therefore to employ respected figures in the colonies—such as Charles Carroll[64] in Maryland or William Beverley in Virginia—to act for them in the necessary negotiation and legal work. (Judicious local representatives were needed since it could be advisable to accept a composition or partial payment rather than litigate for the full claim.)[65] When mortgages were foreclosed, Perrys had no interest in keeping the land but tried to sell it as soon as possible. I have already mentioned the John Lloyd lands that were ultimately sold to Robert Carter. Other such cases could drag on for years before the sums owed could be realized. Dudley Digges mortgaged a tract in Albemarle County to Perrys in 1732 but never paid one penny interest. The mortgage was foreclosed in 1737 and the estates allegedly sold to George Braxton, Jr. This sale proving defective, the Perry brothers resold the estate to Walter King in 1744. A lawsuit ensued which King ultimately won on appeal to the Privy Council in 1754.[66] The important thing about such cases is that assets could be tied up unproductively for many years.

There were other strains on the house's capital resources. The deaths of Thomas Lane in 1710 and Richard Perry in 1720 meant that resources formerly available to or supportive of the firm were thenceforth partially tied up in bequests or trusts for members of their families. Richard's daughter Elizabeth was reported to have brought a fortune of £10,000 on her marriage to Salusbury Cade in 1733.[67] Presumably her sisters Sarah and Mary received near as much. The withdrawal of Phillip Perry with his half-interest in the firm in 1739 was a most serious blow. If the firm's capital had been growing after 1721 as it had earlier, the house could possibly have borne these withdrawals. In the depressed circumstances actually prevailing under Micajah III, the family was helping bleed the firm to death.

7 / The Family after the Fall

T he Perry brothers started out rich enough to bear losses on shipping and uncollectable debts for many years. Since their sister Elizabeth was reported to have brought a fortune of £10,000 on her marriage to Salusbury Cade,[1] the brothers Micajah III and Phillip probably inherited something in the vicinity of £60,000–100,000 from their father, grandfather, Thomas Lane and Mary Lane. At the end, Micajah III did not even leave a will.

But it was not a case of "shirtsleeves to shirtsleeves in three generations." The legal incompetence and relative poverty of Micajah Perry III at the time of his death did not mean that the entire family was destitute. He was outlived by his mother, Sarah Richards, whose marriage settlement had left her with considerable property after the death of her husband, Richard Perry IV. On her death in 1756, mother Sarah left her daughter Sarah Heysham all her plate, linen, furniture and household goods plus her "coach and chariot." The possession of two horse-drawn carriages suggests a significant degree of comfort. To her son Phillip she left all her government annuity stock, money, bonds and bills plus "my estate or mortgage I have on Little Stanbridge in Essex together with the Mannor and quitrents thereunto belonging."[2] When "Phillip Perry of Greenwich, Kent, Esq." died in 1762, he left everything to his sister, the widow Sarah Heysham.[3] When Sarah died the next year, she left £3000 to her niece Sarah Cade and the residue of her estate, real and personal, to her nephew, Philip Cade.[4]

Since no children were born to Alderman Micajah Perry, nor to his brother Phillip, nor to their sister Sarah Heysham, the only known line of descent from Micaiah Perry I and his son Richard was that through Richard's youngest daughter Elizabeth, the sister of

Micajah III, Phillip and Sarah, and wife of Salusbury Cade (1696–1773), also of Greenwich. This Salusbury, the son of a well-known physician of the same name,[5] was educated at Westminster School and Christ Church, Oxford. His only known employment was as paymaster to the Band of Gentlemen Pensioners, a position that does not sound too wearing.[6] The only son of the younger Salusbury Cade and Elizabeth Perry was Philip Cade of Greenwich (1744–1799) who added to his patrimony a substantial inheritance from his aunt Sarah (Perry) Heysham. He was remembered principally as a notable eccentric. He married and divorced Catherine, daughter of Sir Charles Whitworth, an M.P. and customs commissioner. He next married his housekeeper and is reported to have spent the rest of his life a *malade imaginaire*, nursed by his new wife.[7] By his first spouse, he had one surviving son and a daughter. The son, another Salusbury (b. 1767) with a reputation of being "of an extravagant turn of mind," emigrated to Jamaica, where he died.[8] With him ended the male line descended from Dr. Salusbury Cade.

Two female lines of descent from the Cade-Perry marriage survived. Philip Cade's sister Sarah (1739–1810) married a Greenwich neighbor, Benjamin Harenc, of a well-connected Huguenot family. The numerous descendants of this Harenc-Cade marriage over three or four generations included a striking number of officers of both the royal and Indian armies.[9] Philip Cade's daughter Catherine in 1790 married William James Tanzia (de) Savary, from another Huguenot military family also resident at Greenwich. Savary's great-grandfather had emigrated from France following the revocation of the Edict of Nantes and had become a professional officer (colonel) in the army of William III. The colonel's descendants were in the eighteenth and nineteenth centuries also to supply the royal and East Indian armies with many officers, including two sons of Catherine Cade Savary.[10] For students of eighteenth century merchant families in general, as well as of the Perrys and Cades in particular, the career patterns of their Harenc and Savary descendants are interesting and not atypical examples of the way in which the army and East Indian service could provide careers and distinguished social connections for the progeny of once prosperous merchant families.[11]

By the nineteenth century, therefore, the only known descendants of Micaiah Perry I were in the Savary and Harenc military families. There were, however, other lines of descent from the siblings of

Micaiah I. Back in the time of Charles II his sister Mary had married someone named Lowe in Ireland and emigrated to Virginia, where she left offspring. Her granddaughter Elizabeth Jarrett or Garrett married John Tyler and was an ancestor of a numerous descent, including President John Tyler.[12] Micaiah's brother John remained in Ireland, where he gradually acquired a landed estate. In this, he was helped by his kinsmen the Hutchinsons. Richard Hutchinson (a brother of William of Massachusetts) prospered as a London merchant in the 1650s and 1660s and became Treasurer of the Navy under Cromwell. Part of his gains he invested in lands both in England and in Ireland, particularly near Clonmel in County Tipperary.[13] It was, of course to Clonmel that Richard Perry, father of Micaiah I and John, took his younger children in or about 1658.[14] At that time, the Perrys were quite insignificant compared with Richard Hutchinson. By the 1690s, the Perrys' relative position had changed.

Tipperary was grazing country, raising cattle for the big Cork butchers who packed salt beef for export as ship's stores or as provisions for the West Indies. The Irish cattle trade was badly hurt by a serious distemper epidemic in 1688 and by the political-military disturbances of 1689–1691. The Tipperary graziers suffered with the rest of the trade.[15] However, John Perry, then of Newcastle, near Clonmel, who had been gradually building up his landholdings and herds for some years, was able to borrow money from his prosperous brother, Micaiah of London, and quickly rebuilt his herds. By contrast, Edward Hutchinson, eldest son and heir of Treasurer Richard, was jealous that he did not get equivalent help from his own brothers in Ireland or America. Edward had fled from Ireland during the fighting of 1689–1691 and, even after the Battle of the Boyne, preferred to remain in London, leaving his Irish lands in the hands of his manager, "Cousin John Perry," who progressively restored the Hutchinson herds too. When Edward Hutchinson died in 1700, he left bequests to cousin John Perry and the latter's wife Elizabeth Riall, and directed that his executors retain cousin John as manager of his estates.[16]

In 1697, John Perry was able to take advantage of the sales of confiscated Jacobite lands to buy almost two thousand acres jointly with his brother Micaiah of London. This purchase became the core of the family's later Woodrooff estate. When Micajah Perry III got into his final financial difficulties, he (as already noted) sold his inherited half of the property in 1744 to John Perry's son John.[17] It was probably young John who built the splendid Woodrooff House around 1760. In the late eighteenth century, the Perrys of Woodrooff, hitherto Presbyterian, apparently adhered to the Church of Ireland, and became very much part of the local county Ascendancy.[18] (Their distant relations, the Perys of Limerick and the Hely-Hutchinsons of Tipperary, were much more important figures in the greater national or Dublin Ascendancy.) Although there may have been some partition of patrimony to help younger sons or daughters, the surveys of landowners published in the 1870s show the Woodrooff Perrys holding 2768 acres valued at £2873 p.a.[19] The Anglo-Irish writer Molly Keane can remember going to splendid balls at Woodrooff House just before the First World War.[20] More difficult times ensued after Irish independence and the "Troubles" of the 1920s. Both Woodrooff House and Newcastle House are listed as "ruins" in recent architectural surveys.[21] The Perry family was still listed as present in the county in the 1975 edition of *Burke's Irish Family History*, but does not appear to be there any longer.[22]

Conclusion: Choosing a Frame for the Picture

T he rise and fall of the house of Perry, both firm and family, are interesting phenomena in themselves, but, for the historian, take on deeper meaning when viewed in the frames provided by larger-scale developments and broader questions. Such larger contexts can be suggested by questions about the economic evolution of the British-Chesapeake trade during the time of the rise and fall of the Perrys; the social and familial character of failure among their contemporaries; and the psychological or personal components of entrepreneurial success and failure.

The Wider Economic Scene

The business of the firm of Micajah Perry & Co. (under its various styles) grew as part of the growth of trade between England and its American colonies. Between 1663/1669, when Micaiah Perry I was first starting in trade, and 1699–1701, when the prosperity of his firm was at its height, London's trade (combined imports and domestic exports) with the North American and West Indian colonies increased 118 percent.[1] Betwen 1699–1701 and 1752–1754, the time of the death of Micajah Perry III, England's trade (imports, exports and re-exports) with the same area grew 151 percent, while her trade with the Thirteen Colonies alone rose a more impressive 286 percent.[2] Within this pattern of steady, if moderate, increase (closely tied to the growth of population in the colonies), the tobacco trade had a more erratic history. With rapid increases in the seventeenth century in both tobacco consumption in Europe and tobacco production in the English colonies, English tobacco imports increased eighty- or ninety-fold, from 351,925 lb. p.a. in 1622–1631 (when Richard Perry II first ventured into the Virginia trade) to 28 million lb. p.a. in 1686–1688, or 31 million lb. p.a. in 1696–1699, when the business of Perry & Lane was at its peak. (In the 1620s 83.4 percent of these tobacco imports came from Virginia and Maryland; by the late 1690s, 97 percent.)[3]

The quite modest increase in imports between the late 1680s and the late 1690s was symptomatic of a longer term slowing down (1680–1700) and stagnation (1700–1725) in tobacco production and trade that left total British (English and Scottish) imports no higher in 1721–1725 than at the beginning of the century. The wars of 1689–1713 hampered navigation and the regular flow of trade, leading to depressed tobacco prices in the Chesapeake and increased prices in Europe. Production in America was discouraged not only by lower local prices but also by war-induced interruptions in the supply of indentured servants and impediments to rapid growth in alternative slave imports. The restricted labor supply helps explain why low production continued into the peace years 1713–1725.[4] However, the higher prices realized for tobacco in those same postwar years helped planters pay for an increased importation of slaves who, with their progeny, go far to explain the renewed growth in tobaco production and trade after 1725—a growth that raised British tobacco imports in 1771–1775 to three times the level of 1721–1725.[5] The reader curious about the Perrys will note that the stagnation in their firm's imports between 1697 and 1719 paralleled stagnation in the trade as a whole and that when Micajah Perry III took over the firm in 1721 prospects for future growth may well have looked not too promising. That same reader will also note, however, that the firm, under the management of Micajah III and Phillip, did not share in the tobacco trade's resumed expansion after 1725.

The character of the competition facing the Perrys also changed over time. The trade to the American colonies after the dissolution of the Virginia Company in 1624 was open to all Englishmen and Welshmen. Hundreds of small traders like Richard Perry II in the 1620s or young Micaiah in the 1660s eagerly sought to improve their lot by taking a share in an "adventure" to the colonies. However, as prices of tobacco in particular declined in the second half of the seventeenth century, profits were squeezed, competition became sharper and many small venturers were forced to leave the trade. The number of firms or individuals importing tobacco at London was reduced from 573 in 1676 to 117 in 1719. The surviving firms were much larger. In 1676 firms importing over 250,000 lb. of tobacco accounted for 31 percent of London imports; but in 1719, for 68 percent.[6] We appreciate the achievement of Perry & Lane all the more when we realize that they pushed to the top at a time when hundreds of their early competitors were being forced out of the trade.

Little is known about the financial history of the Perry firms, but the silence in the records suggests that in old Micaiah's time they could not have had too much trouble borrowing as needed. They were, of course, helped by the large deposits left in their hands by wealthy planters like "King" Carter and John Custis. By contrast, in young Micajah's time, the disappearance of the planter deposits and the loss of access to Bank of England discounts and other loans must have meant a more straitened situation (or "cash-flow" problems) and help explain the large cash sales to the French agents for which the firm was criticized. Similarly, the absence of references in the lawsuits to their purchasing policies in England suggests that Perry & Lane got along rather well with their hundreds of suppliers, as was implied by James Puckle. This inferred cordiality would have arisen originally more from volume of business given than from generous prices paid. At the beginning of the century Anderson reported that the firm made purchases at the lowest possible prices, though Alderman Perry in the 1730s was accused of buying dear.

Much more is known about the house's success at the American end of their trade, which, the evidence suggests, owed much to the flexibility and adaptability of the heads of the firm. Perry & Lane used all the organizational modes or operational strategies then known in the trade. They divided their ship-owning risks among many vessels and were market-wise in their division of their freighting business between vessels they owned or chartered (in whole or in part) and vessels on which their agents merely took freight. By contrast, Micajah Perry III after 1721 seems much more rigid in pushing the firm's consignment business with major planters and in preferring to own or charter whole vessels. Such preferences left his firm liable to major losses on planter credit and shipping and in the end destroyed the house. The alderman's political "successes" created a Potemkin façade of prosperity behind which the decay of Micajah Perry & Co. proceeded apace.

The decline of the firm also reflects conditions more fundamental than the commercial and managerial misjudgments of Alderman Perry. The older factor system preferred in his grandfather's time still had a great viability, as Scottish firms showed after 1740 with their networks of stores throughout the Chesapeake (eventually accounting for almost half the region's tobacco exports). These later Scottish stores of 1740–1775 differed from their London predecessors of the seventeenth century in that they were entrusted to salaried factors, usually supervised closely by a partner resident in the colonies. Real success for such a factor meant becoming a partner in his employers' firm. By contrast, the little we know of the London "Sot-weed Factors" of 1660–1720 suggests that they most often worked on commission without supervision and all too frequently engaged in private, clandestine trade on the side. Success for them appears to have meant setting up as an independent merchant in the Chesapeake. Thus the later success of the Scots involved not copying the Londoners but developing a new form of merchant firm with many partners, a large capital and managerial and accounting procedures effective in controlling the activities of staff overseas. Had Alderman Perry and many other Londoners continued with their fathers' kind of stores and factors after 1720, they most likely would not have had success comparable to that of the later Scots because their mode of operation was so different. In 1719, when Micajah Perry & Co. was still the largest tobacco importer in London, their closest rival was Bradley & Co. Unlike Perrys, Bradleys continued with stores and factors in the Chesapeake in the 1720s. They were still near the top of the trade in the early 1730s but had failed by 1737.[7] Merely continuing with stores was not enough to guarantee survival.

A problem common to Perrys and Bradleys and other firms in the trade was the previously noted pattern price movements. The high European prices of the war years, 1689–1713, continued into the peace down to 1725, primarily because of stagnant production in the Chesapeake. However, the growth of the slave population there was eventually felt in tobacco production and shipments. Increased British tobacco imports after 1725 had an immediate depressing effect on prices which tended (except for a few wartime years) to remain low down to the start of the Seven Years War in 1756. Depressed British prices reduced commissions, discouraged consignments and made speculative purchases in the Chesapeake very risky. Many smaller ports and weaker firms gave up the trade entirely. The Perrys were simply the most conspicuous among the firms that had prospered in the era of high European prices, 1689–1725, but could not adjust to the harsher climate of 1726–1755.

The Social Character of Failure

An awareness of the depressed market conditions for tobacco between 1726 and 1744 makes it easier to understand that the failure of Micajah Perry III was unlikely to have been an isolated event. In fact, of the 177 individuals or firms importing tobacco at London in 1719, only 11 can definitely be found still active (personally or via their successors) on a 1747 list of London merchants with tobacco duty bonds outstanding. A less problematic comparison between two similar lists shows that the number of merchant importers at London with tobacco bonds outstanding declined from 42 in 1733 to 19 in 1747. Not all who disappeared from the lists had necessarily failed; some had died; others (for example, the very sober Quaker, Thomas Hyam, governor of the London Lead Company) had left the Chesapeake business for more attractive endeavors. Yet some of the decline does represent the failure of firms in the lifetime of the founder (for instance, John Bezeley, Thomas Brooke, Thomas Colmore, Robert Cruikshank, John Peele, Daniel Quare or Charles Rogers). What is perhaps even more striking is the numbers of family firms in the London Chesapeake trade in these decades which, like the Perrys, failed in the second or third generation: Bradleys, Buchanans, Falconars, Hydes, Philpots, Smiths. Other trades too had examples as striking as that of the Chesapeake houses. In 1719, when the Perrys led the tobacco import business, the leading sugar importers in London were the Tryons; they too like the Perrys failed in the third generation in the 1740s.[8] The difficulty of transmitting commercial success from one generation of a family to another has hardly been confined to any one trade, place or time.

Some readers might well wonder, however, whether politics might not have been the decisive factor in the Perry failure. Relevant, of course; decisive, I rather doubt. As suggested in the introduction, politics was more the symptom than the cause of the alderman's decline. On the one hand, many of his contemporaries in the Chesapeake trade (such as those mentioned in the previous paragraph) failed without going anywhere near politics.[9] On the other, the reader will remember that the two Parliaments in which Micajah Perry III sat each contained over fifty merchants, the vast majority of whom clearly knew how to combine political activity with business prudence and success. In the end, the greatest weight dragging down Micajah Perry III was the alderman himself.

The Psychology of Failure

The business of Perry & Lane around 1700 was, as has been frequently noted, extremely complex. For their direct trade, premises had to be acquired and factors engaged and instructed regularly; decisions had to be made each year about what goods should be sent to each store. For the consignment trade as well as the direct trade, return carrying capacity had to be chartered in good time on many vessels (fifty such vessels in 1719) so that tobacco from each river could be returned to London with minimum delays. Difficult decisions had constantly to be made and reassessed about the amount of credit to be allowed to correspondents in America, particularly merchants. Supervising the operations of such a firm required sound business judgment, a willingness to take justifiable risks and an intellectual capacity for keeping a thousand details under constant control. These were all qualities eminently possessed by Micaiah I if not by his grandson. As Robert Carter shrewdly observed in 1721, "I'm afraid the grandson hath not a head calculated to [get] through a multitude of business with that dexterity that they [the firm] have hitherto done."[10]

Having neither a taste nor an aptitude for such "a multitude of business" nor the "spirit" to make the intractable move, Micajah III from the first year of his inheritance proceded to simplify the operation of the firm: stores were closed, factors dismissed and a relatively few owned vessels substituted for chartered space on many vessels. The time saved could be devoted to other interests. Almost immediately, however, it proved difficult to fill even the few vessels sent to Virginia if the firm didn't have the right sort of agent on each river with authorization to purchase when necessary. Micajah III sought to compensate by cultivating more assiduously the larger planter-consigners. But there was a limit to how much credit he could give them and, in patronage matters, he proved less adept than his grandfather, who never held public office. In the end he appears to have lost his bearings and made his political career almost an end in itself without any discernible utility to his business. Very likely, though, the business would have foundered even without the politics for, like most failures, Micajah III and Phillip Perry were not the businessmen their business required. A flair for their trade was something their grandfather could not leave them.

Perry, Tryon, Hyde, Falconar! The withering away and fall of such houses make sad tales, but the firms and people themselves are of interest to less sentimental students of the eighteenth century not because of their ultimate failure, but because for a time they were successful. In their hour of success, they helped keep the wheels of commerce turning, directed hundreds of vessels busy on the seas between Britain and America, and through themselves let the market play its role for good or bad in the working and building of British and colonial economy and society. Thus, if the weight of failure was for most merchant families a private woe, the implications of success may well have involved hundreds and thousands of others, happily or unhappily, including many in remote lands across wide oceans.

Abbreviations

Appendices

Selected Bibliography

Notes

Index

Abbreviations

APC Col.	*Acts of the Privy Council, Colonial Series*
BL	British Library, London
Cal.S.P.Col.AWI	*Calendar of State Papers, Colonial: America and West Indies*
Cal.S.P.Dom.	*Calendar of State Papers, Domestic*
Cal.T.B.	*Calendar of Treasury Books*
IGI	International Genealogical Index
Journal C.T.P.	*Journal of the Commissioners of Trade and Plantations*
LC	Library of Congress, Washington
LCRO	City of London: Corporation Record Office
MdHR	Maryland Hall of Records, Annapolis
P.C.C.	Prerogative Court of Canterbury (at PRO)
PRO	Public Record Office, London
VaHS	Virginia Historical Society, Richmond
VaSL	Virginia State Library, Richmond
VMHB	*Virginia Magazine of History and Biography*
UVa	University of Virginia Library, Charlottesville

Appendix A

Draft service agreement (1684) between a London merchant (William Paggen) and his prospective Virginia factor (John Hardman)

[Hardman was to reside in Virginia and follow instructions sent out by Paggen. Hardman's duties were to include:] takeing care of, buyeing, selling and disposeing of such men and women servants, goods, w[ares] and other merchandizes as shall be from time to time consigned to him and in the buying, receiving in, and shipping, transporting, disposing and tak[ing] care of, preserveing and sending to England all such Tobaccoe, skinns and Furs as shall be by him bought in Virginia for the use of the said William Paggen and his Assignes, [while goods] consigned to the said John Hardman shall by him be laid out, bartered, sold, exchanged and disposed of for bright Tobacco, skinns or Furs and good Bills of exchange[,] and also that he the said John Hardman shall receive all the said Tobacco, skinns and Furs himselfe and shall not nor will imploy any other person or persons whatsoever in, for or about the receaveing of the same. And that the said John Hardman shall from time to time make out returnes [?] and once at least in every year without any request, and oftner if the same be required, Transport, send or convey unto the said William Paggen, his Exec[uto]rs, Administrators and Assignes true, full and perfect accompts in writing of all such sums of mony and bills of exchange as shall by him be received and paid and of all men and women servants, Tobaccoe, goods, wares, merchandizes and other [effects?] as shall be by him in any manner or wise received, sold, bought, consigned, transported or otherwise by him disposed of, with the dayes and times when and the names of what goods shall at such time remaine unsold and undisposed of, and of all other actings, dealeings, doeings and proceedings whatsoever of him the said John Hardman in and about the concernes of the said William Paggen and his Assignes; and that hee the said John Hardman shall from time to time make his returns in such shipp or shipps as the said William Paggen and his Assignes shall order and direct. And it is especially covenanted and agreed that the said John Hardman shall not nor will neither directly nor indirectly at any time or times dureing or within the said Term of [blank] yeares or such further time as is before agreed upon doe or negotiate any affaires or businesse as Factor or Agent or deale for himselfe or any other person or persons whatsoever other than the said William Paggen and his Assignes. In consideration whereof, the said William Paggen for himselfe, his heires, Exec[uto]rs, Administrators and Assignes doth covenant, promise, grant and agree to and with the said John Hardman, his Exec[uto]rs, Adminis[trato]rs and Assignes by these pr[e]sents in manner and forme following (that is to say) That he the said William Paggen shall and will yearly and every year dureing the aforesaid [blank] yeares and untill the End of one year after notice shall be given by either of t[he] said parties to the other as aforesaid transport, convey or consigne unto the said John Hardman such goods, merchandizes, wares and comodityes as At the time of the embarqueing and shipping thereofe shall be worth in value [blank] At the least[;] And that he the said William Paggen and his A[ssigns] shall and will for the consideracons aforesaid pay and allow unto the said John Hardman [blank] p[er] Cent of lawfull money of England [of the] neate produce above all charges of all such Tobaccoes, skinns or furrs and [blank] pounds [sterling] p[er] Cent for bills of exchange arriveing [damaged] [as] shall be returned for servants, goods and other comodityes sold in Virginia . . .

Source: Bodleian Library, Oxford: MS. Aubrey 4 fo. 1 (punctuation modernized but spelling left unchanged). William Paggen & Co. were in 1686 the third largest tobacco importers in London (after Jeffreys and Perry & Lane). See Jacob M. Price and Paul G. E. Clemens, "A Revolution of Scale in Overseas Trade: British Firms in the Chesapeake Trade, 1675–1775," *Journal of Economic History*, XLVII (1987):15.

Appendix B

Goods exported by Perry, Lane & Co. to Virginia and Maryland in year ending Lady Day 1697/8

Note: Almost all goods listed were entered for export between December 1697 and March 1697/8. QU = quantities unspecified. *foreign good re-exported.

		Estimated Value
Woollen Cloth		
"cotton"	14,130 goad (21,195 yards)	£770
plains	4,990 " (7485 yards)	250
flannel	4,281 yards	285
frieze	688 "	72–137
kerseys	761 pieces	1255–1522
minikin baize	232 "	1740–2088
serge	638 "	1053
short cloth	67 "	536–737
Spanish cloth	1 piece	6–13
stuffs	546 pieces	685
wool-cloth	454 lb.	34–45
Other Textiles		
(cotton) *Bengals**	1 piece	
*callicoe**	3 pieces [84 yards?]	1–2
*muslin**	6 "	15
hair-cloth	19 "	13
linen, fustians	710 " [12,425 yds?]	532
other English	63 " + QU	95
*Scotch cloth**	6 "	8
*ozenbrigs**	4,700 ells	147
other German*	26,200 ells	1572
*diaper**	8 pieces	7–9
lawns*	27 " [432 yards?]	7–17
*crocus**	2 "	1
other foreign*	2,354 ells	90

canvas*	200 ells	7
sail cloth	6 pieces [198 yards?]	12
wrought silk	175 lb.	262–350

Leather Goods

bridles	20 doz.	12
horse-collars	133 items	10
saddles	546 items	700
gloves	417.5 doz. pair	167
shoes, wrought leather	19,133 lb. wt.	2152
whips	QU	

Other Personal Attire

"apparel"	QU	
bugle (beads)*	33 lb. wt.	2
canes	QU	
caps	QU	
caps, Monmouth	41 doz. (492)	12
dresses	QU	
haberdashery	9,674 lb. wt.	173
hats, felt and straw	5,889 items	470
castor	1,146 items	620
hose, Irish*	195 dozen	88
thread	QU	
wool	477 dozen	286
worsted	155 dozen	170
lace and laced linnen	QU	
last	QU	
necklaces	QU	
periwigs and wigs	QU	
towers (lady's head-dress)	QU	

Reading, Writing and Music

books	3,129 lb. wt.	112
paper, domestic	2 reams	1
imported*	170 reams	34
ink in bottles	QU	
ink horns	QU	
spectacles	QU	
violins	QU	
violin-strings	QU	
wax (sealing ?)	QU	
weather-glasses	QU	

Comestibles

anchovies*	2 bbl.	1
apothecary wares	1381 lb. wt.	25
aqua vitae*	10 hogsheads [540 gal.]	60
beer	990 gallons	27
butter	31 firkins [1736 lb. net]	28–35
capers*	4 cwt.	13
cheese	143 cwt.	143
chocolate*	63 lb. wt.	12
cinnamon*	26 lb. wt.	9
cloves*	27 lb. wt.	11
coffee*	102 lb. wt.	10
currants*	50 lb. wt.	19
grocery*	4 cwt.	8
mace*	28 lb. wt.	34
malt	2,171 bu.	326
nutmeg*	129 lb. wt.	51
oil*	219 gallons	27
pepper*	961 lb. wt.	56
raisins*	38 cwt.	47
rice*	29 cwt.	54
salt	694 bu.	173
sugar*	46 cwt.	60–130
vinegar*	1 cask	2
wine*	1,561 gallons	312

Other Household and Plantation Consumables

bags	52.5 dozen	16
candles	20 dozen	4
cordage	59.5 cwt.	71
corks	QU	
flints	QU	
gunpowder	50 cwt.	105
shot	335 cwt.	
soap, foreign*	70 cwt.	147
domestic	7 firkins [392 lb.]	6
starch	QU	
tobacco pipes	916 gross	46
wash-balls	QU	

Household Furnishings

beds (feather)	10 items	
blankets	16 pr.	
chairs, couches, tables	QU	
curtains	1 suit	
diaper table cloths*	8 items	1
fringe and nets	QU	
glass (panes)	34 chests	31
glassware and earthenware	18,350 pieces	60
gravestones	QU	
joinery	QU	
napkins*	8 doz.	
pictures	13 items	
pulpit cloth	1 item	
roundles*	14 items	
rugs	1274	446–510
screens	1 pr. and QU	
"tikes" (bed-ticks)*	34 items	
trunks	QU	
turnery ware	QU	
upholstery ware	QU	

Hardware

brass (ware?)	71.5 cwt.	336
iron pots*	348 items	83
iron, wrought	658 cwt.	1842
nails	781 cwt.	1405
pewter	107.5 cwt.	430
press, iron	2 and QU	
shovels	12 dozen	7
tin (ware?)	QU	

Other Capital Goods and Industrial Raw Materials

alum*	2 cwt.	2
brimstone*	358 lb. wt.	4
colours, colouring	QU	
copper	1 cwt.	5
grindstone	20.5 chaldrons	14
iron (foreign)*	22 cwt.	13
plows	QU	
quern stones*	32 pr.	13

smalts (a dye)	14 lb. wt.	1
smith-bellows	QU	
whale-bone*	12 lb.	1
wheels	QU	
wool-cards	40 doz.	20

Other
coaches	2 items	45

Source: Printed bills of entry, 1697, for port of London in Beinecke Library, Yale University. Values derived from official prices in PRO CUST 2/2 and (a few woolen items only) C.O.390/8 ff. 129–149.

Appendix C

The Hutchinson Connection

Both Micaiah Perry I and his partner Thomas Lane were related to the Hutchinson family, noteworthy in the history of England, Ireland and Massachusetts. Students of American history are familiar with William Hutchinson, one of the founders and earliest settlers of Massachusetts, and his wife, Anne Hutchinson, the noted antinomian preacher. They were founders of a prominent colonial family which was to include Thomas Hutchinson, governor of Massachusetts on the eve of the Revolution. William Hutchinson had a brother, Richard, who remained in England and prospered as a merchant of London and as Treasurer of the Navy under Cromwell. Richard invested a good part of his growing fortune in lands in county Tipperary, Ireland, which he left to his son Edward. Students of Irish history are aware of Edward as the ancestor of the Hutchinson and Hely-Hutchinson families (including the earls of Donoughmore), later so prominent in Irish affairs.[1]

Richard Hutchinson of London also had a daughter Mary, who in 1652 married William Puckle (uncle of James Puckle, the London notary and man of letters). Their daughter, Mary Puckle (1661–1727), became the wife of Thomas Lane. Among the Donoughmore papers in the library of Trinity College, Dublin, are a few letters between Mary (Puckle) Lane and her Irish Hutchinson kin, suggesting that a meaningful connection between the families survived into the early decades of the eighteenth century.[2]

The connection of the Perrys to the Hutchinsons is just as certain but much more difficult to explain with precision. In his will of 1699, Edward Hutchinson left bequests to his "kinsman" John Perry of Newcastle, county Tipperary (the brother of Micaiah Perry), and to his "kinswoman" Elizabeth (Riall), wife of said John. He also directed his executors to continue John Perry's employment as manager of his Tipperary estates. There also survive among the Donoughmore papers some Hutchinson family correspondence of the 1690s in which reference is made to "cousin John Perry."[3] The connection with the Hutchinsons of the brothers Micajah and John Perry may well have been through one of their grandmothers: either Dunes Hicks, wife of Richard Perry II, or—more likely—the wife of Richard Malbon referred to but not named in the records of the New Haven colony. Such a connection may help explain, inter alia, the migration of Richard Perry III and family to county Tipperary in or about 1658.

Appendix D

The Early Perys and Perrys: Some Problems

The Betham Version

Figure 3 summarizes the family tree of the early Perys and Perrys as reconstructed in the early nineteenth century for the first earl of Limerick by Sir William Betham, Ulster King of Arms. This table is useful in showing the relationship of the London and Limerick Pery/Perry families, their common origin in Exeter and their probable (possible?) derivation from the Pery family of Water. However, it leaves unexplored the relationship of these families to the Pery/Perry families of Plymouth, Buckland Monachorum and Virginia who are mentioned or suggested as their kin in surviving records.

It is really not possible in the 1990s to conduct a totally rigorous critique of the work of Sir William Betham, inasmuch as several major bodies of records used by him are no longer in existence. Most Irish wills and many other records were destroyed when the Four Courts were blown up during the "Troubles" of 1922. Most Devon wills were concentrated at Exeter and destroyed by aerial bombardment during the Second World War. We also do not know exactly what family records were made available to Betham by the first earl of Limerick. More recently, the late earl of Limerick deposited most of his early family papers in the National Library of Ireland, where they have not yet been catalogued. Some sixteenth and seventeenth century items shown in an inventory prepared for the earl prior to the transfer cannot now be located, though it is hoped that the missing material will turn up later when the cataloguing of this deposit is finished.

Nevetheless, it is possible from the annotations left by Sir William Betham to reconstruct the chain of inductive reasoning he employed in making the early family tree. He knew that the first William Pery of Limerick in his will (proved 1633) remembered his cousin Richard

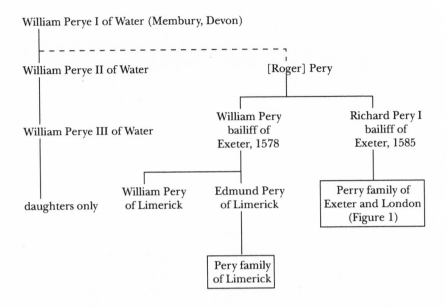

Source: Muniments of earl of Limerick: Pedigree prepared for 1st earl of Limerick by Sir William Betham, deputy Ulster King of Arms, 1815. Registered copy in Genealogical Office, Dublin, G.O. 169 pp. 45–64. See also John L. Vivian, *The Visitations of the County of Devon* (Exeter, ca. 1895), p. 591, which differs from some other versions.

Figure 3. The Early Perys and Perrys According to Betham

Pery of London and that William's nephew, Edmund Pery of Limerick, in his will (proved 1655) left a £5 bequest to his kinsman Peter Pery/Perry of London and £2 to Peter's sister Susanna (son and daughter of the aforementioned Richard II and siblings of Richard III of New Haven). (He probably also knew that John Pery of London in his will—proved 1628—left a small bequest to Ruth White, sister and administratrix of William Pery of Limerick.)[1] He knew that, by their arms (and assertions relating thereto), both the Limerick Perys and the London Perrys claimed some relationship with the older Pery family of Water in Devon. He knew also that the second William Pery of Water was described in a Heralds Visitation of 1564 as the "eldest" son of the first William Pery of Water, implying that he had at least two younger brothers.[2] Betham concluded therefore that one of these younger Pery of Water brothers had settled in Exeter and was the father of William and Richard Pery, both bailiffs of Exeter, with William the ancestor of the Limerick Perys and Richard the progenitor of the London branch. We can now identify the father of bailiff William as Roger Pery, freeman and merchant of Exeter, but still face the problem of fitting in the Plymouth and other known Perry kin absent from Betham's family tree.

The Plymouth-Buckland Link

An alternative pedigree of the early Perrys can be suggested that accepts most (if not all) of Sir William Betham's reconstruction but offers suggestions for fitting in the neglected branches (Figure 4). My account accepts Betham's exposition of the London descendants of bailiff Richard Pery but differs in the matter of the descendants of Richard's brother William Pery.

William Pery, bailiff of Exeter in 1578, had an important link with Plymouth through his wife, Alice, the daughter of John Ilcomb, merchant of Plymouth. William died ca. 1590 and his widow had by 1592 settled in Plymouth, where she had inherited some property from her father.[3] It is therefore not surprising that some of her sons should be active in the Plymouth area. Her son William (christened at Exeter, 1563) emigrated at an unknown date to Limerick in Ireland. (This migration may well reflect the opening in 1585 of the long-lasting hostilities with Spain—hostilities which should have blocked the family's previous trade with that country.) A younger son of bailiff William and Alice is a probable description of the Henry Pery who in 1587 married Richarda Platyr of Buckland Monachorum (a few miles to the north of Plymouth) and settled in that parish.[4] He was described as a merchant, probably connected with the cloth trade, but owned no real estate.[5]

By his wife Richarda, Henry Pery of Buckland Monachorum had four sons: William (christened 1592), Thomas (1595), Henry (1597) and Edmond (1599). The youngest, Edmond, emigrated to Limerick (probably in the 1620s) probably to assist his uncle William, who had come to divide his time between Limerick and London. On his death in 1633, William named his nephew Edmond as his executor, residuary legatee and principal heir.[6] The third son, Henry, appears to

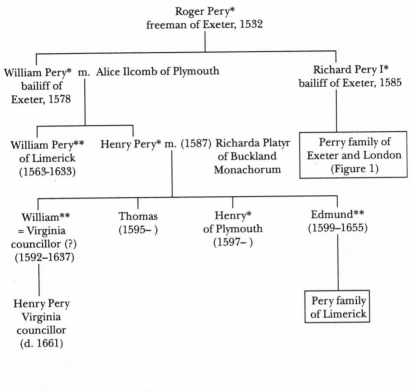

Roger Pery*
freeman of Exeter, 1532

William Pery* m. Alice Ilcomb of Plymouth
bailiff of
Exeter, 1578

Richard Pery I*
bailiff of Exeter, 1585

William Pery**
of Limerick
(1563-1633)

Henry Pery* m. (1587) Richarda Platyr
of Buckland
Monachorum

Perry family of
Exeter and London
(Figure 1)

William**
= Virginia
councillor (?)
(1592–1637)

Thomas
(1595–)

Henry*
of Plymouth
(1597–)

Edmund**
(1599–1655)

Henry Pery
Virginia
councillor
(d. 1661)

Pery family
of Limerick

* merchant in external trade
** emigrant

Figure 4. The Early Perys and Perrys: An Alternative Account

have settled in Plymouth and is probably the Henry Pery we find there in the 1620s trading to Virginia.[7] The eldest son, William, could be the William Pery who settled in Virginia in 1611. There is little direct confirmation for this suggestion, but we do know that Captain William Pery, the Virginia councillor (d. 1637), named his son Henry and that the son called his estate "Buckland."[8] When John Pery of the London family visited Virginia in the 1620s, he stayed with Captain William at Perry's Point on the James River and asked William to witness his will.[9] A family connection would be highly likely.

It will be noted that (almost) every male shown in Figure 4 was either a merchant trading abroad or an emigrant from England. The orientation of the family toward the seaborne frontier was clear by the beginning of the seventeenth century.

Other Kin of the Exeter Perrys

The Exeter Pery family would appear to have been part of an extensive cousinhood which may have some relevance to the Virginia trade. This cousinhood was spread out all over the southwest.

The liberty of Breamore in Hampshire near the Wiltshire border (consisting solely of the parish of Breamore) belonged to the priory of the same name at the beginning of the sixteenth century. At the dissolution of the monasteries, the lands and jurisdictions of the priory came into the possession of the king's cousin, the marquess of Exeter. In the entourage of the marquess, we find two persons who appear to have been attached to each other in something of a patron-client relationship. A list prepared in 1538 of the "servants" of the marquess included Anthony Harvey, a Devon gentleman, described as bailiff of Tappishame (Topsham, Devon), keeper of the king's park of Mee(?), surveyor to the marquess and keeper of his lordship's Chymley (Chumleigh) Park, also in Devon. At a lower level, among the fourteen "yeoman waiters" was one William Pury, keeper of the marquess's Bedewell (Bedwell Park, Herts) and receiver (for the marquess) of the late priory of Breamore. On the downfall and execution of Exeter in 1538, both Harvey and Pury appear to have managed to transfer their loyalties to the lord privy seal, Thomas Cromwell. A "William Perry" was listed in 1538 among the "Gentlemen of my lord Privy Seal's mete [i.e., those who dined at his table] to be preferred unto the King's Majesty's service." William Pury shortly received a grant of the priory of Breamore as well as appointment as "sewer" (headwaiter) of the king's chamber. Harvey for his services was made the king's surveyor of the lands seized from the marquess of Exeter and received major land grants himself. In 1544 he was escheator of Devon and Cornwall.[10]

When William Pury or Pirry of Breamore, sewer of the king's chamber, died in 1547, he left a life interest in Breamore to Anthony Harvey, with the reversion going to his own cousin, John Pury of Warminster (Wilts), yeoman.[11] When John Pury died in 1555, he left most of his property, including real estate in Somerset, to his sons, but the reversion of Breamore (not yet realized) he left to William, son of Roger Pirry, merchant of Exeter.[12] Roger Pirry or Pery is, of course, the ancestor of all the Perys and Perrys treated in this book, while his son William was most probably the progenitor of the Buckland Monachorum and Limerick branches of the family. The story of the Breamore succession suggests that the Exeter Perys were part of a rather extensive clan reaching into Hampshire, Wiltshire and Somerset, while the mention of a sewer of the king's chamber suggests that the family may have had connections more valuable than we might otherwise have thought likely. Some of these connections may have been in families which sent offspring to Virginia. The southwestern counties over which the clan was spread was the origin of much emigration to the Cheapeake in the seventeenth century.[13]

Selected Bibliography

Manuscripts

London Repositories

Public Record Office, London and Kew

Audit Office
A.O.1891/7, 9
A.O.13/32 Loyalist Claims, Walter King

Chancery bills and answers
C.2/Charles I/	P52/20 Perrye v. Latham (1626)
	P53/13 Perry v. Ball (1626)
	P68/60 Perry v. Lowe
	P96/26 Perry v. Lowe (1628)
C.6/257/3	Andrews v. Perry (1686)
C.6/321/45	Cox v. Perry (1701)
C.6/345/70	Doyley v. Perry (1706)
C.6/409/70	Freeman v. Perry (1712)
C.6/434/3,11	Jeffreys v. Jeffreys (1706)
C.7/267/34	Perry v. Flower (1698)
C.7/280/31	Perry v. Godart (1692)
C.7/568/71	Perry v. Flower (1695)
C.7/571/19	Perry v. Flower (1695)
C.8/355/15	Perry v. Bland (1693?)
C.8/355/233	Williams v. Perry (1693)
C.8/550/16	Perry v. Pattison (1691)
C.8/628/61	Minge v. Perry (1706)
C.9/17/62	Hale v. Perry (1655)
C.9/188/70	Perry v. Minge (1708)
C.9/241/121	Perry v. Hale (1655)
C.9/283/61	Perry v. Mills (1695)
C.9/322/42	Phillips v. Perry (1698)
C.9/345/24	Perry v. Mohun (1712)
C.9/443/77	Perry v. Bathurst (1705)
C.10/30/21	Ayling v. Perry (1653)

C.10/328/3	Perry v. Barnes (1713)
C.10/328/6	Perry v. Lane (1713)
C.10/384/16	Sandford v. Perry (1708)
C.11/18/8	Latham v. Perry (1715)
C.11/233/39	Andrews v. Perry (1714)
C.11/292/18	Perry v. Custis (1712)
C.11/307/66	Perry v. Bennett (1748)
C.11/767/68	Carruthers v. Perry (1719)
C.11/967/14	Lloyd v. Perry (1716)
C.11/968/12	Sherrard v. Perry (1717)
C.11/1383/6	Barnes v. Perry (1714)
C.11/1597/8	Perry v. Parker (1745)
C.11/1607/29	Perry v. Nutt (1742)
C.11/1667/15	Beckford v. Perry (1751)
C.11/1672/31	Beckford v. Perry (1755)
C.11/1884/33	Parker v. Perry (1745)
C.11/1971/2	Bellon v. Perry (1714)
C.11/2051/24	Thomlinson v. Duntz
C.11/2286/114	Sherrard v. Perry (1714)
C.11/2287/75	Willis v. Perry (1718)
C.11/2420/8	Perry v. Seaman (1729)
C.11/2626/29	Barry v. Perry (1714)
C.11/2649/41	Leigh v. Perry (1717)
C.12/296/16	Bennett v. Perry (1747)
C.12/307/6	Perry v. Bennett (1748)
C.12/1449/32	Bennett v. Perry (1747)
C.12/1450/83	Hanbury v. Perry (1751)

Other Chancery material

C.22/117/11, 36	Country Depositions
C.24/698(ii)/38	Depositions
C.24/1215, 1351	Depositions
C.33/389, 391	Orders
C.38/296, 300, 304	Reports
C.54/5407, 5539	Close Rolls: Indentures, 1730, 1735
C.107/161	Masters' Exhibits: Lloyd v. Nicholson

Colonial and Board of Trade
Board of Trade in-letters, 1706-
  C.O.5/1305, 1309, 1313, 1315, 1318–1320, 1337
Board of Trade entrybooks
  C.O.5/1362

Board of Trade, Commercial
    C.O.388/17, 24
    C.O.390/4, 8

Exchequer, Court of
    E.112/697/1175 (bills)
    E.122/196/24 (London customs accounts)
    E.127/36, 37 (decrees)
    E.134 (depositions)
    Port books:
    E.190/29/4 London, 1626
    E.190/31/1   1627
    E.190/43/1   1640
    E.190/52/1   1668
    E.190/56/1   1672
    E.190/58/1   1672
    E.190/64/1   1676
    E.190/68/1   1677
    E.190/143   1686
    E.190/152   1695
    E.190/934/4 Exeter, 1582–1583
    E.190/1037/17 Plymouth, 1666
    E.190/1038/8   1668
    E.190/1039/3   1672
    E.190/1041/1   1675

High Court of Admiralty
    H.C.A.13/80, 83, Examinations
    H.C.A.15/18, Case papers
    H.C.A.26/1, 3, 15, 19, Letters of Marque Declarations

Prerogative Court of Canterbury (pr. = will proved)
    PROB 6/133 (Administrations, 1757)
    PROB 8/51 (Probate orders, 1657)
    PROB 11/155 (PCC 32 Ridley) John Perry (pr. 1629)
    PROB 11/211 (PCC 9 Pembroke) Richard Perry (pr. 1650)
    PROB 11/236 (PCC 170 Alchin) Dunes Perry (pr. 1654)
    PROB 11/243 (PCC 33 Aylett) Peter Pery (pr. 1654)
    PROB 11/247 (PCC 231 Aylett) Edmund Pery (pr. 1655)
    PROB 11/268 (PCC 374 Ruthven) Susanna Whittle (pr.1657)
    PROB 11/292 (PCC 328 Pell) Wm. Whittle (pr. 1659)
    PROB 11/308 (PCC 67 Laud) Benjamin Kaine (pr. 1662)

PROB 11/351 (PCC 57 Bench) Maurice Thomson (pr. 1676)
PROB 11/354 (PCC 86 Hale) William Puckle (pr. 1677)
PROB 11/393 (PCC 150 Exton) John Jeffreys (pr. 1688)
PROB 11/421 (PCC 138 Box) George Richards (pr. 1694)
PROB 11/487 (PCC 45 Eedes) Christopher Morgan (pr. 1706)
PROB 11/518 (PCC 250 Smith) Thomas Lane (pr. 1710)
PROB 11/521 (PCC 112 Young) Daniel Parke (pr. 1710)
PROB 11/574 (PCC 118 Shaller) Richard Perry (pr. 1720)
PROB 11/581 (PCC 185 Buckingham) Micajah Perry (pr.1721)
PROB 11/617 (PCC 237 Farrant) Mary Lane (pr. 1727)
PROB 11/821 (PCC 77 Glazier) Sarah Perry (pr. 1756)
PROB 11/877 (PCC 267 St Eloy) Phillip Perry (pr. 1762)
PROB 11/892 (PCC 473 Caesar) Sarah Heysham (pr. 1763)
PROB 11/988 (PCC 240 Stevens) Salusbury Cade (pr. 1773)
PROB 11/1160 (PCC 539 Major) Elizabeth Cade (pr. 1787)
PROB 11/1325 (PCC 422 Howe) Philip Cade (pr. 1799)

Treasury Books and Papers
T.1/297   Treasury Board papers (inwards)
T.29/26, 28   Treasury Board Minutes
T.38/362   trade accounts
T.70/269–71,
273, 276–81   Royal African Company
T.70/1199   Royal African Company

Bank of England Archives (City and Roehampton)

Court of Directors Minutes
General Ledgers
Drawing Office Ledgers (Roehampton)

British Library

Additional MSS. 14,831, Heraldic collection of Charles Townley
Additional MSS. 35,336, Heraldic book of John Washburton
Additional MSS. 41,803, Middleton papers: internal security
Additional MSS. 61,510, Blenheim Papers: re Madeira
Harley MSS. 1238, Miscellaneous commonplace book on tobacco
Harley MSS. 6834, Gregory King's genealogical papers
Loan 29/88/Misc. 85, Harley family papers

City of London. Corporation Record Office

Court of Aldermen. Repertories, vols. 151–156
Mayor's Court. Depositions, box 51

Guildhall Library

Weavers Company records (ms. 4657A/2)
Merchant Taylors' records (microfilm)
Haberdashers Company records

Society of Genealogists Library. Charterhouse Buildings

Bernau Index to Chancery Proceedings (microfilm)
Martin Nail, ed., "The Graveyard and Church Monuments of Epsom"
    (typescript)
Notes by late Major G. S. Parry on Parry and Perry families

OUTSIDE OF LONDON

Cambridge University Library

Cholmondeley(Houghton) MSS. 29/4/2; 29/13; 29/22; 29/29/3; 43;
    81/25,26 (Sir Robert Walpole's papers)

Chelmsford. Essex Record Office

D/DU 190/16 and 19 Manor of Little Stambridge, court rolls

Exeter. Devon Record Office

Parish records of St. Petrocks and St. Edmunds, Exeter (film)

Leeds City Library, Sheepscar Branch. Archives Department

NH2440 (Newby Hall MSS.) London port book, inward, 1719

Oxford. Bodleian Library

Aubrey MSS. 4 Virginia factor's contract, 1684

Plymouth. West Devon Record Office

Miscellaneous deeds: W.720/3; W.720/6; W.720/7

REPUBLIC OF IRELAND

Dublin. National Library of Ireland

Reports on Private Collections, no. 13 (Perry papers, Mallow)
Earl of Limerick's deposit

Dublin. Registry of Deeds

V. 7 p. 6 (no. 1611) John Perry's will, 1710
V. 41 pp. 230–231 (no. 25536)
V. 118 pp. 226–228 (nos. 80570, 80571) Sale of part of Woodrooff, 1743/4

Dublin. Trinity College

Earl of Donoughmore's deposit (Hely-Hutchinson papers)

UNITED STATES

Annapolis. Hall of Records, Maryland State Archives

Provincial Court. Land Records

Charlottesville. University of Virginia Library

Robert Anderson Jr. letterbook
R. Carter letterbook (transcripts)
R. Carter estate letterbook

New Haven, Connecticut. Beinecke Library (Yale University)

Printed *bills of entry*, London, 1697–1698

New York City. New York Public Library

William Beverley papers

Richmond. Virginia Historical Society

R. Carter letterbook
Custis Papers (C9698)
D. P. Custis Estate Papers
Lee Papers (L51)

Richmond. Virginia State Library

Middlesex County will book, 1713–1734
York County deeds

San Marino, California. Huntington Library

Blathwayt (BL) papers

Washington, D.C. Library of Congress

Banks Collection (English transcripts)
John Custis letterbook
Jones family papers

Williamsburg, Virginia. Colonial Williamsburg Foundation

Sir William Gooch correspondence (transcripts)

Printed Materials

PRIMARY SOURCES

Bank of England. *A List of the Names and Sums of all New Subscribers for Enlarging the Capital Stock . . .* London, [1697].

Bannerman, W. Bruce, ed. *The Registers of St. Mary le Bowe, Cheapside . . . and of St. Pancras, Soper Lane, London.* 2 vol. Harleian Society, *Registers,* XLIV–XLV. London, 1914–1915.

Bateman, John. *The Great Landowners of Great Britain and Ireland.* New ed. London, 1879.

Beverley, Robert. *The History and Present State of Virginia,* ed. Louis Booker Wright. Chapel Hill, N.C., 1947.

Billings, Warren M., ed. *The Old Dominion in the Seventeenth Century: A Documentary History of Virginia, 1606–1689.* Chapel Hill, N.C., 1975.

Brock, R[obert] A[lonzo]. *Miscellaneous Papers 1672–1685, Now First Printed from the Manuscripts in the Collections of the Virginia Historical Society.* Collections of the Virginia Historical Society, n.s., VI). Richmond, Va., 1887.

Byrd, William, I, II, and III. *The Correspondence of the Three William Byrds of Westover, Virginia,* ed. Marion Tinling. 2 vols. Charlottesville, Va., 1977.

Byrd, William, I. "Letters of William Byrd, First. (From his Letter Book in the Collection of the Virginia Historical Society)," *Virginia Magazine of History and Biography,* XXV (1917) 250–264; XXVI (1918) 17–31, 124–

134, 247–259, 388–392; XXVII (1919) 167–168, 273–288; XXVIII (1920) 11–25.

Byrd, William, II. *History of the Dividing Line and Other Tracts* . . . , ed. Thomas H. Wynne. *Historical Documents from the Old Dominion,* III. 2 vols. Richmond, Va., 1866.

——. *William Byrd of Virginia: the London Diary (1717–1721) and Other Writings,* ed. Louis B. Wright and Marion Tinling. New York, 1958.

——. *The Secret Diary of William Byrd of Westover, 1709–1712,* ed. Louis B. Wright and Marion Tinling. Richmond, Va., 1941.

——. *The Writings of "Colonel William Byrd of Westover in Virginia Esqr.,"* ed. John Spencer Bassett. New York, 1901.

Calder, Isabel M., ed. *Activities of the Puritan Faction of the Church of England 1625–33.* London, 1957.

Carter, Robert. *Letters of Robert Carter 1720–1727: The Commercial Interests of a Virginia Gentleman,* ed. Louis Booker Wright. San Marino, Calif., 1940.

Chamberlayne, [Edward and] John. *Magnae Britanniae Notitia: or, The Present State of Great Britain.* 22nd ed. 2 vols. London, 1708.

Chapman, Blanche Adams, ed. *Wills and Administrations of Isle of Wight County Virginia 1647–1800.* 3 vols. [Smithfield, Va.], 1938, 1975.

Chester, Joseph Lemuel, and George J. Armitage, eds. *The Parish Registers of St. Antholin, Budge Row, London* . . . Harleian Society, *Registers,* VIII. London, 1883.

Clarke, A. W. Hughes, and Arthur Campling, eds. *The Visitation of Norfolk Anno Domini 1664.* 2 vols. Norfolk Record Society, IV, V. [London?] 1934.

Colden, Cadwallader. *The Letters and Papers of Cadwallader Colden.* 6 vols. Collections of the New-York Historical Society, L–LV. New York, 1918–1923.

Coleman, James, ed. *A Copy of the Names of All the Marriages, Baptisms and Burials* . . . *in the Private Chapel of Somerset House, Strand* . . . *from 1714 to 1776.* London, 1862.

Cook, Ebenezer. *The Sot-Weed Factor: Or, a Voyage to Maryland.* London, 1708 [and later editions].

Dale, T. C., ed. *The Inhabitants of London in 1638* . . . *from Ms. 272 in the Lambeth Palace Library.* 2 vols. London, 1931.

Darnall, Henry. *A Just and Impartial Account of Transactions of the Merchants of London for the Advancement of the Price of Tobacco* Annapolis, Md. [1729].

Des Cognets, Louis, Jr., ed. *English Duplicates of Lost Virginia Records.* Princeton, N.J., 1958.

Dexter, Franklin Bowditch, ed. *New Haven Town Records 1649–1662.* New Haven Colony Historical Society. *Ancient Town Records,* I. New Haven, Conn., 1917.

Donnan, Elizabeth, ed. *Documents Illustrative of the History of the Slave Trade to America*. 4 vols. Carnegie Institution of Washington, Publication no. 409. Washington, D.C., 1930–1935.

Eustace, P. Beryl, ed. *Registry of Deeds Dublin: Abstract of Wills . . . (1705–1745)*. Dublin, 1956.

Exeter. *Exeter Freemen 1266–1967*, ed. Margery M. Rowe and Andrea M. Jackson. Devon and Cornwall Record Society, Extra Series, I. Exeter, 1973.

———. *Tudor Exeter: Tax Assessments 1489–1595*, ed. Margery M. Rowe. Devon and Cornwall Record Society, n.s., XXII. Torquay, 1977.

Firth, Sir Charles Harding, ed. *Scotland and the Commonwealth*. Publications of the Scottish History Society, XVIII. Edinburgh, 1895.

———, ed. *Scotland and the Protectorate*. Publications of the Scottish History Society, XXXII. Edinburgh, 1899.

Firth, Sir Charles Harding, and R. S. Rait, eds. *Acts and Ordinances of the Interregnum, 1642–1660*. 3 vols. London, 1911.

Fleet, Beverley, ed. *Charles City County Court Orders 1655–1665*. Virginia Colonial Abstracts, X–XIII. 4 vols. Baltimore, Md., 1961.

———, ed. *Essex County—Wills and Deeds 1714–1717*. Virginia Colonial Abstracts, IX. Richmond, Va. [1940].

Foster, Joseph, ed. *London Marriage Licenses, 1521–1869*. London, 1887.

Ganter, Herbert Lawrence, ed. "Documents Relating to the Early History of The College of William and Mary," *William and Mary Quarterly*, 2d ser., XIX (1939) 347–375, 446–470.

Glass, D. V., ed. *London Inhabitants Within the Walls*. London Record Society, 2. London, 1966.

Great Britain. *Proceedings and Debates of the British Parliaments Respecting North America*, ed. Leo Francis Stock. 5 vols. Washington, D.C., 1924–1941.

Hallen, A. W. Cornelius, ed. *The Register of St. Botolph, Bishopsgate, London*. 3 vols. London, 1889–1895.

Hartwell, Henry, et al. *The Present State of Virginia, and the College*, ed. Hunter Dickinson Farish. Williamsburg, Va., 1940.

Hazard, Samuel, ed. *Pennsylvania Archives* [1st ser.]. Philadelphia, Pa., 1852.

Hening, William Waller, ed. *The Statutes at Large; being a Collection of all the Laws of Virginia*. 13 vols. Philadelphia, 1823; Charlottesville, Va., 1969.

Hoadly, Charles Jeremy, ed. *Records of the Colony and Plantation of New Haven from 1638 to 1649*. Hartford, Conn., 1857.

Hodson, V. C. P. *List of all the Officers of the Bengal Army 1758–1834*. 4 vols. London, 1927–1947.

Horwitz, Henry, W. A. Speck and W. A. Gray, eds. *London Politics 1713–1717*. London Record Society, 17. London, 1981.

Hutchinson, Thomas. *The Diary and Letters of . . . Thomas Hutchinson Esq.*, ed. Peter Orlando Hutchinson. 2 vols. Boston, 1884.

————. *The History of the Colony and Province of Massachusetts Bay*, ed. Lawrence Shaw Mayo. 3 vols. Cambridge, Mass., 1936.

————. *The Hutchinson Papers*. 2 vols. Publications of the Prince Society, I, II. Albany, N.Y., 1865.

Jacobus, Donald Lines. *List of Officials, Civil, Military, and Ecclesiastical of Connecticut . . . and of New Haven Colony . . .* New Haven, Conn., 1935.

Judd, Gerrit P., IV. *Members of Parliament 1734–1832*. Yale Historical Publications. Miscellany, 61. New Haven, Conn., 1955.

Kingsbury, Susan Myra, ed. *The Records of the Virginia Company of London*. 4 vols. Washington, D.C., 1906–1935.

Labaree, Leonard Woods, ed. *Royal Instructions to British Colonial Governors 1670–1776*. 2 vols. New York, 1935.

Laffan, Thomas, ed. *Tipperary's Families: being the Hearth Money Records for 1665–6–7*. Dublin, 1911.

Le Neve, Peter. *Le Neve's Pedigrees of the Knights Made . . . [1660–1714]*, ed. George W. Marshall. Harleian Society, VIII. London, 1873.

London. Inns of the Court. Middle Temple. *Register of Admissions to the Honourable Society of the Middle Temple*. 3 vols. London, 1944.

————. Royal College of Physicians. *The Roll of the Royal College of Physicians of London*, ed. William Munk. 2d ed. London, 1878.

————. Westminister School. *The List of the Queen's Scholars at St. Peter's College, Westminster*, ed. Joseph Welch. London, 1852.

————. *The Records of Old Westminster: A Biographical List . . . to 1927*, ed. G. F. Russell Barker and Alan H. Stenning. 2 vols. London, 1928.

Longdon, Henry J., ed. *The Visitation of the County of Northampton in the Year 1681*. Harleian Society, LXXXVII. London, 1935.

Luttrell, Narcissus. *A Brief Relation of State Affairs from September 1678 to April 1714*. 6 vols. Oxford, 1857.

McCusker, John J. "European Bills of Entry and Marine Lists: Early Commercial Publications and the Origins of the Business Press. Part I: Introduction and British Bills of Entry," *Harvard Library Bulletin*, XXXI (1983) 209–255.

McGhan, Judith, ed. *Virginia Will Records from the Virginia Magazine of History and Biography . . .* Baltimore, Md., 1982.

Maryland. Council. *Proceedings of the Council of Maryland 1693–1731*. Archives of Maryland, XX, XXIII, XXV. Baltimore, Md., 1900, 1903, 1905.

————. General Assembly. *Proceedings and Acts of the General Assembly of Maryland April 26, 1700–May 3, 1704*. Archives of Maryland, XXIV. Baltimore, Md., 1904.

————. Provincial Court. *Proceedings of the Provincial Court of Maryland 1675–1677*. Archives of Maryland, LXVI. Baltimore, Md., 1954.

Mason, Polly Cary, ed. *Records of Colonial Gloucester County Virginia.* 2 vols. Newport News, Va., 1948.

Matthews, A. G., ed. *Calamy Revised, being a Revision of Edmund Calamy's Account of the Ministers and Others Ejected and Silenced, 1660–2.* Oxford, 1934.

——, ed. *Walker Revised, being a revision of John Walker's Sufferings of the Clergy during the Grand Rebellion 1642–60.* Oxford, 1948.

Minchinton, Walter, Celia King, and Peter Waite, eds. *Virginia Slave-Trade Statistics 1698–1775.* Richmond, Va., 1984.

Moody, Robert E., ed. *The Saltonstall Papers 1607–1815.* Collections of the Massachusetts Historical Society, 80. Boston, Mass., 1972, 1974.

Morant, Philip. *The History and Antiquities of the County of Essex.* 2 vols. London, 1768.

North Carolina. *The Colonial Records of North Carolina,* ed. William L. Saunders. 10 vols. Raleigh, N.C., 1886–1890.

——. Higher Court. *North-Carolina Higher-Court Records 1697–1701,* ed. Mattie Erma Edwards Parker et al. Colonial Records of North Carolina, 2d ser., 3. Raleigh, N.C., 1971.

——. *North-Carolina Higher-Court Records 1702–1708, 1709–1723,* ed. William S. Price, Jr. Colonial Records of North Carolina, 2d ser., IV, V. Raleigh, N.C., 1974, 1977.

Oldmixon, John. *The British Empire in America.* 2 vols. London, 1708; 2nd ed., London, 1741.

Puckle, James. *The Club: or, A Grey Cap for a Green Head,* ed. [Henry] Austin Dobson. London, 1900.

Rylands, W. Harry, ed. *Grantees of Arms Named in Docquets and Patents Between the Years 1687 and 1898.* Harleian Society, LXVII, LXVIII. London, 1916, 1917.

Salley, Alexander S., Jr., ed. *Narratives of Early Carolina 1650–1708.* New York, 1911.

Sherwood, George. *American Colonists in English Records.* 2 vols. London, 1932–1933.

Stout, William. *Autobiography of William Stout of Lancaster, Wholesale and Retail Grocer and Ironmonger . . . A.D. 1665–1752,* ed. J. Harland. London, 1851.

Stow, John. *A Survey of the Cities of London and Westminster.* 2 vols. London, 1720.

Swem, Earl G., ed. "Brothers of the Spade: Correspondence of Peter Collinson, of London, and of John Custis, of Williamsburg, Virginia, 1734–1746," *Proceedings of the American Antiquarian Society,* 51:1 (1948/49) 17–190.

[Thornton, John]. *A New Map of Virginia, Maryland, Pensilvania, New Jersey, Part of New York and Carolina* [2d version]. London, ca. 1702–1720.

Treloar, Sir William Purdie, bart. *A Lord Mayor's Diary 1906–7 to which is Added the Official Diary of Micaiah Perry Lord Mayor 1738–9.* London, 1920.

Trumbull, Benjamin. *A Complete History of Connecticut.* 2 vols. Hartford, Conn., 1797; new ed., New Haven, 1818.

Tucker, Thomas. "Report of Thomas Tucker upon the Settlement of the Revenues of Excise and Customs in Scotland A.D. MDCLVI," *Miscellany of the Scottish Burgh Records Society.* Edinburgh, 1881, pp. 1–48.

United Kingdom. Privy Council. *Acts of the Privy Council of England, Colonial Series,* ed. William Lawson Grant and James Munro. 6 vols. London, 1908–1912.

———. Public Record Office. *Calendar of State Papers Relating to Ireland,* ed. Robert Pentland Mahaffy et al. 13 vols. London, 1870–1910.

———. *Calendar of State Papers, Colonial,* ed. W. N. Sainsbury et al. 42 vols. to date. London, 1860–.

———. *Calendar of the Proceedings of the Committee for Advance of Money, 1642–1656,* ed. M. A. E. Green. 3 vols. London, 1888.

———. *Calendar of the Proceedings of the Committee for Compounding . . . 1643–1660.* 5 vols. London, 1889–1892.

———. *Calendar of Treasury Books,* ed. William A. Shaw. 32 vols. London, 1904–1957.

———. *Calendar of Treasury Books and Papers,* ed. William A. Shaw. 5 vols. London, 1898–1903.

———. *Journals of the Board of Trade and Plantations.* 14 vols. London, 1920–1938.

Virginia. Council. *Executive Journals of the Council of Colonial Virginia,* ed. Henry Read McIlwaine et al. 6 vols. Richmond, Va., 1925–1966.

———. House of Burgesses. *Journals of the House of Burgesses of Virginia,* ed. John Pendleton Kennedy and Henry Read McIlwaine. 13 vols. Richmond, Va., 1905–1913.

Vivian, John Lambrick, ed. *The Visitations of the County of Devon . . . 1531, 1564 and 1620.* Exeter, 1895.

Winthrop Papers. 5 vols. Boston, 1929–1947.

Winthrop, John. *Winthrop's Journal "History of New England" 1630–1649,* ed. James Kendall Hosmer. 2 vols. New York, 1908, 1959.

SECONDARY WORKS

Aylmer, G. E. *The State's Servants: The Civil Service of the English Republic 1649–1660.* London and Boston, 1973.

Banks, Charles Edward. *The Winthrop Fleet of 1630* . . . Boston, 1930.

Baker, George. *The History and Antiquities of the County of Northampton.* 2 vols. London, 1822–1841.

Beaven, Alfred B. *The Aldermen of the City of London.* 2 vols. London, 1908–1913.

Bence-Jones, Mark. *A Guide to Irish Country Houses.* London, 1988.

Boddie, John Bennett. *Historical Southern Families.* 20 vols. Baltimore, Md., 1967–1975.

———. *Southside Virginia Families.* 2 vols. Redwood City, Calif., 1956; Baltimore, Md., 1966.

Bottigheimer, Karl S. *English Money and Irish Land: The 'Adventurers' in the Cromwellian Settlement of Ireland.* Oxford, 1971.

Bruce, Philip Alexander. *Economic History of Virginia in the Seventeenth Century.* 2 vols. New York, 1895, 1935.

Burke, Sir [John] Bernard, et al. *A Genealogical and Heraldic History of the Peerage and Baronetage.* 19th ed. London, 1932 [and other editions].

———. *A Genealogical History of the Dormant, Abeyant, Forfeited and Extinct Peerages of the British Empire.* London, 1883 [and other editions].

———. *The General Armory of England, Scotland, Ireland and Wales.* 2nd ed. London, 1884.

Burke's Presidential Families of the United States of America. London, 1975.

Burke, William P. *History of Clonmel.* Waterford, 1907.

Calder, Isabel MacBeath. *The New Haven Colony.* New Haven, Conn., 1934.

Carr, Lois Green, et al. *Colonial Chesapeake Society.* Chapel Hill, N.C., 1988.

Clemens, Paul G. E. *The Atlantic Economy and Colonial Maryland's Eastern Shore.* Ithaca, N.Y., and London, 1980.

Clode, Charles M. *The Early History of the Guild of Merchant Taylors, London.* 2 vols. London, 1888.

Clutterbuck, Robert. *The History and Antiquities of the County of Hertford.* 3 vols. London, 1815–1827.

[Cokayne, George Edward.] *The Complete Peerage* . . . *Extant, Extinct or Dormant.* New ed., ed Vicary Gibbs et al. 13 vols. London, 1910–1959.

Cotton, William. *An Elizabethan Guild of the City of Exeter.* Exeter, 1873.

Cruikshanks, Eveline. *Political Untouchables: The Tories and the '45.* New York, 1979.

Currer-Briggs, Noel. *The Carters of Virginia.* Totowa, N.J., 1979.

Davies, K. G. *The Royal African Company.* London, 1957.

Davis, Ralph. *Aleppo and Devonshire Square: English Traders in the Levant in the Eighteenth Century.* London, 1967.

———. "English Foreign Trade, 1660–1700," *Economic History Review,* 2nd ser., VII (1954) 150–166.

————. "English Foreign Trade, 1700–1774," *Economic History Review*, 2nd ser., XV (1962) 285–303.

Donnan, Elizabeth. "Eighteenth-Century English Merchants: Micajah Perry," *Journal of Economic and Business History*, IV (1931) 70–98.

Doolittle, I. G. "Walpole's City Election Act (1725)," *English Historical Review*, XCVII (1982) 504–529.

Dorman, John Frederick, ed. *Genealogies of Virginia Families from the William and Mary Quarterly Magazine*, 5 vols. Baltimore, Md., 1982.

Dow, F[rances] D. *Cromwellian Scotland 1651–1660.* Edinburgh, 1979.

Dowdey, Clifford. *The Virginia Dynasties: The Emergence of "King" Carter and the Golden Age.* Boston, 1961.

Dunn, Richard S. *Puritans and Yankees: The Winthrop Dynasty of New England 1630–1717.* Princeton, N.J., 1962.

Dymond, Robert. *History of the Parish of St. Petrock, Exeter.* Exeter, 1882.

Flinn, Michael W. *Men of Iron: The Crowleys in the Early Iron Industry.* Edinburgh University Publications: History, Philosophy and Economics, no. 14. Edinburgh, 1962.

Flippin, Percy Scott. *The Financial Administration of the Colony of Virginia.* Johns Hopkins University Studies in Historical and Political Science, ser. XXXIII, no. 2. Baltimore, 1915.

Foster, Joseph. *Alumni Oxonienses . . . 1500–1714.* 4 vols. Oxford, 1891–1892.

————. *Alumni Oxonienses . . . 1715–1886.* 4 vols. Oxford, 1888.

Ganter, Herbert Lawrence. "Some Notes on 'the Charity of the Honourable Robert Boyle,'" *William and Mary Quarterly*, XV (1935) 1–30, 207–228, 346–348.

Glin, The Knight of, et al. *Vanished Country Houses of Ireland.* [Dublin,] 1988.

Gregory, George C. "Jamestown's First Brick State House," *VMHB*, XLIII (1935) 193–199.

Harrison, Francis Burton. "Harrison in Virginia during the Reign of James I," *VMHB*, LI (1943) 326–338.

Harte, W. J. "Some Evidence of Trade between Exeter and Newfoundland up to 1600," *Transactions of the Devonshire Association for the Advancement of Science, Literature and the Arts*, LXIV (1932/34) 475–484.

[Harrison, Fairfax.] *Landmarks of Old Prince William.* 2 vols. Richmond, Va., 1924.

————. *Virginia Land Grants: A Study of Conveyancing in Relation to Colonial Politics.* Richmond, Va., 1925.

Hemphill, John M. *Virginia and the English Commercial System, 1689–1733.* New York and London, 1985.

Henning, Basil Duke. *The History of Parliament: The House of Commons 1660–1690.* 3 vols. London, 1983.

"Heysham Pedigree," *Miscellanea Genealogica et Heraldica,* n.s., IV (1884) 373–375.

Hill, Christopher. *Economic Problems of the Church from Archbishop Whitgift to the Long Parliament.* Oxford, 1956.

Hillier, Susan E. "The Trade of the Virginia Colony, 1606–1660." Ph.D. thesis, University of Liverpool, 1971.

Hoskins, W. G. "The Elizabethan Merchants of Exeter," in S. T. Bindoff et al., eds., *Elizabethan Government and Society: Essays Presented to Sir John Neale.* London, 1960.

Isham, Sir Gyles. "Pepys' American Dinner Party," *Northamptonshire Past & Present,* III (1965/6) 263–269; IV (1966/7) 25–34.

Jacobus, Donald Lines. *[The American Genealogist:] Families of Ancient New Haven.* 8 vols. New Haven, Conn., 1922–1932; reprinted, 3 vols. Baltimore, Md., 1974.

Jenkins, Alexander. *The History of the City of Exeter and Its Environs.* Exeter, 1806.

Johnson, George. *History of Cecil County, Maryland.* Elkton, Md., 1881.

Jones, D. W. "London Overseas Merchant Groups at the End of the Seventeenth Century and the Moves Against the East India Company." D.Phil. thesis, Oxford, 1970.

——. *War and Economy in the Age of William III and Marlborough.* Oxford, 1988.

Jones, Theophilus. *A History of the County of Brecknock.* Enlarged by Sir Joseph Russell Bailey, bart., baron Glanusk; ed. Edwin Davies. 4 vols. Brecknock, 1909–1930.

Kulikoff, Allan. *Tobacco and Slaves: The Development of Southern Cultures in the Chesapeake, 1680–1800.* Chapel Hill, N.C., 1986.

Langford, Paul. *The Excise Crisis: Society and Politics in the Age of Walpole.* Oxford, 1975.

Lee, Edmund Jennings. *Lee of Virginia.* Philadelphia, Pa., 1895.

Leete, Joseph, and John Corbet Anderson. *The Family of Leete.* 2nd ed. London, 1906.

Lenman, Bruce. *The Jacobite Clans of the Great Glen 1650–1784.* London, 1984.

Liu, Tai. *Puritan London: A Study of Religion and Society in the City Parishes.* London and Toronto, 1986.

MacCaffrey, Wallace T. *Exeter, 1540–1640: The Growth of an English County Town.* Harvard Historical Monographs, XXXV. Cambridge, Mass., 1958.

McCusker, John J., and Russell R. Menard. *The Economy of British America 1607–1789.* Chapel Hill, N.C., 1985.

Marambaud, Pierre. *William Byrd of Westover 1674–1744.* Charlottesville, Va., 1971.

Maurer, Maurer. "Edmund Jenings and Robert Carter," *VMHB* (1947) 20–30.

Mayo, Lawrence Shaw. *The Winthrop Family in America*. Boston, 1948.

Menard, Russell. "British Migration to the Chesapeake Colonies in the Seventeenth Century," in L. G. Carr, ed., *Colonial Chesapeake Society*, pp. 99–132. Chapel Hill, N.C., 1988.

———. "The Tobacco Industry in the Chesapeake Colonies 1617–1730: An Interpretation," *Research in Economic History*, V (1980) 109–177.

Middleton, Arthur Pierce. *Tobacco Coast: A Maritime History of Chesapeake Bay in the Colonial Era*. Newport News, Va., 1953.

Miller, Helen Hill. *Colonel Parke of Virginia*. Chapel Hill, N.C., 1984.

Morgan, Edmund S. *American Slavery American Freedom: The Ordeal of Colonial Virginia*. New York, 1975.

Namier, Sir Lewis. *The Structure of Politics at the Accession of George III*. 2nd ed. London, 1957.

———and John Brooke. *The History of Parliament: The House of Commons: 1754–1790*. 3 vols. London, 1964.

Neill, Edward Duffield. *Virginia Carolorum . . . a.d. 1625–1685*. Albany, N.Y., 1886.

Nolan, William. "Patterns of Living in County Tipperary from 1770 to 1850," in W. Nolan and T. G. McGrath, eds., *Tipperary: History and Society*, pp. 288–324. Dublin, ca. 1985.

Oliver, Vere Langford. *The History of the Island of Antigua*. 3 vols. London, 1894–1899.

Olson, Alison G. "The Board of Trade and London-American Interest Groups in the Eighteenth Century," *Journal of Imperial and Commonwealth History*, VIII (Jan. 1980) 33–50.

———. "The Virginia Merchants of London: A Study in Eighteenth Century Interest Group Politics," *William and Mary Quarterly*, 3d ser., XL (1983) 363–384.

Papenfuse, Edward C., et al. *A Biographical Dictionary of the Maryland Legislature 1635–1789*. 2 vols. Baltimore and London, 1979–1985.

Pares, Richard. *A West India Fortune*. London, 1950.

Pearl, Valerie. *London and the Outbreak of the Puritan Revolution: City Government and National Politics, 1625–1643*. Oxford, 1961.

Phipps, Pownoll W. *The Life of Colonel Pownoll Phipps, K.C., H.E.I.C.S. with Family Records*. London, 1894.

Pinckney, Paul J. "The Scottish Representation in the Cromwellian Parliament of 1656," *Scottish Historical Review*, XLVI (1967) 95–114.

Price, Jacob M. *Capital and Credit in British Overseas Trade: The View from the Chesapeake, 1700–1776*. Cambridge, Mass., 1980.

———. "The Excise Affair Revisited," in Stephen B. Baxter, ed. *England's*

Rise to Greatness 1660–1763, pp. 257–321. Berkeley and Los Angeles, 1983.

———. *France and the Chesapeake: A History of the French Tobacco Monopoly, 1674–1791* . . . 2 vols. Ann Arbor, Mich., 1973.

———. "Glasgow, the Tobacco Trade and the Scottish Customs, 1707–1730," *The Scottish Historical Review*, LXIII (1984) 1–36.

———. "The Last Phase of the Virgina-London Consignment Trade: James Buchanan & Co., 1758–1768," *William and Mary Quarterly*, 3d ser., XLIII (1986) 64–98.

———. "The Maryland Bank Stock Case," in Aubrey C. Land et al., eds., *Law, Society and Politics in Early Maryland*, pp. 3–40. Baltimore, Md., 1977.

———. "One Family's Empire: The Russell-Lee-Clerk Connection in Maryland, Britain, and India, 1707–1857," *Maryland Historical Magazine*, LXXII (1977) 165–225.

———. "Sheffeild v. Starke: Institutional Experimentation in the London-Maryland Trade, c. 1696–1706," *Business History*, XXVIII (1986) 19–39.

———. *The Tobacco Adventure to Russia*. Transactions of the American Philosophical Society, new ser., LI:1. Philadelphia, 1961.

———. "The Tobacco Trade and the Treasury, 1685–1733: British Mercantilism in its Fiscal Aspects", Ph.D. thesis, Harvard, 1954.

———and Paul G. E. Clemens, "A Revolution of Scale in Overseas Trade: British Firms in the Chesapeake Trade 1675–1775," *The Journal of Economic History*, XLVII (1987) 1–43.

Randolph, Robert Lee. *The First Randolphs of Virginia*. Washington, D.C., 1961.

Rogers, Nicholas. "The City Election Act (1725) Reconsidered," *English Historical Review*, C (1985) 604–617.

———. "Resistance to Oligarchy: The City Opposition to Walpole and his Successors," in John Stevenson, ed., *London in the Age of Reform*, pp. 1–29. Oxford, 1977.

Rubinstein, W. D. "Men of Wealth and the Purchase of Land in Nineteenth-Century Britain," *Past and Present*, 92 (Aug. 1981) 125–147.

Rutman, Darrett B., and Anita B. Rutman. *A Place in Time: Middlesex County, Virginia 1650–1750*. New York, 1984.

Savage, James. *A Genealogical Dictionary of the First Settlers of New England . . . who came before May, 1692*. 4 vols. Boston, 1860–1862.

Seaver, Paul S. *The Puritan Lectureship: The Politics of Religious Dissent 1560–1662*. Stanford, Calif., 1970.

Sedgwick, Romney. *The History of Parliament: The House of Commons 1715–1754*. London, 1970.

Sibley, John Langdon. *Biographical Sketches of Graduates of Harvard University. Volume I (1642–1658)*. Cambridge, Mass., 1873.

Simms, J. G. *The Williamite Confiscation in Ireland 1690–1703*. London, 1956.

Smith, R. W. Innes. *English-Speaking Students of Medicine at the University of Leyden*. Edinburgh and London, 1932.

Smyth, William. "Property, Patronage and Population . . . [in] Mid-Seventeenth Century County Tipperary," in William Nolan and Thomas G. McGrath, eds., *Tipperary: History and Society: Interdisciplinary Essays on the History of an Irish County*. Dublin, 1985.

Speck, W. A., and W. A. Gray. "London at the Polls under Anne and George I," *Guildhall Studies in London History*, I (1975) 253–262.

Stanard, W. G. "The Randolph Family," *William and Mary Quarterly*, 1st ser., VII (1898) 122–124, 195–197, VIII (1899–1900) 119–122, 263–265, IX (1900–1901) 182–183, 250–252.

Stearns, Raymond Phineas. *The Strenuous Puritan: Hugh Peter, 1598–1660*. Urbana, Ill., 1954.

Steinman, George Steinman. *The Author of "The Club" Identified*. S.l., 1872.

Stone, Lawrence. *An Open Elite: England, 1540–1880*. Oxford, 1984.

Truxes, Thomas M. *Irish-American Trade, 1660–1783*. Cambridge, 1988.

Tyler, Lyon Gardner. *The Cradle of the Republic: Jamestown and James River*. Richmond, Va., 1900.

United States of America. Bureau of the Census. *Historical Statistics of the United States, Colonial Times to 1970*. 2 vols. Washington, D.C., 1975.

Venn, John, and J. A. Venn. *Alumni Cantabrigienses*, Part I, *to 1751*, 4 vols. Cambridge, 1922–1927; Part II, *1752–1900*, 6 vols. Cambridge, 1940–1954.

The Victoria History of Hampshire and the Isle of Wight. Ed. William Page. 6 vols. London, 1900–1914.

The Victoria History of the County of Hertford. 4 vols. Westminster, 1902–1914.

Wagner, Henry, "The Huguenot Refugee Family of Harenc," *The Genealogist*, new ser., XXXII (1916) 193–195.

Waters, Henry F. *Genealogical Gleanings in England*, 2 vols. Boston, 1901.

Westbury, Susan. "Slaves of Colonial Virginia: Where They Came From," *William and Mary Quarterly*. 3d ser., XLII (1985) 228–237.

Williams, Neville, "England's Tobacco Trade in the Reign of Charles I," *VMHB*, LXV (1957) 403–449.

Withington, Lothrop. *Virginia Gleanings in England*. Baltimore, Md., 1980.

Woodhead, J. R. *The Rulers of London 1660–1689*. London, 1965.

Zuppan, Jo. "John Custis of Williamsburg, 1678–1749," *VMHB*, XC (1982) 177–197.

Notes

Preface

1. This theme is developed in Jacob M. Price and Paul G. E. Clemens, "A Revolution of Scale in Overseas Trade: British Firms in the Chesapeake Trade, 1675–1775," *The Journal of Economic History*, XLVII (1987) 1–43.
2. One such "special circumstance" affecting the American trades were the claims made by British businessmen formerly trading to the Thirteen Colonies for reimbursement of debts made uncollectable by the American Revolution. To substantiate such claims, the petitioning firms submitted to the government's commissioners many volumes of their original accounts and letterbooks. However, only a small fraction of these have survived in the relevant PRO classes, A.O.12 and 13 and T.79.
3. "One Family's Empire: The Russell-Lee-Clerk Connection in Maryland, Britain, and India, 1707–1857," *Maryland Historical Magazine*, LXXII (1977) 165–225.
4. "Eighteenth-Century English Merchants: Micajah Perry," *Journal of Economic and Business History*, IV (1931) 70–98.
5. Richard Pares, *A West India Fortune* (London, 1950); M. W. Flinn, *Men of Iron: The Crowleys in the Early Iron Industry*, Edinburgh University Publications: History, Philosophy and Economics no. 14 (Edinburgh, 1962); and Ralph Davis, *Aleppo and Devonshire Square: English Traders in the Levant in the Eighteenth Century* (London, 1967).
6. George Sherwood, *American Colonists in English Records*, 2 vols. (London, 1932–1933).

Introduction

1. In the first generation, the only Chesapeake merchants among the directors of the Bank of England were Robert Bristow, Jr., 1697–1706, and Richard Perry, 1699–1701. Only Bristow and his father represented the trade among the original subscribers to the Bank in 1694. In later years, Chesapeake merchants William Bowden, William Hunt and Lyonel Lyde became directors of the Bank and Hunt its governor, 1749–1752. He may have achieved this dignity because, in addition to

his own shares, he was trustee for a large block of shares in the bank owned by the province of Maryland as backing for its paper money. See Jacob M. Price, "The Maryland Bank Stock Case," in Aubrey C. Land et al., eds., *Law, Society and Politics in Early Maryland* (Baltimore, Md., 1977) 5–6.

2. From the Chesapeake trade, James Booth, John Cary and Micaiah Perry were among the commissioners for taking the two-million-pound subscription which led to the founding of the new East India Company in 1698; Booth, Cary (and his son Thomas), Peter Paggen and Thomas Starke (but not Perry) were among the major subscribers (£3000–6000 each); John Cary and Peter Paggen were also among the original directors of the company. However, the Carys and Booth were withdrawing from the Chesapeake trade by 1698. None (except possibly Paggen) was active in the affairs of the company after 1700. See Jacob M. Price, *The Tobacco Adventure to Russia . . . 1676–1722*, Transactions of the American Philosophical Society, new ser., LI:1 (Philadelphia, 1961) 33, 35, and sources cited in tables there.

3. For well-known examples of the skeptical school, see W. D. Rubinstein, "Men of Wealth and the Purchase of Land in Nineteenth-Century Britain," *Past and Present*, 92 (August 1981) 125–147; Lawrence Stone, *An Open Elite: England, 1540–1880* (Oxford, 1984).

1. The Early Perrys and Their Wanderings

1. George C. Gregory, "Jamestown's First Brick State House," *VMHB*, XLIII (1935) 199; Lindsay O. Duvall, ed., *James City County 1634–1904* (*Virginia Colonial Abstracts*, ser. 2, v. 4; Washington, D.C., 1957) 20. See also Charles E. Hatch, Jr., *America's Oldest Legislative Assembly and Its Jamestown Statehouses*, rev. ed. (Washington, D.C., 1956) 15–31; and John L. Cotter, *Archaeological Excavations at Jamestown . . . Virginia*, Archaeological Research Series, 4 (Washington, D.C., 1958). For a street map of late seventeenth century Jamestown, showing the locations of the first statehouse (including the Perry unit) and the later third and fourth statehouses, see Charles E. Hatch, Jr., *Jamestown, Virginia: the Townsite and Its Story*, National Park Service Historical Handbook, 2 (Washington, D.C., 1957) 43.

2. Almost all the previous writers on the Perrys have failed to mention the useful if limited pedigree of Micaiah Perry and his immediate family in Vere Langford Oliver, *The History of Antigua*, 3 vols. (London, 1894–1899), 20–24. Oliver, however, knew nothing of the antecedents of Micaiah Perry I and tried needlessly and fruitlessly to tie his family to the Perrys of Antigua and Youghall, co. Cork.

3. Haberdashers' Hall, London, Bindings, 1655–1675 (Oct. 1656).

4. PRO H.C.A.13/80 (25 Mar. 1692).

5. See Appendix D and BL Harley MS. 6834 ff. 121–122; Add. MS. 14,831 fo. 46; J[ohn] L[ambrick] Vivian, *The Visitation of the County of Devon, comprising the Heralds' Visitations of 1531, 1564 and 1620* (Exeter, 1895) 591; Sir Bernard Burke, *The General Armory of England, Scotland, Ireland and Wales*, 2nd ed. (London, 1884) 794.

6. W. J. Harte, "Some Evidence of Trade between Exeter and Newfoundland up to 1600," *Transactions of the Devonshire Association for the Advancement of Science, Literature and Art*, LXIV (1932/34) 473–484. For the connection between the Perrys of Exeter, Plymouth and Buckland Monachorum, see Appendix D.

7. For Roger Pery's possible connection with the Pery family of Water, see Appendix D. "Roger Pirry" of Exeter is referred to as a merchant in the 1552 will (proved 1555) of his kinsman, John Piry of Warminster, Wilts: PRO Prob.11/37 (P.C.C. 21 More).

8. PRO E.190/934/4 fo. 19; E.190/935/11 ff. 12, 19.

9. *Calendar of the Patent Rolls . . . Elizabeth I*, VII, 317–318.

10. For the descendants of William Pery, bailiff of Exeter in 1578, see Appendix D. See also Margery M. Rowe and Andrew M. Jackson, eds., *Exeter Freemen 1266–1967*, Devon and Cornwall Record Society, Extra Series, I (Exeter, 1973) 72, 84; Alexander Jenkins, *The History of the City of Exeter and its Environs . . .* (Exeter, 1806) 127, 130–131; William Cotton, *An Elizabethan Guild of the City of Exeter: An Account of the . . . Society of Merchant Adventurers during the latter half of the 16th century* (Exeter, 1873) 111–113, 119, 140–141; Margery M. Rowe, *Tudor Exeter: Tax Assessments 1489–1595 . . .*, Devon and Cornwall Record Society, new ser., XXII (Torquay, 1977) 51, 62, 64, 68, 71, 76–77. For the Subsidy of 1544, Roger Pery had the lowest tax in his parish; for the assessments of 1577, 1586 and 1593–1595, William and Richard Pery/Perie/Perrye had taxes slightly below the average for their parishes. However, as merchants they may have had effects outside the parish which were exempt from the attention of the assessors. For Exeter bailiffs, see Wallace T. MacCaffery, *Exeter, 1540–1640: The Growth of an English County Town*, Harvard Historical Monographs, XXXV (Cambridge, Mass., 1958) 36, 48. For the Pery peerages, see [George Edward Cokayne,] *The Complete Peerage*, new ed., ed. Vicary Gibbs et al., 13 vols. (London, 1910–1959), s.v. "Pery" and "Limerick."

11. Robert Dymond, *The History of the Parish of St. Petrock, Exeter, as Shown by Its Churchwardens' Accounts and Other Records*, reprinted from *Transactions of the Devonshire Association . . . 1882*, 402–492 (Exeter, 1882) 68; M. Rowe, *Tudor Exeter: Tax Assessments*, 63–64, 71, 76.

12. St. Petrock parish register abstracted in IGI. On Richard Perry I as "merchant," see W. G. Hoskins, "The Elizabethan Merchants of Exeter," in S. T. Bindoff et al., eds., *Elizabethan Government and Society: Essays Presented to Sir John Neale* (London, 1961) 164.

13. St. Edmund parish registers (photocopy) in Devon Record Office, Exeter.

14. John Bennett Boddie, *Southside Virginia Families,* 2 vols. (Redwood City, Calif., 1956; Baltimore, Md., 1966) II, 338; Edward D. Neill, *Virginia Carolorum: The Colony under the Rule of Charles the First and Second A.D. 1625–1685* (Albany, N.Y., 1886) 72, 270; Lyon Gardiner Tyler, *The Cradle of the Republic: Jamestown and James River* (Richmond, Va., 1900) 144; Susan Myra Kingsbury, ed., *The Records of the Virginia Company of London,* 4 vols. (Washington, D.C., 1906–1933) II, 519, 532, IV, 552. It is likely (if not certain) that William Pery of Virginia was the William, son of Henry Pery, who was christened at Buckland Monachorum (Devon) on 27 Aug. 1592 (parish register, IGI). The Exeter (St. Petrock) Perys also had some connection with Buckland Monachorum, where Richard II served his apprenticeship. See Appendix D.

15. PRO C.2/Charles I/P.53/13 and P.52/20. The "merchant-taylor" designation in these documents enables us to identify the Richard Pery mentioned therein with our Richard Pery II.

16. W. Bruce Bannerman, ed., *The Registers of St. Mary le Bowe, Cheapside . . . and of St. Pancras, Soper Lane, London,* 2 vols., Harleian Society, *Registers,* XLIV–XLV (London, 1914–1915), II, 447.

17. See his will, PRO Prob.11/211 (P.C.C. 9 Pembroke); and Guildhall Library, London, Merchant Taylors Records, film 324 (index) and 330 (Court of Assistants Minutes, IX, ff. 182, 185, 214v, 237v). His son Peter was later admitted to the freedom by service to his father. See also Charles M. Clode, *The Early History of the Guild of Merchant Taylors . . .,* 2 vols. (London, 1888) II, 347.

18. Kingsbury, *Virginia Company,* I, 534, II, 518.

19. PRO Prob.11/151 (P.C.C. 41 Skynner) abstracted in Henry F. Waters, *Genealogical Gleanings in England* (Boston, 1901) II, 1016. On James Carter, see Noel Currer-Briggs, *The Carters of Virginia: Their English Ancestry* (Chichester, 1979) 7–8. For details of the partnership between R. Pery and James Carter, see PRO C.2/Charles I/P.68/60 and P.96/26.

20. PRO Prob.11/155 (P.C.C. 32 Ridley). The will was proved in London on 28 Apr. 1629. James Carter had married "Susanne Perrye" in the parish church of St. Andrew, Plymouth, on 1 Aug. 1605 (parish register, IGI). After Carter's death, she married Brian Harrison of Wapping, another sea captain. By her first marriage she appears to have had a daughter, Susanna Carter, to whom John Pery of St. Antholins also left a bequest. See PRO C.2/Charles I/P.68/60 and Francis Burton Harri-

son, "Harrisons in Virginia during the Reign of James I," *VMHB*, LI (1943) 332n.

21. Richard Pery imported 3018 lb. of tobacco in 1627–1628 (1300 from Virginia and 1718 from Bermuda) and 7460 lb. in 1640 (information supplied by Professor Paul Clemens from PRO E.190). See also Neville Williams, "England's Tobacco Trade in the Reign of Charles I," *VMHB*, LXV (1957) 429, 436, 440. Surviving port books indicate that he exported cloth to Virginia in 1626, 1627 and 1640 (PRO E.190/29/4; E.190/31/1; E.190/43/1; E.190/43/4; E.190/44/1). See also PRO Rolls Room catalog 8/58B.

22. BL Harl. MS. 1238 fo. 4.

23. Joseph Lemuel Chester and George J. Armitage, eds., *The Parish Registers of St. Antholin, Budge Row, London . . .*, Harleian Society, *Registers*, VIII (London, 1883) 55–59, 61, 64, 66, 79, 82, 83.

24. T. C. Dale, ed., *The Inhabitants of London in 1638 Edited from Ms. 272 in the Lambeth Palace Library*, 2 vols. (London, 1931) I, 32. From 1621 to his death in 1650, Richard Pery II rented part of the old Muscovy House at the impressive rental of £44 p.a. His children Peter and Sarah occupied the same after his death. See PRO C.9/17/62, C.9/241/121 and C.10/30/21.

25. See Kingsbury, *Virginia Company*, II, 519, 532, IV, 552, and James Savage, *A Genealogical Dictionary of the First Settlers of New England*, 4 vols. (Boston, Mass., 1860–1862; Baltimore, Md., 1977) III, 400; Thomas Hutchinson, *The History of the Colony and Province of Massachusetts Bay*, ed. L. S. Mayo, 3 vols. (Cambridge, Mass., 1936) I, 10; *The Hutchinson Papers*, 2 vols., Prince Society, I, II (Albany, N.Y., 1865) I, 1–25, 117. On the Feoffees for Impropriations and the ultra-Puritan milieu of St. Antholins, see Raymond P. Stearns, *The Strenuous Puritan: Hugh Peter 1590–1660* (Urbana, Ill., 1954) 39; Christopher Hill, *Economic Problems of the Church from Archibishop Whitgift to the Long Parliament* (Oxford, 1956) chap. 11, esp. 254, 259–260; Isabel M. Calder, ed., *Activities of the Puritan Faction of the Church of England 1625–1633* (London, 1957) 28–30, 147; Valerie Pearl, *London and the Outbreak of the Puritan Revolution: City Government and National Politics, 1625–43* (Oxford, 1961) 162–165; Paul S. Seaver, *The Puritan Lectureships: The Politics of Religious Dissent 1560–1662* (Stanford, Calif., 1970) 173, 199, 306; Tai Liu, *Puritan London: A Study of Religion and Society in the City Parishes* (London and Toronto, 1986) 23, 86–87. According to Liu, St. Antholins was led by Presbyterians, while St. Pancras Soper Lane (where Pery was married) was a "known Independent parish." It is likely that Richard Pery II was inclined toward the Presbyterians, while Richard III in his younger years demonstrated definite Independent commitments.

26. *Cal.S.P.Dom., 1640*, 352. Watling Street begins in St. Antholins.

27. See n. 17.

28. *Calendar of the Committee for Advance of Money* II, 844.

29. C. H. Firth and R. S. Rait, *Acts and Ordnances of the Interregnum 1642–1660*, 3 vols. (London, 1911) 1129.

30. Calder, *Activities*, 147; Isabel MacBeath Calder, *The New Haven Colony* (New Haven, Conn., 1934) 1–22, 27–31, 46–47. Before emigrating to America, Richard Malbon(e), woollen-draper, lived in the parish of All Hallows, Bread Street, London, where his son Samuel was christened on 4 Dec. 1631 and his daughter Hanna on 3 Apr. 1634. IGI, London; W. Bruce Bannerman, ed., *The Registers of All Hallows, Bread Street, and of St. John the Evangelist, Friday Street, London*, Harleian Society, Registers, XLIII) (London, 1913) 25; and Boyd's Index 15426 (Society of Genealogists, London). Nothing more is known of his background. His daughter Mary was born before he moved to that parish.

31. Savage, *Genealogical Dictionary*, 400; Donald Lines Jacobus, *[The American Genealogist:] Families of Ancient New Haven*, 8 vols. (New Haven, Conn., 1921–1932) VI, 1439.

32. Calder, *New Haven Colony*, 60, 83–85, 120, 160, 179; Benjamin Trumbull, *A Complete History of Connecticut* (Hartford, 1797) I, 99–101, (New Haven, 1818) I, 104–106; Donald Lines Jacobus, *List of Officials, Civil, Military and Ecclesiastical of Connecticut Colony . . . and of New Haven Colony . . .* (New Haven, 1935) 34; *Winthrop Papers*, 5 vols. (Boston, 1929–1947) IV, 254, V, 119, 121; *[John] Winthrop's Journal "History of New England" 1630–1649*, ed. James Kendall Hosmer, Original Narratives of Early American History, 2 vols. (New York, 1908, 1959) II, 93; Savage, *Genealogical Dictionary*, III, 144; Charles J. Hoadly, ed., *Records of the Colony and Plantation of New Haven from 1638 to 1649* (Hartford, Conn., 1857) 85, 119, 148, 156, 181.

33. Hoadly, *Records of New Haven*, 9, 17, 26, 28, 39, 41, 44, 49, 61, 62, 91, 125, 134, 137–138, 141, 185, 224–225, 228, 230, 268, 274, 302, 304, 320, 327, 333–334, 336, 354, 369–370, 373, 413, 415, 488.

34. Franklin Bowditch Dexter, ed., *New Haven Town Records 1649–1662*, New Haven Colony Historical Society, *Ancient Town Records*, I (New Haven, Conn., 1917) 8n, 58–59, 63–64, 232, 481; Calder, *New Haven*, 158–159, 208.

35. PRO Prob.11/211 (P.C.C. 9 Pembroke) will dated 9 Aug. 1648 and proved 11 Jan. 1649/50. The records of St. Antholins show that Richard Pery was buried on 12 Jan. 1649/50.

36. PRO Prob.11/236 (P.C.C. 170 Alchin), dated 7 Dec. 1653 and proved 25 Feb. 1653/54.

37. PRO Prob.11/243 (P.C.C. 33 Aylett), dated 3 Dec. 1654 and proved 15 Dec. 1654. Peter Pery had continued his father's dealings in wool

products and interest in the trade to Spain, which he visited at least once. See *Cal.S.P.Dom., 1652–53,* 475.

38. PRO Prob.11/268 (P.C.C. 374 Ruthon) dated 10 Nov. 1656, proved 6 Oct. 1657. See also PRO Prob.11/292 (P.C.C. 328 Pell) for the 1659 will of William Whittle, merchant of the parish of St. Dionis Backchurch; and PRO Prob. 8/51 p. 286.

39. Guildhall Library, London MS. 15860: Records of the Haberdashers Company, London: Bindings, 1630–1655 (20 July 1649); 1655–1675 (Oct. 1656).

40. See Currer-Briggs, *Carter of Virginia.*

41. See n. 39.

42. "Report of Thomas Tucker upon the Settlement of the Revenues of Excise and Customs in Scotland, A.D. MDCLVI," *Miscellany of the Scottish Burgh Records Society* (Edinburgh, 1881) 47. For Pery's presence in Glasgow in 1654, see PRO Prob.11/308 (P.C.C. 67 Laud) and Waters, *Genealogical Gleanings,* I, 1. Tucker's report lists John Leete as collector of Leith at £120 p.a. The latter was almost certainly the brother of William Leete, a founding settler of New Haven and governor both of that colony and of Connecticut. Joseph Leete and J. C. Anderson, *The Family of Leete,* 2nd ed. (London, 1906) 128–129, 140, 159–160, 161–164. Their father was of Dodington/Diddington, Hunts, the birthplace of Oliver Cromwell. See also BL Egerton MS. 2519 ff. 10–11 W. Leete to S. Disbrowe, 11 Oct. 1654.

43. PRO A.O.1/891/7 and 9. I am indebted to Dr. Gerald Aylmer for this reference. In April 1656, Richard Pery was also appointed a sequestrator of the estates of those sequestered for nonpayment of arrears of excise. *Calendar of the Proceedings of the Committee for Compounding . . . 1643–1660,* ed. M. A. E. Green, 5 vols. (London, 1889–1892) I, 742.

44. *Cal.S.P.Dom., 1652–1653,* 224; *1657–1658,* 377. For the Hutchinson connection, see Appendix C.

45. For Desborough, Downing and Fenwick, see *Dictionary of National Biography.* For Richard Saltonstall, Jr., see Robert E. Moody, ed., *The Saltonstall Papers 1607–1815,* 2 vols., *Collections* of the Massachusetts Historical Society, 80 (Boston, Mass., 1972, 1974) I, 25–38. See also D. L. Jacobus, *List,* 18; F. D. Dow, *Cromwellian Scotland 1651–1660* (Edinburgh, 1979) 32, 44, 48, 57–58, 122–123, 165, 168–170, 175, 185, 215, 222, 237–238; Sir Charles Harding Firth, ed., *Scotland and the Commonwealth . . . (Publications* of the Scottish History Society, XVIII; Edinburgh, 1895) xxxi, 44; Firth, ed., *Scotland and the Protectorate,* S. H. S., XXXII (Edinburgh, 1899) 311, 315, 387, 390, 411, 414, 416. The committee on sequestrations set up in 1652 was early given reponsibility for customs. When excise was extended to Scotland in 1655, the committee

was reconstituted (with Saltonstall continuing) and given responsibility for that too. Other ex–New Englanders prominent in Scotland at this time included Colonel Stephen Winthrop (son of Governor John Winthrop of Massachusetts), M.P. for the Aberdeen burghs in the Parliament of 1656–58, and his brother-in-law, Colonel Thomas Reade, governor of Stirling Castle. See Bruce Lenman, *The Jacobite Clans of the Great Glen 1650–1784* (London, 1984) 36; *Winthrop Papers*, III and IV; Charles Edward Banks, *The Winthrop Fleet of 1630* (Boston, 1930) 89; Lawrence Shaw Mayo, *The Winthrop Family in America* (Boston, 1948) 63–65, 82; Richard S. Dunn, *Puritans and Yankees: The Winthrop Dynasty of New England 1630–1717* (Princeton, N.J., 1962) 54–55, 98, 126; Paul J. Pinckney, "The Scottish Representation in the Cromwellian Parliament of 1656," *Scottish Historical Review*, XLVI (1967) 95–114. I am indebted to Professor T. C. Smout for help on this point.

46. In the hearth tax returns for County Limerick for 1665–1666, a Richard Perry appears for three hearths and a Richard Perrott for eight hearths, both in Clonmel. Thomas Laffan, *Tipperary's Families: Being the Hearth Money Records for 1665–6–7* (Dublin, 1911) 68. Richard Perrott, whose wife was named Edith, was clearly a different person from Richard Perry. The earliest clear reference to Richard Per(r)y in Clonmel comes in October 1660, when he resigned as "Sergeant at Mace" for the town corporation. This may be interpreted as the withdrawal of a Cromwellian at the Restoration. The post would appear to have been mostly ceremonial and could be held by someone otherwise employed. Burke describes Richard Per(r)y as a merchant after 1660: William P. Burke, *History of Clonmel* (Waterford, 1907) 91, 250, 259. See also n. 50 below. For help on Clonmel I am indebted to Mr. Thomas Power of Trinity College, Dublin. There are two other persons named Richard Perry (or Pery) active in the Chesapeake trade in the 1660s who should not be confused with Micaiah's father Richard, late of Glasgow. One appears in the Plymouth port books, 1664–1675, trading to Virginia. The other was a merchant active on Patuxent River, Maryland, ca. 1668–1674, and then in London from ca. 1679 to his death in 1685. The first was operating on too small a scale; the second's kin do not fit. On the first, see Plymouth port books in PRO E.190/1037/17; E.190/1038/8; E.190/1039/3; E.190/1041/1. On the second, see Edward C. Papenfuse et al., *A Biographical Dictionary of the Maryland Legislature 1635–1789*, 2 vols. (Baltimore and London, 1979–1985) II, 644; MdHR Provincial Court Deeds PL#6, 238–244; WRC#1, 341–44; PRO Prob.11/379 (P.C.C. 26 Cann) and C.10/223/65. He requested to be buried next to his father in the parish church of Thorp, Surrey.

47. For the family connections between the Perys of Limerick and the

Perrys of London, see Appendix D. For the descendants of Edmund Pery, see *Burke's Peerage* (any ed.) s.v. "Earl of Limerick" and *Burke's Extinct Peerage* (1883 ed.) s.v. "Viscount Pery."

48. *Calendar of the State Papers Relating to Ireland . . . 1647–1660,* ed. R. P. Mahaffy (London, 1903) 404, 448, 452, 453, 462, 484, 549, 555, 559; and PRO C.24/698(ii)/38.

49. For Richard Hutchinson of London and Tipperary, see Gerald E. Aylmer, *The State's Servants: The Civil Service of the English Republic 1649–1660* (London and Boston, 1973) 247–250, but see also Savage, *Genealogical Dictionary,* II, 511. For the Perry-Hutchinson connection, see Appendix C.

50. See Chapter 7. See also William Smyth, "Property, Patronage and Population . . ." in William Nolan and Thomas G. McGrath, eds., *Tipperary: History and Society . . .* (Dublin, 1985) 132.

51. Guildhall Library, London, MS. 15857/2 Haberdashers Company Records: Freedoms (1642–1772) p. 107.

52. Joseph Foster, ed., *London Marriage Licences, 1521–1869* (London, 1887) column 1046.

53. On Dr. Richard Owen (1606–1683), see *Dictionary of National Biography;* and A. G. Matthews, *Walker Revised, Being a Revision of John Walker's Suffering of the Clergy during the Grand Rebellion 1642–60* (Oxford, 1948) 54–55.

54. Micaiah's break with his Calvinist New Haven upbringing was not complete. Echoes of his childhood reappear in the language of his later correspondence. See for example the letter of Micaiah and Richard Perry and Thomas Lane to Philip Ludwell Lee, 19 Aug. 1704 (VaHS MSS 1 L51 f8, Lee Papers) in which the safe arrival of the tobacco fleet in wartime is twice seen as a sign "that Gods Providence had a particular regard to our preservation which deserves our . . . thankfullness." Perry was later to exert himself in lobbying against legislation discriminating against colonial Nonconformists.

55. A. G. Matthews, *Calamy Revised, Being a revision of Edmund Calamy's Account of the Ministers and Others Ejected and Silenced, 1660–2* (Oxford, 1934) 333–334; John Langdon Sibley, *Biographical Sketches of Graduates of Harvard University, Volume I, 1642–1658* (Cambridge, Mass., 1873) 550. Ca. 1730, the Perry firm employed a ship captain named Samuel Malbon. Cambridge University Library, Cholmondeley (Houghton) MSS 29/29(3). In the 1660s, a Malbon family of uncertain origin settled in the Norfolk area of Virginia. A branch of this Virginia family was established in Rhode Island in the eighteenth century.

56. Burke, *Clonmel,* 294, 295, 308. The Rialls of Clonmel, the family of John Perry's wife, Elizabeth, were also prominent Presbyterians.

57. John Perry, brother or nephew of Micaiah I, appears in 1700–1701 as one of the co-owners of the very large Virginia trade vessel *Perry and Lane*, whose tobacco carrying capacity was near 900 hogsheads. PRO C.O.5/1441 ff. 33, 84.

58. National Library of Ireland, "Reports on Private Collections," no. 13, pp. 318, 321, 331: Report on "Perry Papers" in custody of Messrs. O'Connor & Dudley of Mallow.

2. The Emergence of Perry & Lane

1. In 1699, Perry deposed in Chancery that he had been active in the Virginia consignment trade "for 34 yeares last past," i.e., since 1665; in 1692, Perry deposed in Admiralty that he "has used the Virginia Trade for almost Twenty six yeares," i.e., since 1666. PRO C.24/1215/63 (Lloyd v. Nicholson); H.C.A.13/80 (25 Apr. 1692). The London port books show him first exporting cloth to Virginia in 1668. PRO E.190/52/1.

2. Donnan, "Micajah Perry," 72.

3. George Baker, *The History and Antiquities of the County of Northampton*, 2 vols. (London, 1822–1841) I, 297; Henry I. Longdon, ed., *The Visitation of the County of Northampton in the Year 1681*, Harleian Society, LXXXVII (London, 1935) 111. For the Randolphs, see W. G. Stanard, "The Randolph Family," *William and Mary Quarterly*, 1st ser., VII (1898) 122–124, 195–197, VIII (1899–1900) 119–122, 263–265, IX (1900–1901) 182–183, 250–252; Sir Gyles Isham, "Pepys' American Dinner Party," *Northamptonshire Past & Present*, IV (1966–67) 30–31; and Robert Lee Randolph, *The First Randolphs of Virginia* (Washington, 1961).

4. Foster, *London Marriage Licenses*, 813.

5. Brother William Puckle in Port Royal, Jamaica, is mentioned in Mary Lane's will of 1723–1727: PRO Prob.11/617 (P.C.C. 237 Farrant).

6. *Cal.S.P.Dom., 1655–1656*, 189, 238–239; *1656–1657*, 41–42; *Cal.T.B.*, I, 554; V(i) 309.

7. Ethel Bruce Sainsbury and William Foster, eds., *A Calendar of the Court Minutes of the East India Company 1674–1676* (Oxford, 1935) xvi, 29, 111, 118, 122, 127, 132, 133. Since Major Puckle was permitted to ship £500 in pieces of eight to India, some sort of private trade was also envisioned. William Puckle's brother James, a merchant at Yarmouth, undertook a confidential mission in Holland for Secretary Williamson during the opening stages of the Third Dutch War (1672–1673). It was at first planned to reward him with a place on the Navy Board; when this did not prove possible, he was given a "free gift" of £1000. *Cal.S.P.Dom., 1668–1669*, 387; *1670*, 255; *1672–1673*, 233, 296, 458, 630, 631; *1673*, 591; *Cal.T.B., 1672–1675*, 367, 416. See also A. W. Hughes

Clarke and Arthur Camplin, eds., *The Visitation of Norfork Anno Domini 1664*, 2 vols. Norfolk Record Society, IV, V (1934) II, 176.

8. Sainsbury and Foster, *Calendar, 1674–1676*, 111; Sir Charles Fawcett, *The English Factories in India*, new ser., vol. II: *The Eastern Coast and Bengal, 1670–1677* (Oxford, 1952) 145n.

9. On the Thomson brothers, see *Cal.S.P.Dom.*, *1659–1660*, 459, *1665–1666*, 457–458; and PRO Prob.11/351 (P.C.C. 57 Bench); on Colonel George Thomson, see *Dictionary of National Biography*, XIX, 720, and Aylmer, *The State's Servants*, 14, 250n.27. On Maurice Thomson, see Pearl, *London and the Outbreak of the Puritan Revolution*, 174–175, 282–283, 310–311; and the forthcoming book on London in the 1640s by Robert Brenner (Princeton University Press). For Major Robert Thomson as navy and victualling commissioner, see *Cal.S.P.Dom.*, *1649–1660*. Four of the Thomson brothers—Maurice, George, William and Paul—had lived for some time in Virginia. W. G. Stanard, "Abstract of Virginia Land Patents," *VMHB*, I (1892–1893) 188–190.

10. Fawcett, *English Factories*, n.s., II, xxi–xxii, 153, 405. One of the "writers" who assisted Puckle on his Bengal inspection was Elihu Yale. William Puckle left each of his daughters Mary and Susannah £100 assigned against both his realty and one-quarter of his personalty. PRO Prob.11/354 (P.C.C. 86 Hale).

11. PRO E.190/56/1 and E.190/58/1. I am indebted to Professor Paul Clemens for this item.

12. See chap. 3 note 55.

13. Guildhall Library, London, MS. 4657A/2 p. 80.

14. PRO E.190/56/1 and E.190/58/1 for 1672 (supplied by Paul Clemens); E.190/64/1 (1676); E.190/143 (1686).

15. See note by Charles Hughes Hamlin in *National Genealogical Society Quarterly*, LXII (1974) 272; will of George Richards in PRO Prob.11/421 (P.C.C. 138 Box). Sarah was still unmarried when her father made his will in 1690, but the first child of her marriage, Micajah III, was christened at St. Katherine Cree church, London, on 30 April 1695 (parish register, IGI). A list of the inhabitants of London in 1695 shows Richard Perry, Sarah, his wife, and Micaiah, their son, in that parish: Guildhall Library MS. 3381 p. 388, printed in D. V. Glass, ed., *London Inhabitants Within the Walls*, London Record Society, 2 (London, 1966). See also PRO C.7/568/71; C.7/571/19; C.9/283/61; C.9/435/111, 117; C.11/967/14. It seems likely that Micaiah Perry had another son named Micajah (whom we shall consider Micajah II), for the register of his parish records the death of a Micajah Perry, aged 22, in 1693. See A. W. Cornelius Hallen, ed., *The Registers of St. Botolph, Bishopsgate, London*, 3 vols. (London, 1889) II, 303.

16. *The Names of the Commissioners Appointed by His Majesty . . . for Taking*

Subscriptions . . . for Raising the Sums of Two Millions . . . [London, 1698]. The names of the subscribers and commissioners are given in the text of the charter of 5 Sep. 1698, printed in *Charters, &c. [of the East India Company]*, 2 vols. in 1, (s.l., n.d.).

17. *A List of the Names and Sums of all the New Subscribers for Enlarging the Capital Stock of the Bank of England, pursuant to the Act of Parliament* [London, 1697] shows that Richard Perry subscribed £1250. See also *Notes and Queries*, CLXXIX (27 July 1940) 59.

18. For example, Bank of England Archives, Bank Court Minutes D p. 99; Minutes I, pp. 16, 152, 226. The current acounts of Richard Perry *solus* and of the firm of Perry & Lane (later Micaiah & Richard Perry, Micajah Perry & Co., etc.) can be followed in the Drawing Office ledgers in the Bank Record Office, Roehampton, starting with Ledger 10 p. 897, which shows Richard Perry opening his account on 20 Dec. 1699, and continuing to Ledger 148 fo. 4181, which noted the deactivation of the account in 1742.

19. For his highest assessment, £600 in 1695, see Glass, ed., *London Inhabitants;* for his £200 assessment earlier in the decade, see the index of tax assessments, ca. 1692–1694, prepared by Dr. J. M. B. Alexander and deposited in LCRO.

20. *The Names of the Commissioners . . . for raising the Sum of Two Millions.* Micaiah I did not subscribe to the company in 1698 though he appears as a small shareholder in 1702. *A list of the names of all the members of the English [new] company trading to the East-Indies who are also Members of The General Society* (s.l., 1702).

21. BL Add. MS. 35,336 fo. 113; Burke, *General Armory*, 794; W. Henry Ryland, ed., *Grantees of Arms in Docquets and Patents between the Years 1687 and 1898*, Harleian Society, LXVII–LXVIII (London, 1916–1917) II, 287.

22. [John Thornton,] *A New Map of Virginia, Maryland, Pensilvania, New Jersey, Part of New York and Carolina* [second version] (London, ca. 1702–1720). A copy is in the William L. Clements Library, Ann Arbor. An earlier version had been published in 1698 without the dedication to Perry.

23. James Puckle, *The Club: or, A Grey Cap for a Green Head*, ed. [Henry] Austin Dobson (London, 1900); G[eorge] Steinman Steinman, *The Author of "The Club" Identified* (s.l., 1872) 11–12. See also entry on Puckle in *Dictionary of National Biography*, and Appendix C for Puckle-Hutchinson connection. As a notary, Puckle received much business from the Perrys and others in the Chesapeake trade both in protesting unaccepted bills of exchange and in making out powers of attorney. For examples, see VaHS MSS. 1 L51 f. 56 (Lee papers) and MdHR Testamentary Proceedings liber 21 ff. 166–171.

24. For the will of Thomas Lane "of Bethnal Green, Stepney," see PRO Prob.11/518 (P.C.C. 250 Smith). See also Baker, *County of Northampton,* I, 294–297; and Longden, *Visitation,* 111. This Thomas Lane (1641–1710) must be distinguished from the contemporary London alderman, Sir Thomas Lane (1652–1709). For Mary Lane's will and estate, see PRO Prob.11/617 (P.C.C. 237 Farrant) and *The British Journal,* no. 265 (21 Oct. 1727) 3. For Mary Lane's kinship to the Perrys through her Hutchinson mother, see Appendix C.

25. John Stow, *A Survey of the Cities of London and Westminster,* 2 vols. (London, 1720) II, bk. 5, 281.

26. For the ownership of Brewers Quay, see will of Richard Perry, PRO Prob.11/574 (P.C.C. 118 Shaller). For the Perry quay business, see PRO C.11/1607/29.

27. See Chapter 1, n. 58. The land in Tipperary transferred from Micaiah I to brother John Perry in 1683 was only part of his holdings. (Micaiah as eldest son would have inherited any land owned by Richard Perry III and not otherwise settled.) In 1743, Micajah Perry III as heir to Micaiah Perry I sold to John Perry of Woodrooff, heir of the late John Perry of Knocklofty, his interest in 1111 acres in the baronies of Iffa and Offa in Tipperary (the heart of John's family's later Woodrooff estate). Registry of Deeds, Dublin, 118/226/80570. I am indebted to Thomas Power for this reference.

28. PRO Prob.11/581 (P.C.C. 185 Buckingham).

29. PRO Prob.11/574 (P.C.C. 118 Shaller). See Philip Morant, *The History and Antiquities of the County of Essex,* 2 vols. (London, 1768) I, 321 for the ownership of Little Stanbridge or Stambridge by Micaiah Perry I. See also PRO C.11/2420/8 for purchase by Richard of messuages in Covent Garden in 1695 for £1580.

30. In later years, Mary's son Micajah Lowe travelled from Virginia to London, where he died in 1703. *Journals of the House of Burgesses of Virginia 1659/60–1693,* ed. H. R. McIlwaine, (Richmond, Va., 1914) xiiii, 289–91, 293, 306, 325; *Cal. S.P. Col. AWI, 1685–1688,* 534; *Executive Journals of the Council of Colonial Virginia,* ed. H. R. McIlwaine et al., 6 vols. (Richmond, Va., 1925–1966) I, 97, 234, 316, 492; Boddie, *Historical Southern Families,* II, 339; *William and Mary Quarterly,* 1st ser., XV (1906–1907) 195–196; XVII (1908–1909) 264–267. Richard Beale Davis would appear to confuse the Virginia firm of Hill, Perry & Randolph with the London firm of Perry & Lane in his edition of *William Fitzhugh and His Chesapeake World 1676–1701: The Fitzhugh Letters and Other Documents,* Virginia Historical Society, *Documents,* III (Chapel Hill, N.C., 1963) 227–228, 234–235. A nephew John Lowe is mentioned in John Perry's will of 1709 (cited in the next note). For an example of Peter Perry in Virginia acting as "attorney" for Perry & Lane in 1687, see John Fred-

erick Dorman, *York County, Virginia, Deeds, Orders, Wills, etc., no. 8: 1687–1691* (Washington, D.C., 1974) 2.

31. On this family, see 1976 ed. of *Burke's Irish Family History;* J. G. Simms, *The Williamite Confiscation in Ireland, 1690–1703* (London, 1956) 182. John Perry's will (February 1709/10) is in the Registry of Deeds, Dublin, vol. 7, p. 60, memorial 1611, and abstracted in P. Beryl Eustace, ed., *Registry of Deeds Dublin: Abstract of Wills, vol. I (1705–1745)* (Dublin, 1956) 15 (no. 35).

32. PRO C.11/2420/8; *Notes and Queries,* v. 179 (27 July 1940) 59; Arthur John Jewers, "Index to Monumental Inscriptions in City Churches", II, 603 (typescript in Guildhall Library, London).

33. PRO Prob.11/574 (P.C.C. 118 Shaller); Guildhall Library, MS. 2480/2 pp. 617–618. On the Heyshams, see "Heysham Pedigree," *Miscellanea Genealogica et Heraldica,* n.s. IV (1884) 373–375; Robert Clutterbuck, *The History and Antiquities of the County of Hertford,* 3 vols. (London, 1821) II, 399; Romney Sedgwick, ed., *The History of Parliament: The House of Commons 1715–1754,* 2 vols. (London and New York, 1970), II, 136–137; and D. W. Jones, "London Overseas-Merchant Groups at the End of the Seventeenth Century and the Moves against the East India Company" (Oxford D.Phil. thesis, 1970) 204–205.

34. V. L. Oliver, *Antigua,* 24; for burial on the 10th, see Hallen, *St. Botolph Bishopsgate,* 474.

35. PRO Prob.11/581 (P.C.C. 185 Buckingham), printed in *William and Mary Quarterly,* 1st ser., XVII (1908–1909) 266–267. That Micajah III owned land in Tipperary inherited from Micaiah I is made clear by the deed cited in n. 27 above. The "sister" Elizabeth Evans mentioned in the will was presumably the sister of his late wife. The lease of Eaton, Bedfordshire, was of the rectory. Through the marriage of Richard's daughter Elizabeth to Salusbury Cade, this passed later in the century to the Cade family. Information supplied by the archivist of Trinity College. See *The Victoria History of the County of Bedford,* 4 vols. (London, 1904–1914) III, 374.

36. Will in n. 35 and Hallen, *Register,* 284.

37. See n. 15 and will in n. 35.

38. Personal inspection and Jewers, "Index," II, 603.

39. Micajah III was christened on 30 April 1694; Phillip on 17 Dec. 1703: St. Katherine Cree parish register (IGI).

40. London port book for 1719 in Leeds City Library, Archives Department (Sheepscar Branch) NH 2440.

41. Sedgwick, *History of Parliament,* II, 341. A careless clerk recorded the marriage of "Michael Parry to Elizabeth Cook" on 19 Sept. 1721: James Coleman, ed., *A Copy of All the Marriages . . . in the Private Chapel of*

Somerset House, Strand . . . from 1714 to 1776 (London, 1862) 5, repeated in Oliver, *Antigua,* 20. See also Martin Nail, ed., "The Graveyard & Church Monuments of Epsom," (typescript, 1963) in library of Society of Genealogists, London (SR/M1/44637).

3. The Business of the Perry Firm

1. Donnan, "Micajah Perry."
2. For the size of plantations in the Chesapeake, ca. 1658–1790, see Allan Kulikoff, *Tobacco and Slaves: The Development of Southern Cultures in the Chesapeake, 1680–1800* (Chapel Hill, N.C., 1986) 331, 338. See also Paul G. E. Clemens, *The Atlantic Economy and Colonial Maryland's Eastern Shore* (Ithaca, N.Y., and London, 1980) 103, 104, 145.
3. For a general view of the economic and social history of the Chesapeake before 1720, one should start with the authoritative bibliography included in John J. McCusker and Russell R. Menard, *The Economy of British America 1607–1789* (Chapel Hill, N.C., 1985) paying particular attention to the works by P. V. Bergstrom, P. A. Bruce, L. G. Carr, P. G. E. Clemens, C. V. Earle, D. W. Galenson, A. Kulikoff, A. C. Land, G. L. Main, R. R. Menard, E. S. Morgan, J. M. Price, J. C. Rainbolt, G. A. Stiverson, T. W. Tate, L. S. Walsh, and T. J. Wertenbaker. Among more recent works, particular attention should be paid to Lois Green Carr et al., *Colonial Chesapeake Society* (Chapel Hill, N.C., 1988), Kulikoff, *Tobacco and Slaves,* and Darrett B. Rutman and Anita H. Rutman, *A Place in Time: Middlesex County, Virginia 1650–1750* (New York, 1984).
4. For early trading conditions and the emergence of the factors, see Susan E. Hillier, "The Trade of the Virginia Colony, 1606–1660" (Ph.D. thesis, University of Liverpool, 1971). For a salaried factor in the 1660s, see *A.P.C.Col.,* I, no. 866. This case is particularly interesting because the factor had in a few years acquired a plantation. For a contract of 1684 between a London merchant, William Paggen, and his intended factor in Virginia, John Hardman, see Bodleian Library, Oxford, MS. Aubrey 4 fo. 1, transcribed in Appendix A below.
5. Philip Alexander Bruce, *Economic History of Virginia in the Seventeenth Century,* 2 vols. (New York, 1895; 1935), esp. chap. 16; Ebenezer Cook, *The Sot-Weed Factor: Or, a Voyage to Maryland,* (London, 1708; and later editions); Jacob M. Price, "Sheffeild v. Starke: Institutional Experimentation in the London-Maryland Trade, c. 1696–1706", *Business History,* XXVIII (1986) 19–39.
6. PRO C.O.5/1318/2. Among the others signing this memorial were John Hyde, William Dawkins and William Hunt.
7. For European prices during the war, see Jacob M. Price, *France and the*

Chesapeake: A History of the French Tobacco Monopoly, 1674–1791. . ., 2 vols. (Ann Arbor, Mich., 1973) II, 852. For American prices and conditions, see Russell R. Menard, "The Tobacco Industry in the Chesapeake Colonies 1617–1730: An Interpretation," *Research in Economic History*, V (1980) 109–177, esp. 159–160; and John M. Hemphill, *Virginia and the English Commercial System, 1689–1733* (New York and London, 1985) 311–314.

8. On Virginia slave imports, see Walter Minchinton, Celia King and Peter Waite, eds., *Virginia Slave-Trade Statistics 1698–1775* (Richmond, Va., 1984); Edmund S. Morgan, *American Slavery American Freedom: The Ordeal of Colonial Virginia* (New York, 1975) 305–306; Susan Westbury, "Slaves of Colonial Virginia: Where They Came From," *William and Mary Quarterly*, 3d ser., XLII (1985) 228–237.

9. The emigration picture is well synthesized and interpreted in Russell R. Menard, "British Migration to the Chesapeake Colonies in the Seventeenth Century," in Carr et al., *Colonial Chesapeake Society*, 99–132. For the slave trade during the war, see Price, "Sheffeild v. Starke."

10. [John Oldmixon,] *The British Empire in America* . . ., 2 vols. (London, 1708) I, 322–323; 2nd ed. (London, 1741) I, x–xi, 453–454. See also Robert Beverley, *The History and Present State of Virginia*, ed. Louis B. Wright (Chapel Hill, N.C., 1947) xvii–xviii. In the related work of Henry Hartwell, James Blair and Edward Chilton, *The Present State of Virginia and the College*, ed. Hunter Dickinson Farish (Williamsburg, Va., 1940; Charlottesville, Va., 1964), is the familiar reference to "Merchants [in Virginia] being . . . seated with their Stores in the Country Plantations, and having their Customers all round them" (p. 12).

11. William Byrd, *History of the Dividing Line and Other Tracts*, ed. Thomas H. Wynne, 2 vols., Historical Documents from the Old Dominion, II, III (Richmond, Va., 1866) II, 163.

12. Clemens, *Atlantic Economy*, 87; Jacob M. Price, "The Last Phase of the Virginia-London Consignment Trade: James Buchanan & Co., 1758–1768," *William and Mary Quarterly*, 3rd ser., XLIII (1986) 64–65, n. 1.

13. *Proceedings of the Provincial Court of Maryland 1675–1677*, ed. Elizabeth Merritt, Archives of Maryland, LXVI (Baltimore, Md., 1954) 197, 437–439. See also MdHR Testamentary Proceedings liber 4B fo. 20 for effort by factor Gunnell to collect 8948 lb. of tobacco owed Bleeke, Perry & Lane by the estate of a deceased planter, 1676.

14. See Chapter 3, n. 5.

15. PRO C.9/443/77 (Perry et al. v. Bathurst). In 1690, Edward Bathurst (d. 1709) had married Susannah Puckle, the sister of Mary (Puckle) Lane. Foster, *London Marriage Licenses*, 96. He later abandoned his wife and daughter Susannah in England and took a new "wife" in Maryland.

See Papenfuse et al., *Dictionary of the Maryland Legislature*, I, 117–118. Some writers have erroneously suggested that the husband of Susannah (Puckle) Bathurst was Lancelot Bathurst of Virginia.

16. [Fairfax Harrison,] *Landmarks of Old Prince William*, 2 vols. (Richmond, Va., 1924) I, 145–146; idem, *Virginia Land Grants: A Study of Conveyancing in Relation to Colonial Politics* (Richmond, Va., 1925) 93–101; Maurer Maurer, "Edmund Jenings and Robert Carter," *VMHB*, LV (1947) 20–30.

17. Louis B. Wright, ed., *Letters of Robert Carter 1720–1727* (San Marino, Calif., 1940) x, 2, 4, 6, 10–15, 29–30, 37–38, 40–43, 52–53, 98.

18. VaSL Westmoreland County Deeds and Wills Book, no. 4, pp. 222–238.

19. The following discussion of William Byrd's relations with Perry & Lane is based on the introduction to John Spencer Bassett, ed., *The Writings of "Colonel William Byrd of Westover in Virginia Esq."* (New York, 1901) and the "Letters of William Byrd First . . .," *VMHB*, XXVI (1918) 17–31, 124–134, 247–259, 338–392, XXVII (1919) 167–168, 273–288, XXVIII (1920) 11–25.

20. PRO C.11/767/68. For some idea of the merchandise carried by a seventeenth century Virginia merchant, see Warren M. Billings, ed., *The Old Dominion in the Seventeenth Century: A Documentary History of Virginia, 1606–1689* (Chapel Hill, N.C., 1975) 192–198.

21. PRO C.9/188/70.

22. PRO C.8/628/61; and Morgan's will in Prob.11/487 (P.C.C. 45 Eedes).

23. UVa Robert Anderson Jr. letterbook.

24. Ibid., to Cuthbert Jones, 10 July 1712.

25. The 1686 London port book (PRO E.190/143) shows tobacco imports of 44,190 lb. by Samuel Clarke and 1082 lb. by Cuthbert Jones. The printed London bills of entry for 1697 (Beinecke Library, Yale University) show tobacco imports of 50 hogsheads by Samuel Clarke and 26 hogsheads by Cuthbert Jones. On Clarke, see J. R. Woodhead, *The Rulers of London 1660–1689* (London, 1965), 48. PRO HCA 15/18 (19 Oct. 1700) refers to Jones as a tobacconist of the parish of St. Paul, Shadwell, Middlesex. By 1719 there were two persons named Cuthbert Jones in Shadwell, a tobacconist and a Virginia merchant, probably father and son; the merchant failed that year. See PRO B4/3 and T.1/140/3.

26. UVa R. Anderson letterbook, to Cuthbert Jones, or Jones & Clarke, letters of 1698–1702.

27. Ibid., to John Lang, 1702.

28. Ibid., to Jones, 28 June 1706.

29. Ibid., to Jones, 27 Aug. 1708.

30. Ibid., to Jones, 10 July 1712, 4 May 1714. In the latter, Anderson ordered goods "for my peoples own ware."

31. Ibid., to Page, 27, 29 Apr., 3 Aug, 12 Sept. 1710.

32. Ibid., to M. Perry & Co., 22 Mar. 1710/1, 4, 10 July 1712, 13 June, 3 July, 14 Oct. 1713. Page should not be confused with John Page of London, a director of the Bank of England, who died in 1711. For the will of John Page of Gloucester County, Virginia, see PRO Prob.11/567 (P.C.C. 14 Browning); and Henry F. Waters, "Genealogical Gleanings in England," *New England Historical and Genealogical Register,* XLIII (1889) 290–310.

33. UVa R. Anderson letterbook, to Jones, 10 July 1712.

34. Ibid, to R. Lee, 9 Apr., 10, 22 July 1712, 1 May, 13 June, 7 July, 15 Aug., 12 Oct. 1713, 11 Jan. 1713/4, 11 May 1715; to Francis Lee (Richard's uncle), 11 Nov. 1713. For the Lees in London, see Edmund Jennings Lee, *Lee of Virginia* (Philadelphia, 1895) 74–83, 83–89, 91–92, and Jacob M. Price, "One Family's Empire: The Russell-Lee-Clerk Connection in Maryland, Britain and India," *Maryland Historical Magazine,* LXXII (1977) 170–171. Anderson also began about this time to have limited dealing with other merchants in London: Gilbert Higginson (1711) and John Maynard (1714).

35. UVa R. Anderson letterbook, to M. Perry & Co., 24 June, 16 Nov., 8 Dec. 1714, 28 Mar. and [May] 1715.

36. Ibid., executors to M. & R. Perry, 23 Mar. 1715/6.

37. See n. 7 above and *Autobiography of William Stout of Lancaster . . . A.D. 1665–1752,* ed. J. Harland (London, 1851) 26, 35.

38. See notes 10 and 11 above.

39. UVa R. Anderson letterbook, to Cuthbert Jones, 28 June 1706.

40. PRO H.C.A.13/83 ff. 575, 578, particularly Response of M. Perry, 17 June 1707. The records of the Royal African Company show large numbers of protested bills ca. 1704. PRO T.70/278 and 279.

41. PRO C.6/345/70 (Doyley v. Perry). Reports (1708–1709) on this case can be found in PRO C.38/296, 300 and 304.

42. PRO E.219/446. See also Price, "Sheffeild v. Starke," esp. 33.

43. PRO T.70/278 and 279, drawn by 65 Virginians. In earlier and some later years, the number of Virginia bills received by the Royal African Company was too small to support any generalizations. See T.70/269–71, 276, 277 and 282.

44. Jacob M. Price, "Credit in the Slave Trade and Plantation Economies," in Barbara Solow, ed., *Slavery and the Rise of the Atlantic System,* (Cambridge, 1991) 293–339.

45. See n. 40 above. Among the bills received by T. Starke were a few whose Chesapeake drawers can almost certainly be identified as merchants, including Richard Bennett, William Edmondson, Robert Gouldesborough (and lawyer), Jacob Moreland, William Phippard, and Philip Smith.

46. LC John Custis letterbook. On him, see Jo Zuppan, "John Custis of Williamsburg, 1678–1749," *VMHB*, XL (1982) 177–197; and Earl G. Swem, ed., "Brothers of the Spade: Correspondence of Peter Collinson of London and of John Custis of Williamsburg, Virginia, 1734–1746," *Proceedings of the American Antiquarian Society*, LVIII:1 (1948–49) 26–33.

47. M. Perry was executor under the will of Daniel Parke Sr., a merchant in Virginia (PRO C.7/280/31; C.7/611/634). Perry & Co. were the London correspondents of Colonel Daniel Parke, Jr. (subsequently governor of the Leeward Islands), whose daughter Frances married John Custis IV, and whose other daughter Lucy married William Byrd II, also a Perry correspondent. PRO C.11/292/18; Prob.11/521 (P.C.C. 112 Young) for will of Col. Daniel Parke (1710); and Lothrop Withington, *Virginia Gleanings in England* (Baltimore, Md., 1980) 164, 335–345.

48. LC Custis leterbook, ff. 6–7.

49. Jacob M. Price, *Capital and Credit in British Overseas Trade: The View from the Chesapeake, 1700–1776* (Cambridge, Mass., 1980) 100–101, 189. Even after the death of John Custis, his son continued to keep substantial deposits in London. In 1757, the estate of Daniel Parke Custis had a balance of £3697.10.8 with Carys plus £1650 in Bank of England stock. VaHS MSS 1 C9698 a 163–186 (D. P. Custis Estate Papers), Robert Cary & Co. to Mrs. Martha Custis, London, 26 Nov. 1757.

50. Invoices of goods shipped to Custis by Perry & Co. after 1723 can be found in VaHS MSS1 C9698 a22 (Custis Papers).

51. See George Johnson, *History of Cecil County, Maryland* (Elkton, Md., 1881) 193–194. The relevant suits include PRO C.6/345/70; C.6/409/70; C.7/280/31; C.8/355/15; C.11/767/68. For examples of the Perrys acting as trustee or executors, see also H. F. Waters, *Genealogical Gleanings*, I, 12, 313–314, 349–350; Withington, *Virginia Gleanings*, 164, 208, 335–345.

52. See Chapter 2.

53. See n. 40 above.

54. See also Chapter 5, n. 18. "Madam Elizabeth Churchill" left a personal estate of £3657.13.2 in 1720, of which £1656.10.10 was on deposit with Messrs. Micaiah and Richard Perry of London, and £923.10.6 with William Dawkins, another London merchant. VaSL Middlesex County Will Book, 1713–1734, fo. 137. For other examples of women leaving money on deposit with Perry & Co. before 1721, see Blanche Adams Chapman, *Wills and Administrations of Isle of Wight County Virginia*, 3 vols. ([Smithfield, Va.], 1938–1975) I, 74; for deposits by men, see Beverley Fleet, *Essex County Wills and Deeds 1714–1717*, Virginia Colonial Abstracts, vol. 9 (Richmond, Va., [1940]) 42.

55. 1697 data from printed London bills of entry (Beinecke Library, Yale); 1719 data from Leeds City Library (Sheepscar branch), Archives Department, Newby Hall MSS. NH 2440 (London port book overseas inward, Christmas 1718–Christmas 1719).

56. The Virginia port books for 1700–1702 do not show any London-bound vessels owned entirely by M. Perry or Perry & Lane. Instead, the Perrys and Lane appear only as co-owners with others. Of such vessels, 16 were from James River, 8 from York River and 3 from Rappahannock. PRO C.O.5/1441.

57. For a 1706 lawsuit involving vessels partly owned by Micaiah Perry I, Richard Perry and Thomas Lane, ca. 1690–1710, see PRO C.6/434/11 (with the Perry & Lane partners holding 3/16, Sir Jeffrey Jeffreys 1/4 and three Brayne brothers 1/4; with James Brayne acting as ship's husband). Both Jeffreys and Perry & Lane had chartered substantial space on the vessel. In another 1708 case (PRO C.10/384/16) Perry & Lane were majority owners of the *Richard and Sarah* and ship's husbands, but their management was challenged by a minority shareholder. PRO C.8/550/16 concerns the pay of sailors on a ship managed by Perry & Lane. In Cox v. Perry, M. Perry acted as managing agent for a ship built in Virginia in which he held no share: PRO C.6/321/45; C.9/322/42.

58. Louis des Cognets, Jr., *English Duplicates of Lost Virginia Records* (Princeton, N.J., 1958) 280–309.

59. PRO H.C.A.26/3 fo. 15. For armed merchantment, see W. R. Meyer, "English Privateering in the War of 1688 to 1697," *The Mariner's Mirror,* LXVII (1981) 259–264.

60. PRO H.C.A.26/1 ff. 52, 64, 68, 76.

61. See Arthur Pierce Middleton, *Tobacco Coast: A Maritime History of Chesapeake Bay in the Colonial Era* (Newport News, Va., 1953) 299–301.

62. For the refusal of the executors of Colonel William Randolph to pay for insurance made before 1710, see Chapter 5, n. 29.

63. D. W. Jones, *War and Economy in the Age of William III and Marlborough* (Oxford, 1988) 164.

64. On convoys, see Middleton, *Tobacco Coast,* chap. 10; on Perry's involvement in the quarrel over convoy timing, see *Cal.S.P.Col.AWI, 1696–1697,* 437; *1702–1703,* 51, 95, 257, 473; *1704–1705,* 303, 313–314, 464; *1705–1708,* 88, 107; *Journal C.T.P. 1704–1709,* 53; PRO C.O.5/1309/14 ff. 25–27; C.O.5/1313/4(i, iii), 5(i); 1313/20, 34; 1315/10, 10(i); on French tobacco prizes during the wars of 1689–1713, see Price, *France and the Chesapeake,* I, 178–181, 184. On the loss of some of the Perrys' tobacco ships, see n. 40 above.

65. See Appendix B for the full list. Prices of manufactures are as given in PRO C.O.390/8 ff. 129–149 and Customs 2. For the uses of alum,

brimstone, etc., see C. H. Kauffman, *The Dictionary of Merchandize*, 2nd ed. (London, 1805).

66. See above for Anderson correspondence and for John Custis's efforts to get discounts for cash. For a general discussion of credit terms, see Price, *Capital and Credit*, chap. 6.

67. See Chapter 2, n. 23.

68. PRO C.O.5/1305 ff. 79–86 (Christmas 1688–Christmas 1689).

69. Jacob M. Price and Paul G. E. Clemens, "A Revolution of Scale in Overseas Trade: British Firms in the Chesapeake Trade, 1675–1775," *Journal of Economic History*, XLVII (1987) 13–15.

70. 1686 data from Price and Clemens, "Revolution of Scale," 11, 15; 1689 and 1690 data from PRO C.O.5/1305 ff. 79–86, 192–196; 1697 data from printed London bills of entry in Beinecke Library (Yale).

71. Jonathan Matthew[s], 44.9%; Timothy Keyser, 64.8%; John Hyde, 73.9%; Peregrine Browne, 75.5%; Anthony Stratton, 77.1%; Samuel Groome, 93.6%.

72. Peter Paggen, 58.9%; Edward Haistwell & Co., 76.6%; J[ohn] Whitty & Co., 78.5%; John Taylor, 79.7%.

73. Robert Bristow, nil; Francis Lee, nil; Edward Lemon, 2.2%.

74. It sometimes happened that the buyer, particularly when a foreigner, asked the importer to make the outward entry in his own name. This facilitated the recovery of the import duties or bonds by the importer and saved the buyer-exporter some paperwork. It does not, however, appear to have been the standard practice.

75. Donnan, "Micajah Perry," 79–80. Perhaps not unrepresentative was an "adventure" of December 1687 in which Perry & Lane took a one-fourth share in a shipment of 33 servants from the Thames to York River. See VaSL York County Deeds, Wills, etc., vol. 8, pp. 208–209, summarized in John Frederick Dorman, *York County, Virginia, Deeds, Orders, Wills, etc., no. 8 1687–1691* (Washington, D.C., 1974) 77–78.

76. Donnan, *Documents*, IV, 59–60; PRO T.70/273 (7 Sept. 1687). The first citation involved Perry & Lane; the second involved an ad hoc adventure by Robert Bristow, Micaiah Perry I and George Richards.

77. PRO T.70/1199 (information supplied by Prof. K. G. Davies).

78. PRO T.70/278–280.

79. PRO C.O.388/17/N.69 (ca. 1710); *Journal C.T.P., 1718–1722*, 15, 19, 30; BL Add. Ms. 61510 f. 136.

80. For London sugar imports by Perry & Co., see 1697 printed London bills of entry and 1719 London port book (n. 55 above). In 1719 the firm imported 3282 cwt. of sugar, primarily from St. Kitts. In a deposition of 3 July 1699, Micaiah Perry alluded to receiving consignments from Barbados and Jamaica. PRO C.24/1215 (Lloyd v. Nicholson). In

1721, Micaiah Perry I and III signed a memorial as merchants trading to Barbados. PRO C.O.28/17 fo. 58.

81. Printed London bills of entry, 1697 (Beinecke Library, Yale).

82. See *Cal.T.B.*, XI, 235, XIX, 224, XXIV, 529, 544; for Pennsylvania, XIV, 148.

83. Mattie Erma Edwards Parker et al., eds., *North-Carolina Higher-Court Records 1697–1701*, Colonial Records of North Carolina, 2nd ser. (Raleigh, N.C., 1971) xxiv–xxv; William S. Price, Jr., ed., *North Carolina Higher-Court Records 1702–1708*, Colonial Records of North Carolina, 2nd ser., IV (Raleigh, N.C., 1974) xxi–xxii, 97–419 passim. The factor sued (pp. 167–169) was John Falconar, who is probably the Quaker of that name who was later a tobacco merchant in London. Pp. 417–419 contain a procuration or power of attorney indicating that the "directors and managers" of the New-Pennsylvania Company included the Londoners Micaiah Perry, Thomas Byfeild, Joseph Marshall, Thomas Cooper, John Frecune (Freame?), Silvanus Grove, Henry Gouldney, John Hodgkins and Samuel Waldenfield, most of them substantial merchants and several of them Quakers. On Byfeild, a London skinner who traded to both North America and the West Indies, see Price, *Tobacco Adventure to Russia . . .*, 31, 32, 36, 105. See also William S. Price, Jr., et al., eds., *North Carolina Higher Court Minutes 1709–1723*, Colonial Records of North Carolina, 2nd ser., V (Raleigh, N.C., 1977) 19–20, 24–26, 44, 67, 73. For the substantial involvement of Perry & Co. with Trent, a Philadelphia merchant, see LCRO Mayor's Court Depositions, box 51 (12 July 1723).

84. John Lawson, *A New Voyage to Carolina*, ed. Hugh Talmage Lefler (Chapel Hill, N.C., 1967) 167. For the analogous Cork provisioning trade, see Thomas M. Truxes, *Irish-American Trade, 1660–1783* (Cambridge, 1988), esp. chap. 8.

85. Price, "James Buchanan & Co.," 73.

86. PRO Prob.11/574 (P.C.C. 118 Shaller) for Richard Perry's will.

87. The questions of who owed what in the Chesapeake trade is discussed in Jacob M. Price, "The Last Phase of the . . . Consignment Trade," 64–98.

4. The Public Role of Micaiah Perry I

1. Jacob M. Price, "The Tobacco Trade and the Treasury, 1685–1733: British Mercantilism in Its Fiscal Aspects" (Harvard Ph.D. thesis, 1954), 2.

2. Ibid. See in particular chap. 10 for a discussion of the success of the tobacco importers (led by Perry, Jeffreys and Richards) in obtaining

concessions from the Treasury on the time allowed for paying the Tobacco Impost and on discounts for prompt or early payment.

3. Middleton, *Tobacco Coast*, chap. 10; Alison G. Olson, "The Board of Trade and London-American Interest Groups in the Eighteenth Century," *Journal of Imperial and Commonwealth History*, VIII:2 (1980) 33–50; idem, "The Virginia Merchants of London: A Study in Eighteenth-Century Interest-Group Politics," *William and Mary Quarterly*, 3rd ser., XL (1983) 363–388. For the efforts of the Chesapeake traders to open up a Russian market for English tobacco and to prevent the sending of skilled English tobacco workers to Russia (in both of which Micaiah Perry tooks a leading role), see Jacob M. Price, *The Tobacco Adventure to Russia . . . 1676–1722*, Transactions of the American Philosophical Society, n.s., LI:1 (Philadelphia, 1961).

4. For the committee in the 1720s, see Henry Darnall, *A Just and Impartial Account of Transactions of the Merchants of London for the Advancement of the Price of Tobacco* (Annapolis, Md., [1729]). The background is discussed in Price, *France and the Chesapeake*, I, 650–655.

5. For this pattern of progressive concentration, see Price and Clemens, "Revolution of Scale," 1–43.

6. The full membership of the committee for 1727–1728 and 1728–1729 is given in Darnall, *Just and Impartial Account*, 5, 54.

7. It is important to distinguish John Jeffreys (originally of Llywel, Brecknockshire), alderman of London, from Col. John Jeffreys of The Priory, Brecon, M.P. The latter is described in Basil Duke Henning, *The History of Parliament: The House of Commons 1660–1690*, 3 vols. (London, 1983) II, 641–642. The former is described in J. R. Woodhead, *The Rulers of London 1660–1689* (London, 1965) 97–98; Alfred B. Beaven, *The Aldermen of London*, 2 vols. (London, 1913) II, 92; and [Peter] *Le Neve's Pedigrees of the Knights Made by King Charles II . . .*, ed. George W. Marshall, Harleian Society, VIII (London, 1873) 470. For both, see Theophilus Jones and Sir Joseph Russell Bailey, bart., baron Glanusk, *A History of the County of Brecknock*, 4 vol. (Brecknock, 1909–1930) esp. II, 141–144, IV, 99, 101–102, 108, 110–113, 273–275, 280. Bevan and Woodhead err in describing the alderman as the M.P. of 1661. Herbert Jeffreys, lieutenant-governor of Virginia, 1676–1679, was the brother of the colonel and not of the alderman. On this there is an error in *Cal.S.P.Col.AWI, 1681–1685*, no. 5.

8. For Jeffreys in 1641–1642, see PRO E.122/196/24; for his activities in the 1650s and later see *Cal.S.P.Col.AWI, 1574–1660*, nos. 397, 418, 426, 430–431; *1661–1668*, nos. 3, 341, 406, 852, 858; *1669–1674*, nos. 98, 176, 934; *1681–1685*, nos. 275, 1037; *A.P.C.Col.*, I, no. 636. For the 1660 committee nomination, see PRO S.P.29/19/22 ff. 42–43, 90.

9. Jones and Glanusk, *Brecknock*, IV, 111n; PRO E.190/56/1 and E. 190/58/1 (1672); E.190/64/1 (1676); E.190/68/1 (1677); and E.190/143 (1686). I am indebted to Prof. Paul Clemens for the 1672 and 1677 data. Jeffreys was also an active exporter, supplying the Royal Tobacco Company of Sweden "for a considerable time, with great quantityes of all sorts of tobacco." BL Add. MS. 41,803 ff. 60–61, J. Lucie and J. Jeffreys to Sir L. Jenkins, 15 Feb. 1683/4.

10. See n. 7 above and his will in PRO Prob.11/393 (P.C.C. 150 Exton).

11. Woodhead, *Rulers*, 97–98; Jones and Glanusk, *Brecknock*, IV, 99, 108–113, 280; Bevan, *Aldermen*, II, 119. There are some inconsistencies in the Jones and Glanusk account.

12. Jones and Glanusk, *Brecknock*, II, 143–144, IV, 99, 108–113, 274–275, 280; Sedgwick, *House of Commons: 1715–1754*, II, 173; Sir Lewis Namier and John Brooke, *The History of Parliament: The House of Commons: 1754–1790*, 3 vols. (London, 1964) II, 673; Sir Lewis Namier, *The Structure of Politics at the Accession of George III*, 2nd ed. (London, 1957) 402–406.

13. See "letter of marque declarations" in PRO H.C.A.26/2 ff. 77 and 128; 26/3 ff. 5, 36, 111, 114, 115, 160.

14. For African trade interests, see PRO T.70/1199; K. G. Davies, *The Royal African Company* (London, 1957) 295, 372, 383; R. A. Brock, ed., *Miscellaneous Papers 1672–1865 . . . in the Collection of the Virginia Historical Society*, Collections of the Virginia Historical Society, n.s., VI (Richmond, Va., 1887) 39–42; Donnan, *Documents*, I, 21, 180 (confusing Alderman John Jeffreys and his nephew of the same name), 183, 392, 393n, 394, IV, 11, 12, 54, 89. See also *Cal.T.B.*, XVII–XXIII, passim, for references to the New York contract, and X, 158–159, 579 for references to the Jamaica contract. See also *Cal.T.B.*, X, 322, 365, XIII, 412, and *Cal.T.Papers, 1697–1702*, 191, *1702–1707*, 269, 326–327, 362; PRO C.O.388/4 and C.O.388/8/D.10 and fo. 231.

15. Jeffrey Jeffreys' name occurs in the printed lists of shareholders in the East India Company for 1690 and 1691 and in similar lists for the Mine Adventure for 1699–1708. On the latter see William Robert Scott, *The Constitution and Finance of English, Scottish and Irish Joint-Stock Companies to 1720*, 3 vols. (Cambridge, 1912) II, 443–458.

16. PRO E.190/152 (1695); T.38/362 (1702); London printed bills of entry (Beinecke Library, Yale).

17. Narcissus Luttrell, *Brief Historical Relation of State Affairs*, 6 vols. (Oxford, 1857) IV, 531.

18. *Dictionary of National Biography*, s.v. Charles Pratt; Jones and Glanusk, *Brecknock*, IV, 110–13.

19. Percy Scott Flippin, *The Financial Administration of the Colony of Virginia*,

Johns Hopkins University Studies in Historical and Political Science, ser. XXXIII, no. 2 (Baltimore, 1915) 59–60, a somewhat jumbled account that does not adequately distinguish the different kinds of agency performed by Perry; *Executive Journals of the Council of Colonial Virginia*, ed. H. R. McIlwaine et al., 6 vols. (Richmond, Va., 1925–1966) III, 6, 12–13, 18, 19; *Proceedings of the Council of Maryland 1693–1696/7*, Archives of Maryland, XX (Baltimore, Md., 1900) 255, 375, 553, *1696/7–1698*, Archives of Maryland, XXIII (1903) 72, 366, *1698–1731*, Archives of Maryland, XXV (1905) 36, 45, 119, *Proceedings and Acts of the General Assembly of Maryland April 26, 1700—May 3, 1704*, Archives of Maryland, XXIV (1904) 27, 74; *Cal. S.P.Col.AWI, 1693–96*, 559, *1696–1697*, 94, 204, 541, *1697–1698*, 126, *1700*, 233, 407, 474, *1701*, 94, 300–301, 743, *1702*, 209, 301, *1702–1703*, 356, *1712–1714*, 128–129.

20. William L. Saunders, ed., *The Colonial Records of North Carolina*, 10 vols. (Raleigh, N.C., 1886–1890) I, 539, 634–640, II, 279–80; Alexander S. Salley, Jr., *Narratives of Early Carolina 1650–1708* (New York, 1911) 348, 353–356 (from Oldmixon); *Cal.S.P.Col.AWI, 1717–1718*, nos. 281, 343, 380.

21. Price, *Tobacco Adventure to Russia* 24, 26, 41n, 42n, 48, 64–65, 83.

22. Price, *France and the Chesapeake*, 514–515, 517, 523, 529.

23. *Archives of Maryland*, XX, 255; Huntington Library, Ms. BL 64 F. Nicholson [to Blathwayt,] 15 June 1693; *Cal.S.P.Col.AWI 1701*, 314; *1702*, 104.

24. *Cal.T.Papers, 1708–1714*, 89, 517; *1714–1719*, 91; *Cal.T.B.*, XX, 154, 287, 371, 435, 498; XXI, 106; XXII, 464; XXIII, 36–37, 483; XXIV, 21–22, 30, 145; XXIX, 418; XXX, 14, 158, 517; *Cal.S.P.Col.AWI, 1699*, 571; *1716–1717*, 93–94, 140, 142–143, 147, 175, 179, 345, 351–352; *Journal C.T.P., 1704–1708/9*, 533; *1708/9–1714/5*, 186, 426, 519; *1714/5–1718*, 110–112; VaHS Mss 1 L51 f72 (Lee Papers) Stephen Fouace to Ph. Ludwell II, 2 Apr. 1711; "Letters and Papers," *VMHB*, XXIII (1915) 357–360; Bassett, ed., *Writings of Colonel William Byrd*, xxi–xxv, xlviii–ix; Lewis B. Wright and Marion Tinling, eds., *William Byrd of Virginia: The London Diary (1717–1721) and Other Writings* (New York, 1958) 55.

25. Perry was an unsuccessful candidate in 1697 for "trustee for circulating exchequer bills." The subscribers elected six and the Treasury chose six from among other candidates unsuccessful on the ballot. Perry received more votes (96) than four of those eventually chosen by the Treasury, including the Whig Sir Henry Furnese (86) and the Tory Sir Joseph Herne (80). The implication is that Perry's inactivity in other matters touching public finance (except for paying duties) reduced his standing with the Treasury. *Cal.T.B.*, XI, 143; for his two millions in customs (presumably paid over three or so decades), see XXIX, 798.

26. John [and Edward] Chamberlayne, *Magnae Britanniae Notitia*, 22nd ed.

(London, 1708) 689–690. For Perry's mild Whiggishness in 1713–1717, see Henry Horwitz , W. A. Speck and W. A. Gray, eds., *London Politics 1713–1717*, London Record Society, 17 (London, 1981) 88, 109.

27. *Cal.S.P.Col.AWI, 1689–1692*, 452–453. The trustees, besides Perry and the bishop of London, were Jeffrey Jeffreys, then Virginia political agent in London, Lord Howard of Effingham, governor of Virginia, and James Blair. The auditors included the bishops of Salisbury and St. Asaph and the merchants Arthur North, John Cary and Francis Lee. See also Herbert Laurence Ganter, "Some Notes on the Charity of the Honourable Robert Boyle . . .," *William and Mary Quarterly*, 2nd ser., XV (1935) 17–19; idem, "Documents Relating to the Early History of the College . . .," ibid., 2d ser., XIX (1939) 352, 371. For the Perrys' later work as London agents of the college, see also *Cal.T.B.*, XXIV, 192 and Donnan, "Micajah Perry," 80–81.

28. *Cal.S.P.Dom.*, *1700–1702*, 307, 327, 335; McIlwaine, ed., *Virginia Council Executive Journals*, I, 227–228, 277; *Cal.S.P.Col.AWI, 1702*, 129.

29. Saunders, *Colonial Records*, I, 986–990. For Cairnes and Janssen, see Price, *Tobacco Adventure*, 105, 108. See also *Cal.S.P.Col.AWI 1706–1708*, 744, 754; *1708–1709*, 1; *1711–1712*, 173.

30. *Cal.T.B.*, XXIII, 36–37, XXIV, 21–22, 30, 157, 341, 456 (1710); *Cal.T.Papers*, *1708–1714*, 151, 387, 398; *Journal C.T.P. 1704–1708/9*, 494, 496, 503–504, 507–511; *1708/9–1714/5*, 227, 318, 319, 321.

5. The Challenge of the Third Generation

1. Leeds City Library (Sheepscar branch), Archives Department, Newby Hall MSS., NH 2440 (London port book, Christmas 1718–Christmas 1719). In that year, Perry & Co. imported 2,719,529 lb. (or 3,419,128 lb. with estimated correction). See Jacob M. Price and Paul G. E. Clemens, "A Revolution of Scale in Overseas Trade, 1675–1775," *Journal of Economic History*, XLVII (1987) 18–20.

2. In 1697, the predecessor firm of Perry, Lane & Co. imported about 4,723,200 lb. of tobacco.

3. Richard's death date is specified as 16 April 1720 in PRO C.11/2420/8. His will was proved in May 1720. It is likely that Richard had a younger brother named Micajah who had died young. The burial on 6 Feb. 1692/3 of a Micajah Perry, aged 22, is noted in the records of St. Botolph Bishopsgate, the parish where the elder Micaiah and family lived. See A. W. Cornelius Hallen, comp., *The Registers of St. Botolph, Bishopsgate, London*, 3 vols. (London, 1889) II, 303.

4. See Chapter 2.

5. Louis B. Wright, ed., *Letters of Robert Carter 1720–1727: The Commercial Interests of a Virginia Gentleman* (San Marino, Calif., 1940) 46–47, 54–55.

6. Ibid. 84–85: R. Carter to J. Carter, 3 Mar. 1720/1.

7. For 1719, see Chapter 5, n. 1. For young Micajah's time in Philadelphia, see *The Letters and Papers of Cadwallader Colden,* 6 vols., Collections of the New-York Historical Society, L–LV (New York, 1918–1923) II, 26–30, 30–34, 45–48, III, 15–16.

8. For trade petitions (etc.) signed by Phillip Perry, see PRO C.O.5/1319/36 fo. 142 (1723); C.O.388/24/R.144 fo. 152 (1724). See also LC J. Custis letterbook ff. 72v-74 [to R. Cary, 1737], to Ph. Perry, 1737; UVa R. Carter letterbooks, IV, 38 to same, 2 Mar. 1731/2.

9. There are scattered references to the Perrys' connections with Madeira and the West Indies in various Chancery suits. For West Indies, see PRO C.11/2051/24; for Madeira, see PRO C.11/1667/15 and C.11/1672/31 and PROB 6/133 ff. 109–114; and Chapter 3.

10. The whole episode is discussed in Jacob M. Price, "Glasgow, the Tobacco Trade, and the Scottish Customs, 1707–1730," *The Scottish Historical Review,* LXIII (1984) 1–36.

11. *Journal of the House of Commons,* XX, 102–109, esp. 102–103; reprinted in Leo Francis Stock, ed., *Proceedings and Debates of the British Parliament respecting North America,* 5 vols. (Washington, D.C., 1924–1941) III, 460–464, esp. 460. There is frequent confirmation of short crops and hard-to-find freights in the early 1720s in the Robert Carter correspondence in the VaHS and UVa.

12. For the trading system of Perry & Lane, see Chapter 3.

13. In October 1721, the Perry firm sold a brick building at Jamestown, owned by them since at least 1696 and most likely used in part as a store. The building adjoined a similar structure earlier used as the state house. As the Perry building was once occupied by John Jarrett, the elder Micajah's nephew (by marriage), it is possible that the building in question was the headquarters of the firm in the colony. When the capital was moved to Williamsburg, it may no longer have been well situated for such a function. George C. Gregory, "Jamestown's First Brick State House," *VMHB,* XLIII (1935) 199; Lindsay O. Duvall, ed., *James City County 1634–1904,* Virginia Colonial Abstracts, ser. 2, vol. 4 (Washington, D.C., 1957) 32.

14. There is much on this in the records of the lawsuit Bennett v. Perry in PRO. See in particular C.12/1449/32 plus C.11/307/66; C.12/296/16; C.12/1450/83. In the early 1720s, when crops were short, the Perrys empowered "agents" and ship captains in the Bay to buy tobacco for them (with bills) to fill ships. These agents do not appear, however, to have been factors or general mercantile correspondents to whom they

sent trading goods. John Custis tried unsuccessfully to persuade Micajah Perry III to follow the example of his London competitor James Bradley (second in the trade in 1719) and employ factors. LC John Custis letterbook, to Perry, 1725 (2 letters).

15. William Byrd, *History of the Dividing Line and Other Tracts,* ed. Thomas H. Wynne, 2 vols., Historical Documents from the Old Dominion, II, III (Richmond, Va., 1866) II, 163.

16. For credits extended by British merchants to local merchants in the Chesapeake in later years, see Jacob M. Price, "The Last Phase of the Virginia-London Consignment Trade: James Buchanan & Co., 1758–1768," *William and Mary Quarterly,* 3rd ser., XLIII (1986) 64–98; idem, "Buchanan & Simson, 1759–1763: A Different Kind of Glasgow Firm Trading to the Chesapeake," ibid., XL (1983) 3–41.

17. PRO C.11/967/14; see also C.11/2287/75. Sometime after 1708, Lloyd conveyed 117 slaves and cattle to Micajah Perry and Francis Willis. Judith McGhan, *Virginia Will Records . . .* (Baltimore, Md., 1982) 294. One way or another, the Perrys appear eventually (after Lloyd's death) to have got control of at least part of Lloyd's Virginia land which was sold to Robert Carter. See UVa R. Carter letterbooks (transcripts) IV, 45, 66 to M. Perry, 12 May, 11 July 1732 in particular; Robert Carter Estate letterbook, pp. 2–3 to W. Dawkins, 30 Aug. 1732. John and Thomas Lloyd also consigned tobacco to Clement Nicholson of Whitehaven in the 1690s; this subsequently involved them in another chancery suit, Lloyd v. Nicholson. On the latter, see PRO C.6/92/40; C.22/117/11 and 36; C.24/1215 (depositions of M. Perry and R. Wise); and C.107/161/1–28.

18. For planters with funds in the firm's hands before 1721, see Chapter 3. For those with such credits or deposits after 1721, see Judith McGhan, *Virginia Will Records* 445–447; John Frederick Dorman, ed., *Genealogies of Virginia Families . . .,* 5 vols. (Baltimore, Md., 1982) II, 250; Blanche Adams Chapman, *Wills and Administrations of Isle of Wight County Virginia 1647–1800,* 3 vols. ([Smithfield, Va.], 1938) II, 52.

19. For the post-1714 discounts or rebates for early payment of tobacco duties, see Jacob M. Price, "The Tobacco Trade and the Treasury, 1665–1733 . . ." (Ph.D. thesis, Harvard University, 1954), chap. X, esp. 807–811. The rate quoted prevailed uniformly after 1723.

20. For John Custis's relations with the Perrys, see his letterbook (1717–1741) in LC, especially the letters to Perry of 1718, 2 Apr. 1723, [10 May], 17 Sept., 10 Dec. 1727, 3 Feb. 1727/8, [1730], 1734 (ff. 7, 14v–15v, 35v, 36, 37, 38–v, 42v–43, 68v–69) and letters to Bell & Dee, 1718, 1721, to R. Cary, [10 May], 17 Sept. 1727, 1731, 1735, 1736 (ff. 36, 37v, 44v–5, 61v–62, 69–70). On Custis, see also Jo Zuppan, "John Custis of Williams-

burg, 1678–1749," *VMHB*, XL (1982) 177–197. For Carter, see Wright, ed., *Letters of Robert Carter*, xi, 31–32; University of Virginia Library, R. Carter letterbook (transcript) I, pp. 25, 47 (N.B.), II, p. 18: to M. Perry, Aug. 1723, 25 Mar. 1723/4, 17 May 1727; VaHS Carter letterbook, III, p. 53 to M. Perry, 7 Aug. 1728. Even though Robert Carter generally had a favorable balance with Perrys, he had to ask Micajah III to lend his son John £1500 to purchase the post of secretary of Virginia. It was to be repaid in two years. Ibid., I, 3–4 to M. Perry, 4 July 1723.

21. For the Parke inheritance, see LC Custis-Lee Papers, correspondence, box 2, M. Perry to J. Custis, 12 May 1711; VaHS Mss 1 C9698.a 3, 41–51 (Custis Papers); Helen Hill Miller, *Colonel Parke of Virginia* (Chapel Hill, N.C., 1989) esp. 205–214; Pierre Marambaud, *William Byrd of Westover 1674–1744* (Charlottesville, Va., 1971) 17, 28; Marion Tinling, ed., *The Correspondence of the Three William Byrds of Westover, Virginia*, 2 vols. (Charlottesville, Va., 1977) I, 195, 200, 252–253, 280–282, 284–285, 285n; William Waller Hening, ed., *The Statutes at Large . . . of Virginia. . .*, 13 vols. (Philadelphia, Pa., 1823; Charlottesville, Va., 1969) IV, 29.

22. As Daniel Parke's executors in England, the Perrys were involved in many years of litigation there concerning Parke's Hampshire real estate and mortgages. Among the Chancery records in the PRO, see C.10/328/3, 6, C.11/233/39, C.11/292/18, C.11/1383/6, C.11/2281/73, C.11/2284/123, C.11/2626/29, C.11/2649/41 and C.24/1351 (3 depositions). For a suit involving Parke as merchant, see C.11/968/12 and C.11/2286/114. For a suit involving an annuity Parke had foolishly purchased from the notorious duellist, Lord Mohun, see C.9/345/24.

23. LC J. Custis letterbook ff. 46–47 to M. Perry, 1731.

24. Louis B. Wright and Marion Tinling, eds., *William Byrd of Virginia: The London Diary (1717–1721) and Other Writings* (New York, 1958).

25. Tinling, ed., *Three William Byrds*, I, 240–241, III, 454, 478–480, 484–485, 499, 547–548; John Spencer Bassett, ed., *The Writings of "Colonel William Byrd of Westover in Virginia Esq[uir]e"* (New York, 1901) xxxii–lxxxv.

26. See Chapter 2 and n. 30.

27. Louis B. Wright and Marion Tinling, eds., *The Secret Diary of William Byrd of Westover 1709–1712* (Richmond, Va., 1941) 49, 72, 82, 83, 86, 87. The letter from Randolph to Perry & Co. is referred to in the "Case" cited in note 29 below.

28. Jefferson Randolph Anderson, "Tuckahoe and the Tuckahoe Randolphs," *VMHB*, XLV (1937) 57. The will of William Randolph of Turkey Island is printed in full in Valentine Museum, *The Edward Pleasants Valentine Papers*, 4 vols. (Richmond, Va., [1927]) III, 1368–1372.

29. "The Case of Sarah Perry Widow and Micajah Perry and Phillip Perry

Merch[an]ts of London on their Appeal ag[ains]t the Randolphs [of] Virginia" in Cambridge University Library, Cholmondeley (Houghton) MSS. 81/25.

30. PRO C.O.5/1320/R.17 Drysdale to Board of Trade, 10 July 1726; R.20 ("The humble Representation of the Council & Burgesses of Virg[ini]a" to the king, 1726); R.34 R. Carter to P. Leheup, 5 Jan. 1726/7; *APC Col.*, III, 69–70; *Cal.S.P.Col.AWI, 1726–1727*, 109–117, 227; Henry R. McIlwaine et al., eds., *Executive Journals of the Council of Colonial Virginia*, 6 vols. (Richmond, Va., 1925–1966) IV, 102–103.

6. The Perils of Politics

1. Edward Chamberlayne, *Magnae Britanniae Notitia*, 22nd ed. (London, 1708) 689–690; Henry Horwitz et al., eds., *London Politics 1713–1717*, London Record Society, 17 (London, 1981) 88, 109.

2. For the political situation in London in the 1720s, see W. A. Speck and W. A. Gray, "London at the Polls under Anne and George I," *Guildhall Studies in London History*, I (1975) 253–262; I. G. Doolittle, "Walpole's City Elections Act (1725)," *English Historical Review*, XCVII (1982) 504–529; Nicholas Rogers, "The City Election Act (1725) Reconsidered," *English Historical Review*, C (1985) 604–617; idem, "Resistance to Oligarchy: The City Opposition to Walpole and His Successors 1725–47," in John Stevenson, ed., *London in the Age of Reform* (Oxford, 1977) 1–29; Romney Sedgwick, *The History of Parliament: The House of Commons 1715–1754*, 2 vols. (Oxford, 1970) I, 279–283. For the Heyshams, see ibid., and "Heysham Pedigree," *Miscellanea Genealogica et Heraldica*, n.s., IV (1884) 373–375.

3. James Puckle, *The Club: or, A Grey Cap for a Green Head*, ed. [Henry] Austin Dobson (London, 1900); G[eorge] Steinman Steinman, *The Author of "The Club" Identified*, (s.l., 1872) 11–12;; notice on James Puckle in *Dictionary of National Biography*.

4. Haberdashers Company records in Guildhall Library: Ms. 15,844/1 fo. 14v (Court of Wardens Minutes, 21 June 1727); MS. 15857/2 p. 373 (Freedoms, 7 July 1727); MS. 15842/5 p. 236 (Court of Assistants Minutes, 14 July 1727).

5. E[veline] C[ruickshanks], "Micajah Perry," in Sedgwick, *History of Parliament*, I, 280, II, 341–342; Alfred B. Beaven, *The Aldermen of the City of London*, 2 vols. (London, 1908–1913) I, 257, 279, 280, II, 126; *Daily Journal*, no. 2029 (15 July 1727) 2; no. 2031 (18 July 1727) 2; no. 2037 (25 July 1727) 2; no. 2110 (23 Oct. 1727) 2; Guildhall Library: MS. 15842/5 pp. 241, 243 (Haberdashers' Court of Assistants Minutes, 2, 6 Dec. 1727).

6. Sedgwick, *History of Parliament*, I, 148, 155.
7. Gerrit P. Judd IV, *Members of Parliament 1734–1832* (New Haven, Conn., 1955) 22, 26; Sir Lewis Namier and John Brooke, *The History of Parliament: The House of Commons 1754–1790*, 3 vols. (New York, 1964) I, 98. The St. Katherine Cree Church parish registers show that Micajah III was christened on 30 April 1694.
8. Sedgwick, *History of Parliament*, I, 435–437, II, 21, 326–327.
9. Ibid., I, 148–150 and passim.
10. Cruickshanks, "Perry"; Jacob M. Price, "The Excise Affair Revisited," in Stephen B. Baxter, ed., *England's Rise to Greatness 1660–1763* (Berkeley and Los Angeles, 1983) 277; Thomas M. Truxes, *Irish-American Trade, 1660–1783* (Cambridge, 1988) 29–33.
11. Stock, *Proceedings*, III, 498–501n; Samuel Hazard, ed., *Pennsylvania Archives* (Philadelphia, Pa., 1852) I, 197. Perry was less successful in obtaining a paper money act desired by Pennsylvania. See ibid., I, 197–198, 206; *Minutes of the Provincial Council of Pennsylvania . . . to the Termination of the Proprietary Government* (Philadelphia, Pa., 1852) III, 377.
12. Stock, *Proceedings*, IV, 56, 58–60, 62, 84–85, 87.
13. Ibid., 12–13, 25–28. On the problem of tobacco "stalks" or "stems," see Price, "The Tobacco Trade and the Treasury", II, 751–784, esp. 766–774.
14. Stock, *Proceedings*, IV, 57, 60–62, 154–155.
15. Ibid., 149, 151, 166. The Commons journals suggest that Perry managed the earlier stages of the coffee bill but that it became a ministerial measure when the drafting committee was chosen to include the chairman of committees, a secretary to the Treasury and four junior lords of the Treasury.
16. *The Letters of Cadwallader Colden*, II, 45–48; Stock, *Proceedings*, IV, 123–126, 139, 181. For the colony's hostility to the sugar bill, see McIlwaine, ed., *Executive Journals of Virginia Council*, IV, 252, 257.
17. On Leheup and the Walpoles, see Price, "Excise Affair," 274–276.
18. PRO T.29/26 p. 158. The man appointed, Josiah Cock, may have been related to Perry's wife, née Cocke.
19. *Cal.S.P.Col.AWI, 1731*, nos. 177, 567; *1732*, nos. 27, 112, 118; *Journal C.T.P., 1728/9–1734*, 269, 316. For Taylor, read "Tayloe."
20. Colonial Williamsburg Foundation, Gooch transcripts, Gov. Gooch to Dr. Thomas Gooch, 28 July 1732; Price, "Excise Affair," 276.
21. For the councillors, see Chapter 4.
22. *Journal C.T.P.*, passim.
23. For the accusations concerning the association and the French buying agent, see Jacob M. Price, *France and the Chesapeake: A History of the French*

Tobacco Monopoly, 1674–1791. . ., 2 vols. (Ann Arbor, Mich., 1973) I, 649–654; based in part on Henry Darnall, *A Just and Impartial Account of the Transactions of the Merchants in London*. . . (Annapolis, 1729), rept. as *Photostat Americana*, 2nd ser., no. 164.

24. See n. 3 above.

25. This ranking based on tobacco import data is confirmed by other data on tobacco bonds outstanding, an important measure of activity for Virginia and Maryland merchants. An account of London merchants' tobacco bonds outstanding as of 27 May 1732 shows Micajah Perry in fourth place, while a similar account as of 6 April 1733 shows him in fifth place. Cambridge University Library, Cholmondeley (Houghton) MSS. 29/13 and 29/22.

26. PRO C.54/5407 membranes 3–6 and 6–9 (indentures of 6 and 9 June 1730) The same or some similar properties on Gravel Lane, part of the estate of Richard Perry IV, were in 1720 sold for £2270 by Sarah and Micajah III to the South Sea Company director Sir John Blunt, bart. *The Particulars and Inventories of the Estates of the late . . . Directors of the South-Sea Company*, 2 vols. (London, 1721) I: Blunt, 38.

27. PRO C.54/5539/6 membranes 34–35 (indenture, 15 Oct. 1735). H. L. Lehmann, *The Residential Copyholds of Epsom from the Records of the Manor of Ebbisham 1663 to 1925* (Epsom, 1987) 15–16, 87–89.

28. Register of Deeds, Dublin, vol. 118, p. 226, no. 80570 (22 Feb. 1743/4); Lehmann, *Epsom Copyholds*, 87–89.

29. Price, "Glasgow, the Tobacco Trade, and the Scottish Customs," 33–35.

30. U.S. Bureau of the Census, *Historical Statistics of the United States, Colonial Times to 1970*, 2 vols. (Washington, D.C., 1975), II, 1168–69, 1172; Walter Minchinton, Celia King and Peter Waite, eds., *Virginia Slave-Trade Statistics 1698–1775* (Richmond, Va., 1984).

31. Price, "Excise Affair," 276–277; John M. Hemphill, II, *Virginia and the English Commercial System, 1689–1733* (New York and London, 1985) 150–173.

32. *Cal.S.P.Col.AWI, 1716–1717*, nos. 140–142, 534; *1717–1718*, nos. 174, 263, 281, 343, 380, 395, 657iii; Saunders, *Colonial Records of North Carolina*, II, 279–280.

33. Leonard Woods Labaree, ed., *Royal Instructions to British Colonial Governors 1670–1776*, 2 vols. (New York, 1935, 1967) I, 338; William Waller Hening, ed., *The Statutes at Large; being a Collection of all the Law of Virginia*. . . , 13 vols. (Philadelphia, 1809–1823; Charlottesville, Va., 1989) III, 333–335, IV, 222–228. The first Virginia act (4 Anne c. xxiii) declared slaves to be real estate for purposes of inheritance but left them liable to be seized for debts as if they were chattel; the second

Virginia act (1 Geo. I, c. xi) increased the discretion of slaveowners but still left slaves liable to seizure for debt.

34. Price, "Excise Affair," 277–279; Hemphill, *Virginia and the English Commercial System*, 174–189; Stock, *Proceedings*, IV, 145, 150.

35. Price, "Excise Affair," 283–292; Paul Langford, *The Excise Crisis: Society and Politics in the Age of Walpole* (Oxford, 1975); Hemphill, *Virginia and the English Commerical System*, 190–286.

36. Ibid.

37. Cruickshanks, "Perry," II, 341–342; Beaven, *Aldermen*, II, 126.

38. Price, "Tobacco Trade and Treasury," 382; *Cal.T.B.& P., 1735–1738*, 341, 388, 468; *1739–41*, 6, 79; PRO T.1/297/20; T.4/10 (Ind. 4625) p. 133; T.29/28 pp. 51, 111; E.127/36 ff. 353v, 387–387v, 394–394v and E.127/37 Easter 1737 nos. 44, 45; *The Political State of Great Britain*, XLIX (January 1735) 22–24; LI (January 1736) 31–32: LII (August 1736) 131; Cambridge University Library, Cholmondeley (Houghton) MSS., 81/26. The crown suit against Perry was for £623.14.4. Presumably, with fines, interest and legal expenses, the final amount involved was much larger. Perry was very active in the house on the "Spanish depredations" issue in 1738, less so thereafter. Stock, *Proceedings*, IV, 367, 405–406, 430, 445–447, 450–509, 509n, 670–672.

39. Colonial Williamsburg Foundation, Gooch transcripts, 35–36, 41–42, 45–46, to brother, 20 July 1733, 8 March 1734/5, 5 July 1735.

40. In the 1720s, Perry had been able to get sixty-day loans or discounts from the Bank for up to L8000 at a time. The last such advance noted was in 1729. Bank of England Archives, Court Minutes I, pp. 16, 152, 226; ADM 7/10 (General Ledger) 49.

41. *Letters and Papers of Cadwallader Colden*, II, 105–106.

42. Wright, ed., *Letters of Robert Carter;* Carter letterbooks of 1720s in UVa (transcripts) and VaHS; letterbook of executors of R. Carter estate in UVa. See also Clifford Dowdey, *The Virginia Dynasties: the Emergence of "King" Carter and the Golden Age* (Boston, 1969) esp. chap. 9.

43. Tinling, *William Byrd Correspondence*, II, 522–533 to Perrys, 4 July 1737, and passim; *VMHB*, XXXVII (1929) 102–104. Nadir Shah, also called Kouli Khan, was the contemporary general who seized the throne of Persia. The rejection by King Rehoboam, son of Solomon, of the advice of his father's old councillors to treat his people gently led to the withdrawal of the allegiance of the ten northern tribes that became the separate kingdom of Israel. Byrd implied that a comparable harshness by Alderman Perry was encouraging the withdrawal of the old friends of his firm in Virginia.

44. New York Public Library, William Beverley Papers; in particular, see

letters to Perry of 4 Aug., 6 Nov., 8 Dec. 1742; 1 Sept., 21 Oct. 1743. For the Perry associations of his father and grandfather, see Dorman, ed., *Genealogies of Virginia Families*, I, 75, 82–83; Polly C. Mason, *Records of Colonial Gloucester County Virginia*, 2 vols. (Newport News, Va., 1948) II, 105–106; VaHS, MSS. 1 B4678 b 9 (Beverley Papers).

45. LC J. Custis letterbook, to Dee & Bell, 1718; ff. 37, 38 to Perry, 17 Sept., 10 Dec. 1727; ff. 44v–45 to R. Cary, 1731; ff. 48v–49 to [Lyonel] Lyde, 1732; ff. 54–54v, 59–60 to Perry, 1733 (2 letters).

46. Ibid., ff. 54–4v to Perry, late 1733.

47. Ibid., ff. 64–4v to Perry, 1735, marked "never sent."

48. Ibid., ff. 68v–69, 72v–73, 73v–74, 84–85, 89v–90 to M. Perry, 1736, 1741; to P. Perry, 1737; to [R. Cary, 1737], to [Peter] Collinson, 1739.

49. For Perry's public activities in his mayoral year, see Sir William Purdie Treloar, bart., *A Lord Mayor's Diary* (London, 1920).

50. *Notes and Queries*, 8th ser., VIII (6 July 1895) 17; Martin Nail, ed., "The Graveyard and Church Monuments of Epsom," no. 99 (typescript in library of Society of Genealogists, London).

51. The withdrawal of Phillip is mentioned in the Bennett and Pope lawsuits (see notes 60 and 61 below) and in Walter King appeal in PRO A.O.13/32.

52. Sedgwick, *History of Parliament*, I, 280, 282; II, 341–342.

53. Ibid., II, 341–342; Eveline Cruickshanks, *Political Untouchables: The Tories and the '45* (New York, 1979) 140.

54. PRO C.11/1667/15 (Beckford v. Perry). PRO T.1/325 f. 137 shows James Johnston as a small importer of tobacco ca. 1747. He may have gone into business for himself, or have been acting as trustee for the realization of assets belonging to the defunct Perry firm.

55. LC Jones Papers, V, ff. 687–688 W. King to Col. T. Jones, 6 Dec. 1743.

56. Perry's "failure" did not result in a formal bankruptcy. See PRO C.12/296/16. However, his creditors appear to have forced him to sue members of his late wife's family for long forgotten debts. PRO C.11/1597/8; C.11/1884/33.

57. LC Jones Papers, V, f. 699 King to Jones, 30 May 1744.

58. See *London Magazine* (1746) 489; Beaven, *Aldermen*, I, 14, 257, 280, II, 126; LCRO Court of Aldermen Repertory 151 pp. 25–26, 32, 402–403; Rep. 152 p. 437; Rep. 153 p. 492; Rep. 154 pp. 504–505; Rep. 155 p. 536; Rep. 156 p. 584. However, *F. Farley's Bristol Journal*, no. 130 (10 Jan. 1746/7) reported "that over and above the 200*l.* per Annum, voted by the Common Council to Micajah Perry, Esq., the Court of Aldermen have likewise voted him the same Sum per Annum more, and the Aldermen agreed to present him with 5*l.* per Annum each, in regard

to the great Services done to this City [London]." I have, though, been unable to find confirmation of any subventions beyond those voted by the Court of Aldermen.

59. PRO C.11/1667/15; *Gentleman's Magazine*, XXIII (1753) 53; *London Magazine*, XXII (1753) 93. *Notes and Queries*, 8th ser., VIII (6 July 1895) 17 states that Perry died at Epsom. He appears, however, to have been buried at East Greenwich.

60. For some of the records of the Chancery suit, Bennett v. Perry, see PRO C.12/296/16; C.12/307/66; C.12/1449/32; C.12/1450/83; C.33/389 ff. 49v, 178v–179; C.33/391 ff. 233v, 342v, 564v. For the countersuit, Perry v. Bennett, see C.11/307/66.

61. On suits conducted after Pope's death, as Beckford v. Perry, see PRO C.11/1667/15; C.11/1672/31. See also PRO Prob.6/133 ff. 109–114 (Administrations, Surrey, Nov. 1757).

62. See Chapter 5, n. 11.

63. LC Custis Family Papers: J. Hanbury to J. Custis, 20 Dec. 1745. See McIlwaine, *Virginia Council Executive Journals*, IV, 249 for the loss in 1729 of a ship owned by Perry and filled with 540 hogsheads of tobacco on his account.

64. In 1702, Perry, Lane & Co. gave to Charles Carroll of Annapolis, sometime attorney-general of Maryland, a general power of attorney to act for them in the colony; after his death, a similar power was given to Thomas Bordley, a leading Annapolis lawyer (1721) and in 1728 to Samuel Chew, a prominent merchant in Anne Arundel County. MdHR Provincial Court Land Records T.P.#4 pp. 41–42, P.L.#5 pp. 472–475; P.L.#6 pp. 342–344.

65. For a Maryland "composition," see MdHR T.P.#4 pp. 52–56; D.D.#2 pp. 44–47.

66. *APC Col.*, IV, 210–211. King's appeal and related papers are in PRO A.O.13/32(i) pp. 9–16. In 1704 Micaiah Perry owned 600 acres in Prince George's County. Gary Parks, ed., *Virginia Tax Records. . .* (Baltimore, 1983) 410. In 1714, the firm of Micaiah Perry & Co. was similarly the temporary proprietor of 2060 acres in Isle of Wight County on the "South Side" of the lower James River. John D. Neville, "An Isle of Wight Quitrent Roll, 1714," *VMHB*, LXXXVII (1979) 180. Other long-drawn-out problems arose from the mortgages of the brothers Augustine and Charles Smith of Essex County on the Rappahannock River. It took an act of the Virginia legislature in 1744 to clear title to a parcel mortgaged by Charles to the Perrys in 1719 so that it could be sold. VaHS MSS. 1 B4678 b 9; Beverley Fleet, ed., *Essex County Wills and Deeds 1714–1717*, Virginia Colonial Abstracts, vol. 9 (Richmond, Va., [1940]) 87; John

Bennett Boddie, *Historical Southern Families*, 20 vols. (Baltimore, Md., 1967–1975) XVII, 183–188; Mason, *Records of Colonial Gloucester County*, II, 105–106; Hening, *The Statutes at Large . . . of Virginia*, V, 287–292.
67. *Gentleman's Magazine*, III (1733) 45; *London Magazine* (1733) 44.

7. The Family after the Fall

1. *London Magazine* (1733) 44.
2. PRO Prob.11/821 (P.C.C. 77 Glazier).
3. PRO Prob.11/877 (P.C.C. 267 St. Eloy).
4. PRO Prob.11/892 (P.C.C. 473 Caesar). The court rolls of the manor of Little Stanbridge or Stambridge, Essex, show that the lordship of the manor passed from Richard Perry IV to his widow Sarah, then to their son Phillip and ultimately to Philip Cade, who sold the same in 1782 or shortly before. Essex Record Office (Chelmsford) D/DU 190/16 and 19. See also Figure 2 above.
5. On Dr. Salusbury Cade, see *Dictionary of National Biography*; Joseph Foster, *Alumni Oxonienses . . . 1500–1714*, 4 vols. (Oxford, 1891–1892) I, 228; William Munk, *The Roll of the Royal College of Physicians of London*, 2d ed. (London, 1878) I, 510.
6. On Salusbury Cade (Jr.), the husband of Elizabeth Perry, see Foster, *Alumni Oxonienses*, I, 228; Joseph Welch, *The List of the Queen's Scholars at St. Peter's College, Westminster . . .* (London, 1852) 251, 262, 263; C. F. Russell Barker and Alan H. Stenning, *The Records of Old Westminster: A Biographical List . . . to 1927*, 2 vols. (London, 1928) I, 155. For his will, see PRO Prob.11/988 (P.C.C. 240 Stevens). He left almost all his personal estate to his wife Elizabeth "in consideration of the neglect shewn her by her own Relations and in the full Confidence I have that she will do Justice to her Children." This reflects the omission of Elizabeth Cade in the will of her brother Phillip Perry and Sarah Heysham's passing over her sister to leave major bequests to Elizabeth's daughter Sarah (£3000) and son Philip (the residue). For the will of Elizabeth (Perry) Cade, proved 10 Dec. 1787, see PRO Prob.11/1160 (P.C.C. 539 Major). She left her son Philip Cade the great tithes of Eyton Rectory in Bedfordshire, held on lease from Trinity College, Cambridge, which had originally been acquired by Micaiah Perry I.
7. On Philip Cade, see *Gentleman's Magazine*, LXIX (1799) 165, 249–250; Russell Barker and Stenning, *Old Westminster*, I, 155; Foster, *Alumni Oxonienses*, I, 208.
8. For the third Salusbury Cade, see Russell Barker and Stenning, *Old Westminster*, I, 155; Welch, *Queen's Scholars*, 410, 411.
9. For the family of the rather affluent Philip Cade, see his will in PRO

Prob.11/1325 (P.C.C. 422 Howe). For the Harenc family, see Henry Wagner, "The Huguenot Refugee Family of Harenc," *The Genealogist*, new ser., XXXII (1916) 193–195; John and J. A. Venn, *Alumni Cantabrigienses . . . to 1900: Part II, from 1751 to 1900*, 3 vols. (Cambridge, 1940–) III, 241; Foster, *Alumni Oxonienses 1715–1886*, II, 607; *Clarke's New Law List* (1839), 33; *Marlborough College Register 1843–1952*, 9th ed., ed. C. Warwick Jones (Marlborough, Wilts [1952]) 49, 132. A member of this family, Henry Benjamin Harenc, lived in London, but ca. 1870 held 5,979 acres in county Kerry (Ireland) with a gross rental of £2121 p.a. John Bateman, *The Great Landowners of Great Britain and Ireland* (Leicester, 1971) 207.

10. *Gentleman's Magazine*, LX (1790) 1146; Huguenot Society of London Library, Wagner Pedigrees: Savary. James Savary and Catherine Cade had two sons who served in the Bengal Army: John Tanzia (1800–1832) and William Tanzia (1802–1855). See Major V. C. P. Hodson, *List of Officers of the Bengal Army*, 4 vols. (London, 1927–1947) IV, 24. William had several sons who became army officers; the youngest, Dalzell, died in 1908: *London Times*, 4 May 1908. See also Henry Wagner, "The Huguenot Refugee Family of De Varenne," *The Genealogist*, n.s., XXIII (1907) 62–63; and notes on Savary family by Mrs. I. V. Pearson in Huguenot Society of London Library.

11. Their families were in no sense socially decayed at the time of the 1790 marriage of Catherine Cade to W. J. Savary. Catherine's mother Catherine, after her divorce from Philip Cade, married the 4th baron Aylmer, an impoverished Irish peer, by whom she had a son, the future 5th baron. Thus at her marriage Catherine (Cade) Savary was the half-sister of an Irish peer, a professional soldier (ultimately a general) and future governor-general of Lower Canada. In addition, her mother's brother Charles, an even more successful soldier-diplomat and viceroy of Ireland, was created baron Whitworth in the Irish peerage (1800) and viscount (1813) and earl Whitworth (1815) in that of the United Kingdom. Similarly, W. J. Tanzia de Savary's mother, Marie Blaquière, was the sister of John Blaquière, who left a London counting-house to become a professional soldier, diplomat and Irish politician. He was created baron de Blaquière in the Irish peerage in 1800. See *The Complete Peerage*, ed. V. Gibbs, I, 369, IV, 107–108, XII(2) 618–619.

12. See Figure 1 above and *Burke's Presidential Families of the United States of America* (London, 1975) 225.

13. For Richard Hutchinson, see G. E. Aylmer, *The State's Servants: The Civil Service of the English Republic 1649–1660* (London and Boston, 1973) 247–250; Peter Orlando Hutchinson, *The Diary and Letters of . . . Thomas*

Hutchinson Esq., 2 vols. (Boston, 1884) II, 446–447, 457–458; Karl S. Bottigheimer, *English Money and Irish Land: The "Adventurers" in the Cromwellian Settlement of Ireland* (Oxford, 1971) 184, 215, 386, 393. For his will see PRO Prob.11/332 (P.C.C. 47 Penn). See also Trinity College, Dublin, Donoughmore Papers, T.3459/Y/2/5 for lease (20 March 1658/9) by Richard Hutchinson to son Edward Hutchinson of all his lands in Ireland; and B/2/6 for Massachusetts connection. Edward had recently returned from New England.

14. See Chapter 1.

15. Thomas M. Truxes, *Irish-American Trade, 1660–1783* (Cambridge, 1988) 24–26.

16. Land acquisition began under John Perry's father Richard. See [11th-15th] *Reports from the Commissioners . . . respecting the Public Records of Ireland* (London, 1829) 403; William P. Burke, *History of Clonmel* (Waterford, 1907) 125; Seamus Pender, *A Census of Ireland circa 1659* (Dublin, 1939) 310–314 (for the thin population of the district then). For will of Edward Hutchinson, see Trinity College, Dublin, Donoughmore Papers T.3459/B/1/6. For correspondence re John Perry's managing Hutchinson's Irish lands, see ibid., B/2/1–4. For land acquisition by John Perry, see ibid., B/1/5, 10, 11. The name of John Perry's wife is incorrectly given in the most recent edition of *Burke's Landed Gentry of Ireland* and *Irish Family History*. For the Riall family, see Pownoll R. Phipps, *The Life of Colonel Pownoll Phipps . . .* (London, 1894) appendix 12. For the Presbyterian affiliations of the Rialls, see Nolan, "Tipperary," 300.

17. Registry of Deeds, Dublin, vol. 118, pp. 226–228, no 80570 (22 Feb. 1743/4); Mark Bence-Jones, *A Guide to Irish Country Houses* (London, 1988) 286. John Perry (Jr.) was the second son of John Perry. An older brother, Richard, mentioned in his father's will of 1710, had died by 1723. See Registry of Deeds, Dublin, vol. 7, p. 6 (no. 1611); and v. 41 pp. 230–231 (no. 25536). His third son, Edward, inherited Newcastle House near Clonmel but was also dead by 1723. His fifth son, Samuel, became a merchant in Cork. Registry of Deeds doc. nos. 28/342/17832 and 40/12/23868.

18. Prior to 1780, the only observable higher educational attainments of the Clonmel Perrys were the admission of John Perry's eldest son Richard to the Middle Temple in 1694 and younger son Micajah to the Leyden and possibly Reims medical faculties. See H. A. C. Sturgess, *Registers of Admissions to the Honourable Society of the Middle Temple*, 3 vols. (London, 1949); R. W. Innes Smith, *English-Speaking Students of Medicine at the University of Leyden* (Edinburgh and London, 1932) 181. From 1780, however, we find numerous young men from the Woodrooff

family entering such Ascendancy institutions as King's Inn and Trinity College, Dublin. See Edward Keane et al., eds., *King's Inn Admissions Papers 1607–1867* (Dublin, 1982) 399; George Dame Burtchaeli and Thomas Ulick Sadleir, *Alumni Dublinenses (1593–1860),* new ed. (Dublin, 1935) 664; *Middle Temple Admissions,* II, 414.

19. U. H. Hussey de Burgh, *The Landowners of Ireland* (Dublin, ca. 1878) 365; John Bateman, *The Great Landowners of Great Britain and Ireland,* 4th ed. (London, 1883) 357; both based on C. 1492 in parliamentary papers.

20. Mary D. Kierstead, "Profiles: A Great Old Breakerawayer," *The New Yorker* (October 13, 1986) 97–112, esp. 102–104. Molly Keane collaborated in writing a number of plays with the actor, playwright and theatre manager, John Perry, a member of the Woodrooff family. He also collaborated with Elizabeth Bowen in writing *Castle Anna,* a play about a decayed Irish country house and family. On him, see *Who's Who in the Theatre,* 14th ed. (London, 1967) 1059; and Victoria Glendinning, *Elizabeth Bowen* (New York, 1978) 163, 226–227.

21. Bence-Jones, *Irish Country Houses,* 286; The Knight of Glin et al., *Vanishing Country Houses of Ireland* ([Dublin,] 1988) 136.

22. According to the 1989–1990 Irish telephone directory.

Conclusion

1. Ralph Davis, "English Foreign Trade, 1660–1700," *Economic History Review,* 2nd ser., VII (1954) 164–165.

2. Ralph Davis, "English Foreign Trade, 1700–1774," *Economic History Review,* XV (1962) 300–303; U.S. Bureau of the Census, *Historical Statistics of the United States, Colonial Times to 1970* (Washington, D.C., 1975) II, 1176–1177.

3. *Historical Statistics of the United States,* II, 1189–1191; Neville Williams, "England's Tobacco Trade in the Reign of Charles I," *VMHB,* LXV (1957) 403–449; PRO Customs 2.

4. See Russell R. Menard, "The Tobacco Industry in the Chesapeake Colonies, 1617–1730: An Interpretation," *Research in Economic History,* V (1980) 109–117.

5. See n. 3 above.

6. Jacob M. Price and Paul G. E. Clemens, "A Revolution of Scale in Overseas Trade: British Firms in the Chesapeake Trade, 1675–1775," *Journal of Economic History,* XLVII (1987) 1–43, esp. 11.

7. Cambridge University Library, Cholmondeley (Houghton) MSS. 29/13; 29/22. The firm was then in its second generation. Brother James died in 1733, leaving his brother Benjamin to fail in 1737.

8. E. A. Webb, G. W. Miller and J. Beckwith, *The History of Chislehurst Its Church, Manors, and Parish* (London, 1899) 276–279.
9. Sedgwick, *History of Parliament*, 154 lists several dozen "ruined men" among those who sat in Commons between 1715 and 1754. Only Perry and Sir Thomas Johnson, M.P. for Liverpool, had any active connection with the Chesapeake trade.
10. Wright, *Letters of Robert Carter*, 84–85, R. Carter to J. Carter, 3 Mar. 1720/1.

Appendix C

1. Peter Orlando Hutchinson, *The Diary and Letters of His Excellency Thomas Hutchinson, Esq.*, 2 vols. (Boston, 1884) II, 446–447, 457–458. For the 1669 will of Richard Hutchinson, see PRO Prob.11/332 (P.C.C. 47 Penn). For his service as Treasurer of the Navy, see G[erald] E. Aylmer, *The State's Servants: The Civil Service of the English Republic 1649–1660* (London and Boston, 1973) 247–250. See also *Dictionary of American Biography*, s.v. William, Anne and Thomas Hutchinson; and *Dictionary of National Biography*, s.v. Anne and Thomas Hutchinson and the Hely-Hutchinsons.
2. William Puckle is mentioned in the will of Richard Hutchinson. See also IGI, London; A. W. Hughes Clarke and Arthur Camplin, eds., *The Visitation of Norfolk Anno Domini 1664*, 2 vols., Norfolk Record Society, IV, V (1934) II, 176; *Dictionary of National Biography*, s.v. James Puckle; Trinity College, Dublin, Donoughmore Papers (T.3459) B/2/4 and 5.
3. For will of Edward Hutchinson (19 Jan. 1698/9), see Trinity College, Dublin, Donoughmore Papers (T.3459) B/1/6, plus B/2/1–4.

Appendix D

1. PRO Prob.11/247 (P.C.C. 23 Aylett) and will notes in Genealogical Office, Dublin.
2. A fairly clear idea of the sources used by Sir William Betham can be obtained from his annotation of the Limerick pedigree (Genealogical Office, Dublin, G.O. 169 pp. 45–64; copy in the possession of the earl of Limerick) and from related notes in the Genealogical Office. I am indebted to Mr. John Grenham of Dublin for help on this point. See also Chapter 1, n. 5.
3. West Devon Record Office, Plymouth, W.720/3; W.720/6; and W.720/7, particularly 169/10(a) and (e).
4. IGI.

5. PRO E.134/39 Eliz., Trin. 10; LC Banks Collections: Transcript of Devon Subsidy Roll 1624 (PRO subsidy roll 102/463) fo. 63.

6. Genealogical Office, Dublin, G.O.226 p. 31.

7. Hillier, "Virginia Trade," 297.

8. Among the numerous references to Captains William and Henry Pery/Perry in Virginia, see in particular "Minutes of the Council and General Court 1622–1679," *VMHB*, XXIV (1916) 245; Conway Robinson, ed., "Notes from the Council and General Court Records," ibid., XIV (1906–1907) 191.

9. PRO Prob.11/155 (P.C.C. 32 Ridley). Captain Henry Pery's heirs were his two surviving daughters, both married and living near London. This suggests that Captain Henry had close connections there to whom he could send or bring his daughters. Henry Pery himself may have returned to England, at least for a visit, for someone of that name signed a 1659 London "Petition of Merchants, Planters & Traders to the English Plantations in America, but more especially to Virginia": BL Loan 29/88/Misc. 85.

10. *Letters and Papers Foreign and Domestic of the Reign of Henry VIII*, IV, 794, 1678 and no. 1377(27); VIII, 303–304; X, 159, XIII(i), 441; XIII(ii), 175, 292–294, 400, 429, 497; XIV(i), 262, 610; XV, 177, 563, 565; XVI, 321, 327, 427; XVII, 114, 159, 163; XVIII, 124; XXI(ii), 429; William Page, ed., *Victoria History of Hampshire and the Isle of Wight*, 6 vols. (London, 1900–1914) IV, 596–602; William Page, ed., *The Victoria History of the County of Hertford*, 4 vols. (Westminster, 1902–1914) III, 429, 460–461. A "sewer" is defined in the *Oxford English Dictionary* as "an attendant at a meal who superintended the arrangement of the table, the seating of the guests, and the tasting and serving of the dishes."

11. PRO Prob.11/31 (P.C.C. 31 Alen).

12. PRO Prob.11/37 (P.C.C. 21 More).

13. See n. 10. The eldest son of John Piry was Nicholas "Perrie" of Warminster, clothier.

Index

Adams, Joseph, 79
Admiralty, 52; High Court of, 8
"Adventure" trading system, 30, 49
Africa, trade to, 47, 55. *See also* Slave
   trade; Royal African Company
Albemarle County, Virginia, 90
Alum, exported, 44
Amsterdam, English congregation at,
   18
Anderson, Robert, Jr., 35–37, 44, 97,
   156n34
Anderson, Robert, Sr., 35
Annapolis, Maryland, 173n64
Anne Arundel County, Maryland,
   173n64
Annuities, government, 67
Army: parliamentary, 15–16; royal, 92;
   East India Company, 92
Artisans, emigration of, 57
Attorneys (agents) in Virginia, 25,
   165n14
Aylmer, Henry (Aylmer), 4th baron,
   175n11

Baltic Sea littoral, 45
Band of Gentlemen Pensioners, 92
Bank of England, 3, 22, 25, 59, 67, 74,
   75, 85, 97, 139n1, 156n32, 157n49,
   171n40
Barbados, 19, 47, 159n80
Barnard, Sir John, 74
Bath, Somerset, 87
Bathurst, Edward, 33, 154n15
Bathurst, Lancelot, 155n15
Bathurst, Mrs. Susannah (Puckle), wife
   of Edward, 154–155n15
Bathurst, Susannah, daughter of
   Edward, 154n15
Bayonne, France, 84

Bedwell Park, Hertfordshire, 118
Beef, exported, 93
Bengal, 20
Bennett, Richard, 41, 65, 88, 156n45
Bernard family of Virginia, 20
Betham, Sir William, 114–115
Beverley, Robert, 86
Beverley, William, 86, 89
Bezeley, John, 99
Bills of exchange, 31, 34, 37–39, 43,
   47, 56, 64, 66, 87, 150n23, 165n14
Black, William, 79
Blair, James, 164n27
Blaquière, John (Blaquière), baron de,
   175n11
Blaquière, Marie. *See* Savary, Mrs. Marie
Blathwayt, William, 57
Bleeke, Edward, 32–33
Blofield, Norfolk, 18
Blunt, Sir John, bart., 170n26
Board of Trade, 7, 52, 57, 77, 80, 81
Bolingbroke, Henry (St. John),
   viscount, 84
Bonds: mercantile, 35, 41, 66, 89, 99;
   customs, 82–83, 170n25
Books, exported, 108
Booth, James, 140n2
Bordley, Thomas, 173n64
Boston, Massachusetts, 13
Bowden, William, 139n1
Bowen, Elizabeth, 177n20
Boyne, battle of the, 93
Bradby, Capt. James, 69
Bradley, James, & Co., 84, 98, 99,
   166n14
Brassware, exported, 110
Braxton, George, Jr., 90
Brayne, James, 158n57
Breamore, Hampshire, 118–119

Brecknockshire, 54, 161n7
Brecon, 54, 161n7
Bremen, 45, 46
Brewers Quay, London, 24
Bridger, Col. Samuel, 35
Brimstone, exported, 44
Bristol, 30, 65, 81, 85
Bristow, Robert, Sr. and Jr., 139nl,
    159n73
Brooke, Thomas, 99
Browne, Peregrine, 159n71
Buchanan & Hamilton, 99
Buckland Monachorum (Devon): Pery
    family of, 8, 9, 114–117; Richard
    Pery II at, 11, 14, 142n14
Burwell family, 20
Byfeild, Thomas, 160n83
Byrd, Mrs. Lucy (Parke), 68
Byrd, William, I, 32–34, 43, 47, 57
Byrd, William, II, 31, 32, 37, 57, 66,
    68–70, 78, 85, 157n47

Cade, Mrs. Catherine (Whitworth), 92,
    175n11
Cade, Mrs. Elizabeth (Perry), 25, 26,
    63, 90–92, 174n6
Cade, Catherine. See Savary, Mrs.
    Catherine
Cade, Philip, 91, 92, 174n6
Cade, Dr. Salusbury, I, 92
Cade, Salusbury, II, son of Salusbury I,
    63, 90–92, 174n6
Cade, Salusbury, III, son of Philip, 92
Cade, Sarah. See Harenc, Mrs. Sarah
Cadiz, 11, 84
Cairnes, Sir Alexander, bart., 59
Canada, Lower, 175n11
Canvas, exported, 108
Capital, 40–41
Carroll, Charles, 89, 173n64
Carter, Capt. James, 11, 142n20
Carter, John, of Middlewich, Cheshire,
    15
Carter, John, secretary of Virginia, 64,
    167n20
Carter, Robert, London haberdasher,
    15
Carter, Robert, Virginia councillor, 33,

34, 41, 47, 57, 63, 67, 71, 78, 85, 90,
    97, 167n20; executors of, 85
Carter, Susanna, daughter of Capt.
    James, 142n20
Carter, Mrs. Susanne (Pery), wife of
    Capt. James, 11, 142n20
Cary, John, 140n2, 164n27
Cary, Robert, 84, 85
Cary, Thomas, 140n2
Cattle raising and trade, Ireland,
    16–17, 93
Chancery, Court of, 88
Charles City County, Virginia, 34
Charlestown, Massachusetts, 13
Charwelton, Northamptonshire, 23
Chesapeake, trade in, 30–32
Chester's Quay, London, 23–26, 80
Chew, Samuel, 173n64
Christ's Hospital, London, 23, 27
Chumleigh Park, Devon, 118
Church of England, 17; archbishop of
    Canterbury, 58; bishops: London,
    58; Bristol, 76; Norwich, 76; Ely, 76;
    Salisbury, 164n27; St. Asaph, 164n27
Church of Ireland, 94
Churchill, Madam Elizabeth, 157n54
Clarke, Samuel, 35, 155n25
Clemens, Paul, 29
Clonmel, co. Tipperary, 16, 18, 93,
    146n46
Coaches, 44, 91, 111
Cocke, Elizabeth. See Perry, Mrs.
    Elizabeth
Cocke, Richard, 27
Cocke, William, 57
Coffee, 75, 169n15
Colden, Cadwallader, 76
College of Arms, London, 8, 22, 115
College of William and Mary
    (Virginia), 58
Colmore, Thomas, 99
Comestibles, exported, 109
Commissions on sales and purchases,
    49–50
Connecticut, returnees from, 16. See
    also New Haven
Consignments by planters, 30–33,
    36–40, 64, 66, 97, 100

Contractors, government, 75
Cooleagh, co. Tipperary, 24
Cooper, Thomas, 160n83
Corbett, Richard, 84
Corbin & Lee, 36
Corbin, Thomas, 33
Cordage, exported, 109
Cork, Ireland, 16, 48
Correspondence trade between
    merchants, 32, 34, 35
Cottons, exported, 107
Cowes, Isle of Wight, 45
Credit, 44, 66, 97, 100–101; legal rights
    of creditors, 56. *See also* debt
Cromwell, Oliver, 16, 145n42
Cromwell, Thomas, 118
Crookshanks (Cruikshanks), Robert, 79
Crowley family, 75
Custis, Daniel Parke, estate of, 157n49
Custis, Mrs. Frances (Parke), 48
Custis, John, III, 57
Custis, John, IV, 39–40, 67–68, 78,
    86–87, 89, 97, 157n47, 166n14
Customs: service, 7; in Scotland,
    15–16; duties paid by Perry & Co.,
    23, 49–50, 64, 67, 78; duties on
    tobacco, 52, 82–83; commissioners,
    80; warehouses, 82–83; procedures,
    155n74, 170n25
Customs House Quay, London, 24

Dartmouth, Devon, 54
Davenport, Rev. John, 12, 13
Dawkins, William, 84, 85, 153n6,
    157n54
Debts: to firm, 49–50, 66–71, 88, 89;
    interest on, 70–71; legislation, 81–82
Dee & Bell, 39, 40, 67
Deerskins, 47, 105
Denbighshire, Wales, 66
Deposits, with merchants, 97
Desborough, Maj.-Gen. John, 16
Desborough (Disbrowe), Samuel, 16
Desmadril, J. C., 84
Devon, sheriff of, 12
Digges, Dudley, 90
Donnan, Elizabeth, 28
Dorsey, John, 57

Downing, Sir George, bart., 15–16
Doyley, Rev. Cope, 38
Dublin, 16
Dunckley, Robert, 33
Dyes, exported, 44

Earthenware, exported, 44
East India Company: new, 3–4, 22, 56,
    59, 74, 140n2; old, 20, 55; United, 75
Eaton, Theophilus, 12
Eaton (or Eyton) Bray, Bedfordshire,
    24, 26, 152n35
Edinburgh, governor of, 16
Edmondson, William, 156n45
Eliot family, of Cornwall, 74
Elizabeth I, charter of, 9
Epsom, Surrey, 80, 87, 173n59
Essex, lands in, 24
Essex County, Virginia, 173n66
Evans, Elizabeth, 152n35
Exchequer, Court of, 84
Exchequer bills, 163n25
Excise service: at Glasgow, 15; national,
    15, 20; crisis of 1733, 82–83
Exeter: Society of Merchant
    Adventurers, 8; Pery family of, 8–10;
    bailiffs of, 9, 116; parish of St.
    Edmund, 9, 11, 14; parish of St.
    Petrock, 9, 14
Exeter, Henry (Courtenay), marquess
    of, 118
Exports to Chesapeake: 33, 37, 43–44,
    107–111; prices of, 37
Eyles, Sir John, 2d bart., 74

Factors, in Chesapeake, 30–33, 98
Fairfax, Catherine (Colepeper),
    baroness, 33
Falconar family, of London, 99
Falconar, John, 160n83
Fenwick, George, M.P., 16
Feoffees for the Purchase of
    Impropriations, 12
Figs, imported, 8
Flanders, tobacco exports to, 46
France: wartime trade with, 57;
    commercial treaty with, 57; tobacco
    monopoly of, 77, 97

Freame, John 160n83
Fur trade, 34, 47–48, 105
Furnese, Sir Henry, bart., 163n25

Galley Quay, London, 24
Galloway, John (Stewart), 5th earl of,
    80
George I, 73
Germany, tobacco exports to, 45
Glasgow: municipal government, 4;
    Perys in, 8; Chesapeake traders of,
    64, 85
Glassware, exported, 44
Godwin, Edmond, 35
Gooch, Dr. Thomas, 76
Gooch, Sir William, bart., 76–77, 80,
    81, 85
Gouldesborough, Robert, 156n45
Gouldney, Henry, 160n83
Greenwich (East), Kent, 87, 91, 92,
    173n59
Grindstones, exported, 44
Grocers Company, London, 54
Groceries, exported, 44
Groom(e), Samuel, 45, 159n71
Grove, Silvanus, 160n83
Grymes, John, 85
Gunnell, Edward, 33
Gunpowder, exported, 109

Haberdashers Company, London, 8,
    15, 17, 73–74
Haberdashers, wholesale, 44
Haberdashery, exported, 33, 108
Haistwell, Edward, & Co., 159n72
Hamburg, 45, 46
Hampshire, 68, 118
Hanbury, John, 79, 88, 89
Hardman, John, 105–106
Hardware, exported, 110
Harenc, Benjamin, 92
Harenc, Henry Benjamin, 175n9
Harenc, Mrs. Sarah (Cade), 91, 92,
    174n6
Harrison, Brian 142n20
Harrison, Nathaniel, 57
Harvard College, 18
Harvey, Anthony, 118

Hats, exported, 44, 108; made in
    colonies, 76
Heathcote, Sir Gilbert, bart., M.P., 74
Hely-Hutchinson family, 94, 112
Henrico county, Virginia, 34
Henshaw, Essex, 18
Heralds. See College of Arms
Herne, Sir Joseph, 163n25
Heysham, Robert, M.P., 25, 72–73
Heysham, Mrs. Sarah (Perry), 25, 63,
    73, 90–92, 174n6
Heysham, William, M.P., 25, 63, 72–73,
    78
Hicks, Dunes. See Pery, Mrs. Dunes
Higginson, Gilbert, 156n34
Hill, Edward, Jr., 25, 69
Hill, Perry & Randolph, 25, 69, 151n30
Hodgkins, John, 160n83
Holland, tobacco exported to, 45
Hose, exported, 108
Household furnishings, exported, 110
Howard of Effingham, Thomas
    (Howard), 6th baron, 164n27
Huguenot refugees, 58
Hunt, William, 139nl, 153n6
Hutchinson, Mrs. Anne (Marbury), 112
Hutchinson, Edward, 17, 93, 112
Hutchinson, Richard, 15–17, 20, 93,
    112
Hutchinson, Thomas, 112
Hutchinson, William, 16, 93, 112
Hutchinson family, 16–17, 112–113;
    Irish lands, 17
Hyam, Thomas, 99
Hyde, John, 58, 79, 89, 153n6, 159n71
Hyde family, of London, 99

Iberia, traders to, 55
Ilcomb, Alice. See Pery, Mrs. Alice
Ilcomb, John, 116
Independents (Congregationalists), 12
India, interloping trade to, 20
Indian trade in Virginia, 34, 47
Ireland: Perys in, 16–17; "adventurers"
    in, 16; lands in, 27, 151n27; refugees
    in, 58; plantation trade, 75; tobacco
    smuggling in, 84. See also Clonmel;
    Limerick; Tipperary
Iron, wrought, exported, 110

Ironmongers, wholesale, 44, 73
Isham family, of Virginia, 20
Isle of Wight county, Virginia, 173n66

Jamaica, 19, 20, 47, 55, 81, 92, 159n80
Jamestown (James City), Virginia, 7, 30, 165n13
Janssen, Sir Theodore, 59
Jarrett, Elizabeth. *See* Tyler, Mrs. Elizabeth
Jarrett, Mrs. Johanna (Lowe), 25
Jarrett, John, 7, 10, 165n13
Jeffreys, Edward, 54–55
Jeffreys, Herbert, 161n7
Jeffreys, (Sir) Jeffrey, 21, 54–55, 158n57, 162n9, 164n27
Jeffreys, Col. John, M.P., 161n7
Jeffreys, Alderman John (I), 21, 54–56, 160n2, 161n7, 162n9
Jeffreys, John (II), nephew of John (I), 21, 54–55
Jeffreys, John (III), son of John (II), 54
Jeffreys, John, & Co., 21, 54–55
Jeffreys, Walter (Watkin), 54
Jeffreys Street, Camden Town, 55
Jenings, Edmund, 33
Johnston, James, 87, 172
Jones, Cuthbert, 35–37, 155n25
Jones, Col. Thomas, 87

Keane, Molly, 94, 177n20
Keith, Governor William, 57
Kennet, Dean White, 59
Kent, Mrs. Sarah, 66
Keyser, Timothy, 159n71
King, Walter, 87, 90
King's Inn, Dublin, 177n18
Koulikun (Kouli Khan), or Nadir Shah, 85, 171n43

Lancashire, 77
Lancaster, 25
Lane, Mrs. Mary (Puckle), 20, 22, 23, 112, 154n15
Lane, Thomas, I, 19
Lane, Thomas, II, son of Thomas I: family, 19–20, 33; activity in Perry &

Lane, 21–27; marriage 20, 112; land purchases, 23; death and will, 23, 25, 90
Lane, Alderman Sir Thomas, 151n24
Lane, Valentine, brother of Thomas II, 23
Lane, Valentine, nephew of Thomas II, 23–24
Lang, John, 35
Lawsuits: Lloyd v. Perry, 66; Beckford v. Perry, 88, 173n61; Bennett v. Perry, 88, 173n60; Lloyd v. Nicholson, 166n17
Leather goods, exported, 44, 108
Lecturers, evangelical, 12, 14
Lee, Francis, 159n73, 164n27
Lee, Richard III, 36
Lee, Thomas, 33
Leete, John, 145n42
Leete, William, 145n42
Leeward Islands, 68
LeGendre, Thomas, 23
Leheup, Peter, 71, 75–77, 80, 83
Lemon, Edward, 159n73
Leigh, Col. William, 35
Leith, Scotland, 116
Letters of marque, 42, 55
Leyden, University of, 176n18
Lightfoot family, of Virginia, 20
Limerick, Ireland: Pery family of, 9, 16, 114, 116; trade at, 16
Linens, exported, 33, 44, 107
Linendrapers, wholesale, 44, 73
Little Stanbridge (or Stambridge), Essex, 24, 91, 174n4
Liverpool: municipal government, 4; merchants of, 66, 81, 85
Lloyd, John, 66–67, 90, 166n17
Lloyd, Philemon, 57
Lloyd, Thomas, 66, 166n17
Loans, to Perry & Co., 41
London, City of: political life, 4, 72–77; members of Parliament, 25, 72–87; lord mayor, 54, 84, 87; aldermen, 54, 73, 74, 88, 172–173n58; auditor, 54; lieutenancy, 54, 58, 72; sheriff, 54, 84; train bands, 54, 84; Court of Common Council, 73, 172n58; tradesmen voters, 73

London, Diocese of: St. Paul's Cathedral, 17; parishes of St. Pancras Soper Lane, 11; St. Antholins, 11, 12, 14; St. Mary-le-Bow, 17; St. Swithin, 17; St. Botolph Bishopsgate, 27; St. Katherine Cree, 27; All Hallows Bread Street, 144n30; St. Paul Shadwell, 155n25

London, Port of: port book, 20; Chesapeake and tobacco merchants, 30–31, 65, 79, 81, 105–106

London, topography of: quays, 23–25, 80; Aldgate Ward, 74; Leadenhall Street, 24, 25, 27; Hatton Gardens, 24; Moorfields, 24; Jeffreys Square, 55; Petticoat Lane, 79; Stony Lane, 79; Gravel Lane, 79, 170n26; warehouses, 79–80; Mansion House, 87

London Lead Company, 99

London Workhouse, Bishopsgate Street, 23, 27

Lowe, Christopher, 77

Lowe, John, 151n30

Lowe, Mrs. Mary (Perry), 13, 14, 25, 93, 151n30

Lowe, Micajah, 151n30

Ludwell, Philip, 57, 58

Luttrell, Narcissus, 55

Lyde, Sir Lyonel, bart., 139n1

Lyme Regis, Dorset, 85

Madeira, trade to, 47, 64; merchant of, 88

Madras, 20

Malbon(e), Hanna, 144n30

Malbon(e), Mary. See Pery, Mrs. Mary

Malbon(e), Richard, of London and New Haven, 12–15, 144n30

Malbon, Samuel, uncle of Micaiah Perry I, 18, 144n30

Malbon, Samuel, sea-captain, 147n55

Malbon(e) families, of Virginia and Rhode Island, 147n55

Malt, exported, 109

Mann, Thomas, Buddenbrooks, 3

Mark-ups, retail, 49

Marlborough, Wiltshire, 54

Maryland: adventure to, 33; tobacco of, 45, 46; merchants trading to, 46, 53; export duties on tobacco, 56; governor of, 57; council, 57, 77; press, 78; merchants in, 88; paper money, 140n1

Marshall, Joseph, 160n83

Massachusetts Bay Company, 12

Massachusetts: returnees from, 15; Hutchinsons in, 16, 112

Maynard, John, 156n34

Merchant-planters in tobacco colonies, 29, 32, 33, 67–71

Merchant Taylors Company, London, 11, 12

Merchants in Chesapeake, 30, 31, 33, 35, 65, 66, 89, 173n64

Merchants of London: 11, 99; in Chesapeake trade, operations, 29–32, 82, 105–106, number of, 96–97, 170, lobbying organization ("association"), 53, 56, 77, lobbying activity, 81, 84; political participation, 74, 100

Mine Adventure, the, 55

Mint, Warden of the, 55

Molasses, 75

Moreland, Jacob, 156n45

Morgan, Capt. Christopher, 35, 41, 42

Mortgages, 66, 68, 90

Muscovy Company, 56

Muscovy House, London, 143n24

Nails, exported, 44, 110

Namier, Sir Lewis, 54

Navy Board, 148n7

Navy, Treasurer of, 15, 16, 93, 112

Navy, victualling of, 55

Newcastle, co. Tipperary, 93–94, 112

New England: Perys in, 8, 12; returnees from, 15–17

Newfoundland, trade to, 8

New Haven, town and colony, 12, 13, 16; First Church, 13; returnees from, 16

New Kent County, Virginia, 35

New Pennsylvania Company, 47–48, 160n83
New York, 47, 55, 59, 75
Nicholson, Clement, 166n17
Nicholson, Francis, governor of Maryland and Virginia, 57
Nonconformists, 56. *See also* Presbyterians; Independents
Norfolk, Virginia, 147n55
North, Arthur, 34, 45, 164n27
Northamptonshire, emigration from, 19–20
North Carolina, 47–48, 59, 64; laws of, 56
Northern Neck (Virginia), proprietary, 33, 57

Oronoco tobacco, 45
Orton, Capt. W., 42
Owen, Ann. *See* Perry, Mrs. Ann
Owen, Richard, D.D., 17, 18
Oxford University, 17–19, 92
Ozenbrigs, exported, 44

Page, John, merchant-planter of Virginia and London, 36, 156n32
Page, John, director of the Bank of England, 156n32
Page, Mann (?), 69
Paggen, Peter, 58, 140n2, 159n72
Paggen, William, 45, 105–106
Palatine refugees, 58–59
Parke, Daniel, Sr., 157n47
Parke, Col. Daniel, Jr., 39, 68–69, 157n47, 167n22
Parke, Frances. *See* Custis, Mrs. Frances
Parke, Lucy. *See* Byrd, Mrs. Lucy
Parliament, acts of: 21 James I, 81; emigration of artisans (1719), 57; Tobacco Act (1723), 65, 76; London Act (1725), 73; Carolina Rice Act (1730), 75; New York Salt Act (1730), 75; Irish Trade Act (1731), 75; American Coffee Act (1732), 75; Molasses Act (1733), 75; Colonial Debts Act (1732), 81–83, 86
Parliament, commissioners named by, 12

Parliament, House of Commons: elections, 73–74; composition, 74, 100; lobbying of, 81
Parsons, Humphry, M.P., 75
Patronage, colonial, 76–77
Patuxent River, Maryland, 146n46
Peddlers, in Chesapeake, 30
Peele, John, 79, 99
Pennsylvania, 42, 75
Pennsylvania Company, 42
Perrott, Richard, 146n46
Perrie, Nicholas, 179n13
Perry family, of Clonmel, 10, 17, 18, 93–94
Perry family, of London (post-1660), 18, 22, 114
Perry, Mrs. Ann (Owen), 17, 18, 24
Perry, Ebenezer, 14, 25
Perry, Edward, 176n17
Perry, Elizabeth, daughter of Richard IV. *See* Cade, Mrs. Elizabeth
Perry, Mrs. Elizabeth (Cocke), wife of Micajah III, 27, 87
Perry, Mrs. Elizabeth (Riall), wife of John, of Clonmel, 93, 112
Perry, Grace, 13, 14, 25
Perry, John, of Clonmel and Newcastle, brother of Micaiah I, 13, 14, 17, 24, 25, 93–94, 112–113, 148n57, 151n27, 176n17
Perry, John, Jr., of Woodroof, 94, 148n57, 151n27, 176n17
Perry, John, playwright, 177n20
Perry, Mary, sister of Micaiah I. *See* Lowe, Mrs. Mary
Perry, Mary, daughter of Richard IV, 25, 26, 63, 90
Perry, Micaiah I: on family, 7–8, 10, 22, 24; early years and marriage, 13–15, 17, 18, 24; rise in business, 19–27; land purchases, 24; death and will, 25–27, 63–64; descendants, 26; as lobbyist, 31; share in business, 48; public role, 52–59, 140n2; as surety, 66; as executor, 68; on debts, 70; politics, 72. *See also* Perry & Lane
Perry, Micajah II, son (?) of Micaiah I, 25, 149n15, 164n3

Perry, Micajah, III, son of Richard IV: birth and inheritance, 23, 25–28, 63–64, 91, 149n15; lobbying by, 65, 68; in politics, 4, 72–84, 87, 99–100; sale of real estate, 79–80, 93–94, 151n27; loss of friends, 85–87; decline and death, 87–90; pension, 172–173n58. See also Perry, Micajah & Phillip

Perry, Micajah & Phillip (firm): policies, 64–66, 89–90, 95–101; problems with debtors, 66–71; tobacco imports, 78, 79; earnings, 79; export sales, 84; decline, 85–90

Perry, Micajah, of Clonmel, medical student, 176n18

Perry, Peter, brother of Micaiah I, 14, 25, 69

Perry, Phillip, son of Richard IV (and partner in Micajah & Phillip Perry), 25–28, 63–64, 87, 90, 91, 174n4

Perry, Richard, IV, son of Micaiah I, 22, 23, 25–27, 31, 48, 58, 65, 66, 68, 69, 139n1, 149n15; death, 63, 64, 90, 91; estate, 170n26, 174n4

Perry, Richard, of Clonmel, 176n17

Perry, Richard, of Maryland and London (fl. 1668–1685), 146n46

Perry, Richard, of Plymouth (fl. 1664–1675), 146n46

Perry, Samuel, brother of Micaiah I, 13, 14, 25

Perry, Samuel, of Cork, 176n17

Perry, Mrs. Sarah (Richards), wife of Richard IV, 21–22, 24–26, 63, 66, 70, 77, 87, 91, 149n15, 174n4

Perry, Sarah, daughter of Richard IV. See Heysham, Mrs. Sarah

Perry & Lane: as leading importer, 2; in Virginia, 7; formation and rise, 19–27; business activities, 28–48, 88, 95–99, 100; earnings and profits, 48–51; provides tobacco for Russia, 56; as London agents, 57

Perry, Lane & Co., 22

Perry's Point, Virginia, 11, 117

Pery family: of Buckland Monachorum, 114–117; of Exeter, 10, 114–117; of Limerick, 9, 16, 18, 44, 114–117; of London (to 1660), 16, 114–117; of Plymouth, 114–117; of Virginia, 114–117; of Water (Devon), 8, 114–115

Pery, Mrs. Alice (Ilcomb), 116

Pery, Mrs. Dunes (Hicks), 11, 12, 14

Pery, Edmund, of Limerick, 9, 115–117

Pery, Henry, of Buckland Monachorum, 116, 142n14

Pery, Henry, of Plymouth, 116–117

Pery, Capt. Henry, of Virginia, 117, 179n9

Pery, John, I, of London, 9–11, 115, 117, 142n20

Pery, John, II (infant), 12

Pery, Mrs. Mary (Malbon), wife of Richard III, 13

Pery, Peter, 12, 14, 16, 115, 144n37

Pery, Richard, I, of Exeter, 8–11, 116, 141n10

Pery, Richard, II, of London, 9–12, 14, 19, 114–115, 142n14, 143n21, n24, n25, 144n35, 145n43

Pery, Richard, III, of London, 12, 143n25; of New Haven, 13, 14, 115; of Glasgow, 15, 16; of Tipperary, 16–17, 93, 146n46

Pery, Mrs. Richarda (Platyr), wife of Henry of Buckland, 116

Pery, Roger, of Exeter, 8–10, 115–116, 119, 141n7, n10

Pery, Susanna. See Whittle, Mrs. Susanna

Pery, Susanne. See Carter, Mrs. Susanne

Pery, Thomas, of Buckland Monachorum, 116

Pery, William, of Exeter, son of Roger, 8, 9, 11, 116, 118–119, 141n10

Pery, William, of Limerick, 9, 16, 114–116

Pery, William, of Virginia, 9, 11, 116–117, 142n14

Pery, William, I and II, of Water, 115

Peter the Great, 56–57

Pewter, exported, 110

Philadelphia, 47, 64, 76, 160n83

Philpot family, of London, 99

Phippard, William, 156n45
Pigeon Swamp, Surry County, Virginia, 70
Planters in tobacco colonies, 28–32, 66–71; consignments by, 30–33, 36–40, 66; deposits with firm, 41, 157n54
Platyr, Richarda. See Pery, Mrs. Richarda
Plows, exported, 44
Plymouth, 11; Pery families of, 7, 8, 114, 116–117, 146n46
Pope, James, 88
Pork, trade in, 48
Portugal, Pery trade with, 9
Pratt, Charles, 1st earl Camden, 55
Presbyterians, 12, 18, 94, 147n56
Prince George's County, Virginia, 173n66
Privateers, 42, 43, 55
Privy Council (British), 52; committee of, 54; orders-in-council, 57, 71; judicial appeal to, 70–71, 90; disallows colonial laws, 81
Profits reinvested and distributed, 47–49
Provisions, ships', 48
Puckle, James, notary of London, 22, 44, 73, 112, 150n23; author of The Club, 22
Puckle, James, brother of Maj. William, 148n7
Puckle, Mary. See Lane, Mrs. Mary
Puckle, Susannah. See Bathurst, Mrs. Susannah
Puckle, Thomas, 20
Puckle, Maj. William, 20, 112, 148n7
Pulteney, William, M.P., 84
Puritans, 12; from New England, 15
Pury (or Piry), John, of Warminster, 118, 141n7, 179n13
Pury (or Pirry), William, of Breamore, 118–119

Quakers, 160n83
Quare, Daniel, 99
Quern stones, exported, 44

Radnorshire, 54

Raisins, imports of, 8
Randolph, Henry, 70
Randolph, Isham, 82
Randolph, (Sir) John, 75, 83
Randolph, Mrs. Mary, wife of Col. William, 69–70
Randolph, Thomas, 70
Randolph, Col. William, 25, 69–70, 83; estate of, 70–71, 82
Randolph, William, son of Col. William, 70
Randolph family, of Virginia, 20
Reade, Col. Thomas, 146n45
Rehoboam, king of Israel, 85, 171n43
Rhode Island, 147n55
Riall, Elizabeth. See Perry, Mrs. Elizabeth
Riall family, 147n56
Rice, Carolina, 75–76
Richards, George, 21–23, 45, 66, 159n76, 160n2
Richards, Phillip, 21, 66
Richards, Sarah. See Perry, Mrs. Sarah
Richards family, 24
Richmond County, Virginia, 66
Rogers, Charles, 99
Ropemakers, 73
Rotterdam, 45, 46
Royal African Company, 38, 55, 75, 156n43
Rum, 36, 47
Russia, tobacco trade in, 56–57

Sail-cloth, exported, 108
Sailmakers, 73
Sailors, wartime quotas, 53
St. Germans, Cornwall, 74
St. James's Park, ranger of, 55
St. Kitts, 47, 159n80
St. Mary's City, Maryland, 30
St. Thomas's Hospital, Southwark, 23
Salt, 75
Saltonstall, Richard, Jr., 15, 16
Sandford, Samuel, 15
Savary, Mrs. Catherine (Cade), wife of William James, 92, 175n10
Savary, Dalzell, 175n10
Savary, John Tanzia de, 175n10

Savary, Mrs. Marie (Blaquière) de, 175n11
Savary, William James Tanzia de, 92, 175n10
Savary, William Tanzia de, son of William James, 175n10
Savoy Military Hospital, London, 15
Sayer (Sayres), Joseph, 33
Scotland: Commissioners for Sequestrations, 16, 145–146n45; New Englanders in, 15–16
Scottish traders in Chesapeake, 64, 98
Scrope, John, M.P., 82
Secretaries of state, 52
Servants, indentured, 28, 31, 46, 96, 159n75
Sewer of king's chamber, 118
Sexton, Stephen, 9
Sheffeild, John, 38
Shipping in Chesapeake trade, 34; convoys, 34, 35, 43, 52; freight rates, 34, 35, 42; marine insurance for, 35, 37, 41–43, 70; Perry firm's, 41–42, 88–89, 97, 158n57; armed merchantmen, 42; managers (ship's husbands) 42; agents, 42; crew size, 42; war losses, 43; quotas, 52–53
Ships and other vessels: *Phoenix,* 13; *America,* 42; *Exeter Merchant,* 42; *London Merchant,* 42; *Pennsylvania Merchant,* 42; *Perry and Lane,* 42, 148n57; *Richard and Sarah,* 158n57
Shoemaking, in Virginia, 36
Shoes, exported, 33, 44, 108
Sibrey, Jonathan, 33
Silks, exported, 44, 108
Slaves, 28, 29, 31, 80, 81, 98, 170n33
Slave trade, 31, 34, 38, 39, 47, 96; "guarantee" in, 34
Smith, Augustine and Charles, 173n66
Smith, Philip, 99, 156n45
Soap, exported, 109
Society for the Propagation of the Gospel in Foreign Parts, 59
Somerset, 118
"The Sotweed Factor," 30
Southampton, 21
South Carolina, 47, 75–76

South Sea Company, 74, 75, 170n26
Spain: Pery trade with, 8–9; tobacco exports to, 46; convention with, 87; war with, 116
"Spanish Company," 9
Starke, Thomas, 38, 140n2, 156n45
Stegge, Thomas, Sr. and Jr., 34
Stepney, Middlesex, 16
Stockings, exported, 33
Stone family, of Virginia, 20
"Stores" in tobacco colonies, 33, 98
Stratton, Anthony, 159n71
Sugar, 47, 109, 159n80
Sussex, lands in, 24
Sweden, Royal Tobacco Company, 162n9

Tayloe, John, 77
Taylor, John, 159n72
Tenant farmers, in tobacco colonies, 28
Thomson, Col. George, M.P., 20, 149n9
Thomson, Maurice, 20, 149n9
Thomson, Paul, 149n9
Thomson, Maj. Robert, 20
Thomson, William, 149n9
Tibbott, Capt. R., 42
Tilghman, Richard, 57
Tipperary, county, 16–18, 24, 25, 80, 93–94, 112, 151n27, 152n35
Tobacco: trade in, 2, 11, 31–32, 95–99, 105–6; importers, 21–22, 34, 45, 55, 58, 143, 155, 170; customs duties and procedures, 24, 52, 55, 82–83; prices, 31, 37, 49, 64, 79, 80, 96, 98–99; home market, 40, 45; varieties, 44; export markets, 45–46, 57; skilled workmen in, 57; crops, 64, 80; manufacturers, 84
Topsham, Devon, 8, 118
Tories, 54–55, 58, 72, 74, 75
Totnes, Devon, 12
Traders, country, in Chesapeake, 30
Train(ed) bands, New Haven, 13
Treasury (British), 7, 52, 54–55, 57, 59, 77, 82, 84, 163n25
Trinity College, Cambridge, 24, 174n6
Trinity College, Dublin, 177n20
Tryon family, of London, 99

Tyler, Mrs. Elizabeth (Jarrett), wife of John, 10, 93
Tyler, John, colonist, 10, 93
Tyler, John, U.S. president, 25, 93

Utrecht, commercial treaty of, 57

Vintners, 84
Virginia: lands in, 11; traders to, 11, 19–27, 40, 53; settlers in, 19–20, 117; map of, 22; social structure, 28–32; legislature, 32, 71, 83; justices and officials, 32, 77; auditor-general, 34, 57; council, 39, 58, 77, 83; financial agents, 41, 56, 85; juries, 43; export duties, 56; political agents, 56, 75–76, 164; laws of, 56, 68, 80–82, 170–171; governor, 57; receiver-general, 57, 85; refugees in, 58; General Court, 70. *See also* Merchants; Planters
Virginia Company of London, 11, 12

Waldenfield, Samuel, 160n83
Wallace, James, 35
Walpole, Horatio, elder, 76
Walpole, Sir Robert: London policy, 73; excise scheme, 83–84; opposition to, 87
War, effects on trade, 34, 35, 37, 43, 52–53
Warminster, Wiltshire, 118, 179n13
Washington family, of Virginia, 19–20
Waterford, 16
Weavers Company, London, 21
West Indies: trade to, 25, 55, 64, 81, 93; Perry correspondents in, 47; estate in, 68; "Spanish depredations" in, 75

Westminster School, 92
Westover, Virginia, 34
Weymouth, 85
Whigs, 56, 58, 72–74
White, Mrs. Ruth, 115
Whitehaven, Cumberland, 166n17
Whittle, Esther, 14
Whittle, Mrs. Susanna (Pery), 12, 14, 115
Whittle, William, 14
Whitty, John, & Co., 159n72
Whitworth, Catherine. *See* Cade, Mrs. Catherine
Whitworth, Sir Charles, M.P., 92
Whitworth, Charles (Whitworth), baron and earl, 175n11
Wilkins, Capt. Thomas, 42
Williamsburg, Virginia, 38
Williamson, Sir Joseph, 148n7
Willis, Francis, 66, 166n17
Wilson, Samuel, 35
Wilson, Col. William, 35
Wine Islands, 55
Wine: imports of, 8, 11; exports of, 47, 109; taxation, 83
Winthrop, John, governor of Massachusetts, 146n45
Winthrop, Col. Stephen, M.P., 146n45
Woodroof, co. Tipperary, 93–94, 151n27
Wool-cards, exported, 44
Woolen cloth, exported, 11, 33, 44, 107
Woolendrapers, wholesale, 44, 73
Wynn, Capt. J., 42

Yale, Elihu, in India, 149n10
York County, Virginia, 25
York River, Virginia, 35, 39, 40, 45, 67